W9-BOD-442

Contemporary's

Number Power

GED Math for the Casio fx-260

Robert Mitchell and Judy Reagan

McGraw-Hill Contemporary

McGraw-Hill/Contemporary

*A Division of The **McGraw·Hill** Companies*

Send all inquiries to:

McGraw-Hill/Contemporary
4255 W. Touhy Ave.
Lincolnwood, IL 60712

ISBN: 0-07-251697-6

Printed in the United States of America.

1 2 3 4 5 6 7 8 9 10 QWD 07 06 05 04 03 02 01

Table of Contents

GEOMETRY AND MEASUREMENT 143

To the Student

Welcome to *Calculator Power for the GED*.

Calculator Power for the GED is designed to help you master the use of the Casio *fx*-260 calculator for all types of basic math problems. You will learn to use the calculator to add, to subtract, to multiply, and to divide. You'll discover how a calculator can simplify your work with whole numbers, decimal numbers, fractions, percents, and more. You'll learn how a calculator can help you gain confidence in solving all kinds of word problems.

Calculator Power for the GED will help make using a calculator more enjoyable. Step-by-step examples will show how to use the Casio *fx*-260 to solve math problems you're most likely to come across in daily life and on the GED Mathematics Test.

A calculator icon, 🖩 , is used throughout *Calculator Power for the GED*. The calculator icon alerts you to procedures that are in Contemporary's *Calculator Reference Cards*.

An important skill for anyone who uses a calculator is to be on the lookout for keying errors, such as entering incorrect digits or accidentally pressing a digit twice. The most important skill for noticing keying errors is to anticipate about how large an answer should be. To develop that skill, *Calculator Power for the GED* emphasizes estimation and mental math throughout the book.

To get the most out of your work, do each exercise carefully. Check your answers with the answer key at the back of the book. A Practice Test similar to the GED Mathematics Test will help you determine your ability to use the Casio *fx*-260 in a testing situation. The accompanying Evaluation Chart will show you which areas you may need to review.

Number Sense and Operations

BECOMING FAMILIAR WITH THE CALCULATOR

To **calculate** is to work with numbers. You calculate each time you add, subtract, multiply, or divide. You also calculate each time you estimate, perform mental math, or write arithmetic problems using paper and pencil.

In this section, you will learn the basics of using the Casio *fx*-260 scientific calculator. By the end of this book, you will see that the best way to calculate combines estimation, mental math, and calculator use.

Calculator Basics

A **calculator** is an electronic device that makes it easy to work with numbers. When used carefully, a calculator is amazingly quick and accurate. The calculator pictured below is the Casio *fx*-260. This is the calculator that will be used on the first half of the GED Mathematics Test.

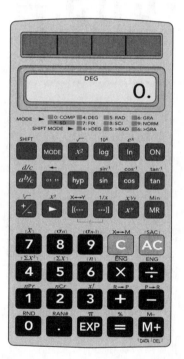

This calculator is an example of a scientific calculator. The four **operation keys** are $+$, $-$, $\times$, and $\div$. The **memory keys** are $M+$ and MR.

You'll soon learn about all the keys shown above. For now, notice the group of ten **digit keys**: 0, 1, 2, 3, 4, 5, 6, 7, 8, and 9. Digit keys let you enter numbers on a calculator.

The Calculator Display

Your calculator displays a zero and a decimal point when it is turned on. You will see "DEG" in the display. If your calculator does not display a "0." when you press the ON key, or if you do not see "DEG" in the display, then your calculator has a problem.

The maximum number of digits a calculator can work with is determined by the size of its display. Press the ON key on your calculator. Press the digit keys one at a time until the display will not hold any more digits. How many digits are displayed on your calculator? You should see 10 digits in your display. Your calculator has a 10-digit display.

DEG	0.

An "ON" display

9024857394.

A displayed 10-digit number

Clear Keys

To start a new calculation or to change the number shown in the display, you use special erasing keys called **clear keys.** Learn the meaning of the clear keys on your calculator.

Key	Meaning	Function
AC	All Clear	The All Clear key erases the display.
ON	On/Clear	Pressing ON turns the calculator on. It also erases the display, all parts of a calculation stored in the calculator, and any number stored in the memory.
C	Clear	The Clear key erases the display only. It does not erase any calculations stored in the calculation or in memory.
►	Backspace	The backspace key erases digits in an entry starting with the digit farthest to the right.
+, −, ×, ÷	Overide	To change an operation key (+, −, ×, or ÷), press the correctoperation key to override.

Answer each of the following questions about your calculator.

1. Press the following keys in order: 1, 2, 3, 4, 5. Press the backspace key 2 times. What number is on the display?

2. Press ·. Enter 4 and 5 again. What number is on the display?

3. What is the largest number you can display on your calculator?

4. Which key do you press to erase your calculator's display?

5. Enter 5. Press +. Press −. Enter 4. Press =. Did your calculator add or subtract?

The Decimal Point Key

The ⟦·⟧ key is the **decimal point** key. One use of the decimal point key is to enter an amount of money. For example, to enter 14 dollars and 29 cents, you use the decimal point to separate dollars from cents. Cents always appear as 2 digits to the right of the decimal point.

dollars ⟶↓   ↓⟵cents

$14.29

↑
decimal point

Here are some points to remember.

- No dollar sign is displayed on a calculator.
  The amount $14.29 is entered as ⟦1⟧ ⟦4⟧ ⟦·⟧ ⟦2⟧ ⟦9⟧ and is displayed as

  | 14.29 |

- When you enter cents only, the calculator displays a 0 to the left of the decimal point.
  The amount $0.18 is entered as ⟦·⟧ ⟦1⟧ ⟦8⟧ and is displayed as

  | 0.18 |

- When you enter an amount between 1¢ and 9¢, put a 0 between the decimal point and the cents digit. As examples, you enter 4¢ as ⟦·⟧ ⟦0⟧ ⟦4⟧
  and you enter $3.08 as ⟦3⟧ ⟦·⟧ ⟦0⟧ ⟦8⟧.

  | 0.04 |
  | 3.08 |

- If you perform a calculation and the answer is a dollar amount ending in 0, the calculator does not display the 0. For example, $6.80 is displayed as

  | 6.8 |

Enter each of the following money amounts on your calculator. Then, below each amount, write how that value appears on the calculator display. (Clear the display before each entry.)

6. four dollars and nineteen cents   six dollars and twelve cents

7. twenty-seven cents   forty-two cents

8. one cent   eight cents

9. one dollar and six cents   two dollars and seven cents

More About Displayed Numbers

Think for a moment about things you've discovered about your calculator.

- Digit keys are used to enter numbers.

- You enter a number one digit at a time, starting with the left-hand digit.

- You can set the display to "0" by pressing a clear key.

- You press the decimal point key ⟨ · ⟩ to separate dollars from cents.

Here's an interesting fact: The Casio *fx*-260 does not have a comma (,) key. For example, to enter 1,960, you press ⟨1⟩ ⟨9⟩ ⟨6⟩ ⟨0⟩. *You do not enter a comma.*

EXAMPLE 1   To enter 82,500 on your calculator, press keys as shown below.

Press Keys	Display Reads
8	8.
2	82.
5	825.
0	8250.
0	82500.

> **Discovery**
> - Calculators display a decimal point to the right of a whole number.
> - The Casio *fx*-260 does not display commas.
> - The calculator will omit zeros at the right of a decimal number. The display 1367.5 means $1367.50.

EXAMPLE 2   To enter $1,367.50 on your calculator, press these keys.

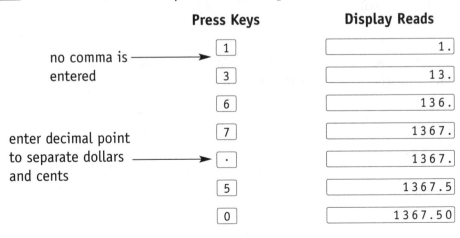

	Press Keys	Display Reads
no comma is entered →	1	1.
	3	13.
	6	136.
	7	1367.
enter decimal point to separate dollars and cents →	·	1367.
	5	1367.5
	0	1367.50

Rewrite each of the numbers. If the number is greater than 999, write it with a comma. The first is completed as an example.

no decimal point

1. `2450.` 2,450

2. `875.` _____

3. `4056.` _____

4. `39450.` _____

5. `1832.` _____

6. `29609.` _____

Write these money amounts with a dollar sign and comma if the amount is $1,000 or more.

7. `18.32` $18.32

8. `2471.60` _____

9. `649.09` _____

10. `5038.18` _____

Choose how each of the displayed numbers and money amounts would be written.

11. `340.`

   a. thirty-four
   b. three hundred forty
   c. three thousand, four hundred

12. `900.`

   a. nine
   b. ninety
   c. nine hundred

13. `3.07`

   a. thirty-seven cents
   b. three dollars and three cents
   c. three dollars and seven cents

14. `0.20`

   a. twenty cents
   b. two dollars
   c. twenty dollars

Enter each of the following numbers on your calculator. Write how each displayed number looks. Be sure to write the decimal point in the display.

15. ninety-five `95.`

16. two hundred forty-three

17. three thousand, five hundred twenty-nine

18. eight thousand, four hundred six

19. fifteen dollars and eighty-two cents

20. two hundred four dollars and nine cents

WHOLE NUMBERS AND MONEY

Much of the math around us involves whole numbers and money. Calculators can help us work more effectively with large numbers and with groups of whole numbers. Calculators can also help us focus our efforts on thinking about how to solve problems.

In this part of the book, besides the digit keys, you will use the decimal point key $\boxed{\cdot}$, the Clear (correct) key $\boxed{C}$ or $\boxed{AC}$, the backspace key $\boxed{\blacktriangleright}$, and the $\boxed{+}$, $\boxed{-}$, $\boxed{\times}$, $\boxed{\div}$, and $\boxed{=}$ keys to solve problems.

The first step in using the Casio *fx*-260 for any problem is to press either the All Clear key $\boxed{AC}$ or $\boxed{ON}$. This clears the calculator and allows you to enter a new number. Be sure to clear your calculator's display as your first step in working all the problems in this book.

Adding Numbers

The Add Key and the Equals Key

The $\boxed{+}$ key is called the **add key** and is used to add numbers. The $\boxed{=}$ key is called the **equals key** and, when pressed, tells a calculator to display the answer to a calculation.

To see how the $\boxed{+}$ key and the $\boxed{=}$ key work together in a calculation, start by clearing the display. Then press the following keys in order:

What answer does your calculator display show?

Adding Two Numbers

If your calculator displayed 8, you already know how to add two numbers. The answer to an addition problem is called the **sum**. (**Remember:** Always clear your calculator display before beginning each new problem.)

EXAMPLE 1 To add 37 and 28 on your calculator, press the keys as shown.

Press Keys	Display Reads
3 7	37.
+	37.
2 8	28.
=	65.

ANSWER: 65

Discovery

- The display will not show a + sign.
- The answer appears only after you press =.
- You must clear your calculator before you start a new problem.

EXAMPLE 2 To add \$2.38 and \$1.09 on your calculator, press the keys as shown.

Press Keys	Display Reads
2 . 3 8	2.38
+	2.38
1 . 0 9	1.09
=	3.47

ANSWER: \$3.47

Fill in the numbers and operations to show what keys you would press to solve each problem. Do not write the solution.

1. 8 + 4 = 8 + 4 =
2. 39 + 17 = ☐☐☐☐☐☐
3. 2,063 + 989 = ☐☐☐☐☐☐☐☐☐
4. \$5.09 + \$4.26 = ☐☐☐☐☐☐☐☐☐☐
5. 128 + 89 ☐☐☐☐☐☐☐
6. \$7.90 + 3.78 ☐☐☐☐☐☐☐☐☐☐

7. thirty-five plus fourteen

☐ ☐ ☐ ☐ ☐ ☐

8. the sum of one hundred fifty-seven and sixty-one

☐ ☐ ☐ ☐ ☐ ☐ ☐

9. five thousand, two hundred nine plus two thousand, four hundred

☐ ☐ ☐ ☐ ☐ ☐ ☐ ☐ ☐

10. four dollars and fifty cents added to six dollars and twelve cents

☐ ☐ ☐ ☐ ☐ ☐ ☐ ☐ ☐

Use your calculator to solve each of the following problems. Remember to clear your calculator before you start a new problem.

11. $41 + 18 =$ $450 + 207 =$ $1{,}950 + 872 =$

12. $\$0.98 + \$0.67 =$ $\$34.09 + \$20.98 =$ $\$245.75 + \$169.99 =$

13. $348 + 121 =$ $658 + 469 =$ $635 + 122 =$

14. $\$886 + \$527 =$ $\$4.23 + \$2.45 =$ $\$6.93 + \$4.58 =$

15. What is the combined weight of the pickup and trailer?

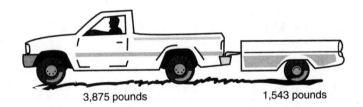

3,875 pounds   1,543 pounds

Keying Errors

Pressing the wrong key is called a **keying error.** When people use calculators, keying errors are very common. In fact, keying errors are so common that you must always be alert to them!

There are three main types of keying errors.

- pressing the wrong key
  Example: Pressing [8] [2] instead of [9] [2].

- double keying—accidentally pressing the same key twice
  Example: Pressing [4] [7] [7] instead of [4] [7].

- transposing digits—pressing keys in the wrong order
  Example: Pressing [3] [5] instead of [5] [3].

As you practice your calculator skills throughout this book, be careful to check your display so you avoid each type of keying error. If you make a keying error, use the Clear key [C], All Clear key [AC], or backspace key [▶] to correct the error.

For each problem below, indicate by a check (✓) which type of error was made. Then fill in the blank keys to show the correct way to key each problem.

Problem to Solve	Keys Pressed	Wrong Key	Double Keying	Transposing Digits
1. 27 + 18 =	[2] [7] [+] [1] [1] [8] [=]	_____	_____	_____
Correct:	( ) ( ) ( ) ( ) ( ) ( )			
2. $20 + $39 =	[2] [0] [+] [9] [3] [=]	_____	_____	_____
Correct:	( ) ( ) ( ) ( ) ( ) ( )			
3. 153 + 89 =	[1] [4] [3] [+] [5] [9] [=]	_____	_____	_____
Correct:	( ) ( ) ( ) ( ) ( ) ( )			
4. $0.67 + $0.49 =	[·] [7] [6] [+] [·] [4] [9] [=]	_____	_____	_____
Correct:	( ) ( ) ( ) ( ) ( ) ( ) ( )			

Note: When you have a number such as $20, as in problem 2 above, you can enter 20 or 20.00 on your calculator. If you enter 20.00, the Casio *fx*-260 displays [20.] as soon as you press the [+] key. When you have a number such as $0.67, as in problem 4 above, the calculator displays [0.67] whether you enter .67 or 0.67.

Adding Three or More Numbers

To add three or more numbers, a calculator adds the first two. Then it keeps adding the next number to the previous sum.

EXAMPLE   Add $24.87 + $12.99 + $8.35.

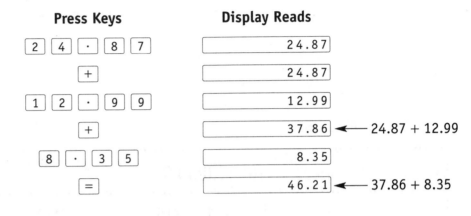

Press Keys	Display Reads	
2 4 . 8 7	24.87	
+	24.87	
1 2 . 9 9	12.99	
+	37.86	← 24.87 + 12.99
8 . 3 5	8.35	
=	46.21	← 37.86 + 8.35

ANSWER: $46.21

> **Discovery:** The Casio *fx*-260 displays a value each time the ⊞ key is pressed. That value is the result of the calculations up to that moment.

Estimating: Spotting Keying Errors Using Rounded Numbers

Suppose you use your calculator and find the sum at the right. A quick check to identify keying errors is to round each number and use mental math to add the rounded values.

$$\begin{array}{r} 59 \\ 81 \\ +\ 37 \\ \hline 147 \end{array}$$

	rounds to	
59	→	60
81	→	80
+ 37	→	+ 40
	Estimate is:	180

The estimated value 180 is not close to 147, so use your calculator and try the problem again.

$$59 + 81 + 37 = 177$$

The value 177 agrees with the estimate of 180. The value 147 was incorrect, probably due to a keying error.

For each problem, first estimate the value. Then use your calculator to find the sum. Remember to clear your calculator before each problem.

1. $354 + 227 + 100 =$

2.
$$\begin{array}{r} \$8.43 \\ 3.57 \\ +\ 0.98 \\ \hline \end{array}$$

3. $\$7.56 + \$0.08 + \$124.90 =$

4.
$$\begin{array}{r} 649 \\ 1,334 \\ 1,610 \\ +\ 2,930 \\ \hline \end{array}$$

5. $\$330 + \$590 + \$2,450 + \$420 =$

6. Complete the Production Log.

Production Log		
	2/11–2/18	**2/21–2/28**
Monday	965	3,001
Tuesday	4,216	2,333
Wednesday	3,139	2,060
Thursday	1,116	1,575
Friday	782	2,906
Weekly Total		

A student used the Casio *fx*-260 to solve the following problems. Because of keying errors, four of the problems have *wrong answers*. Use estimation to spot the four problems with wrong answers. Then use your calculator to find correct answers.

7.
$$\begin{array}{r} 28 \\ 17 \\ +\ 9 \\ \hline 54 \end{array}$$

8.
$$\begin{array}{r} 354 \\ 227 \\ +\ 100 \\ \hline 681 \end{array}$$

9.
$$\begin{array}{r} \$8.43 \\ 3.57 \\ +\ 0.98 \\ \hline \$15.98 \end{array}$$

10.
$$\begin{array}{r} \$365 \\ 154 \\ +\ 116 \\ \hline \$935 \end{array}$$

11.
$$\begin{array}{r} 231 \\ 106 \\ +\ 53 \\ \hline 290 \end{array}$$

12.
$$\begin{array}{r} \$28.90 \\ 17.83 \\ +\ 13.58 \\ \hline \$60.31 \end{array}$$

13.
$$\begin{array}{r} \$6.90 \\ 8.23 \\ +\ 4.50 \\ \hline \$19.63 \end{array}$$

14.
$$\begin{array}{r} 5,675 \\ 1,476 \\ +\ 850 \\ \hline 2,794 \end{array}$$

Subtracting Numbers

The [–] key is called the **subtract key** and is used to subtract one number from another, or to find the difference between two numbers. The answer to a subtraction problem is called the **difference.**

<u>EXAMPLE 1</u> To subtract 37 from 108 on your calculator, press keys as shown.

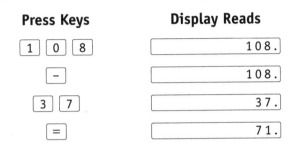

Press Keys	Display Reads
1 0 8	108.
–	108.
3 7	37.
=	71.

ANSWER: 71

You can use your calculator for an expression such as 20 – 3 – 5 – 3 by pressing [–] before each new subtraction. Press [=] only once, after you enter the last number.

<u>EXAMPLE 2</u> Stan paid $11.98 for a hammer plus $0.60 tax. How much change did Stan get from a $20 bill?

To solve, start with $20 and subtract each amount.

Press Keys	Display Reads
2 0 . 0 0	20.00
–	20.
1 1 . 9 8	11.98
–	8.02
. 6 0	0.60
=	7.42

ANSWER: $7.42

> **Reminder:** When you have numbers such as $20, you can enter 20.00 or just 20. Many people prefer to enter all of the 0s as a reminder that they are working with dollars and cents.

> **Discovery:**
> Try the following subtraction problem on your calculator:
>
> | You subtract | The display reads |
> |---|---|
> | $0.35 – $0.15 | 0.2 |
>
> The answer is $0.20, but the display reads 0.2.
> • A calculator does not display a 0 that is at the right-hand end of the decimal part of an answer.
> • When you write an answer in money, remember to write two digits in the decimal part.

Fill in the numbers and operations to show what keys you would press to solve each problem. Do not write the solution.

1. the difference between eighty-six and forty-nine

   ☐ ☐ ☐ ☐ ☐ ☐

2. two hundred seventeen subtracted from five hundred eight

   ☐ ☐ ☐ ☐ ☐ ☐ ☐ .

3. ten dollars minus seven dollars and ninety-two cents

   ☐ ☐ ☐ ☐ ☐ ☐ ☐

4. eight dollars minus three dollars and eleven cents

   ☐ ☐ ☐ ☐ ☐ ☐ ☐

5. Show another set of numbers and operations for problems 3 and 4.

Use your calculator to solve each of the following problems. Remember to clear your calculator before each problem.

6. $119 - 57 - 28 =$

7. $\$20.00 - \$13.89 - \$3.19 =$

8. As pictured at the right, how many pounds heavier than the sports car is the van?

4,138 pounds

2,869 pounds

9. Mari paid for her lunch, shown at the right, with a $10 bill. If her tax is $0.35, how much change should Mari be given?

Coffee $1.25

Ham & Cheese Sandwich $4.45

10. The last time this water meter was read, it read 61,357 gallons. How many gallons have been used recently?

gallons

Calculators and Word Problems

Have you ever thought, "Wow, that calculator is really fast!" Yet, as fast and amazing as it is, a calculator can't tell you

- which numbers are important
- whether to add or to subtract
- whether the answer you compute is correct

Five Steps for Solving Word Problems

When solving word problems, you may find it useful to follow this problem-solving approach.

STEP 1 Read the word problem and find the key information.

STEP 2 Estimate an answer.

STEP 3 Choose the operation (add, subtract, multiply, or divide) and set up a calculation.

STEP 4 Perform and check the calculation(s).

STEP 5 Reread the word problem and see if your answer makes sense.

Word Clues

You can use word clues to help you decide which operation to use when solving a problem.

Addition: Look for items or values that need to be combined. Look for words that indicate addition, such as:

combined with	sum	added to	total
in all	plus	altogether	

Subtraction: Look for items or values that are taken away. Look for words that indicate subtraction, such as:

how much more	how much less	what is the difference	take away
less	minus		

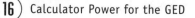

Read the paragraph below and answer each question.

Nathan traded in his Ford for a new Honda. Although the sticker price was $23,450, the salesperson lowered this price by $1,875. Nathan was also given a trade-in allowance of $7,250, although the Ford was only worth $6,525. Using his trade-in as a down payment, Nathan wanted to know how much he still owed for the Honda.

1. What is the key information?

2. What rounded numbers should you use to estimate an answer?

3. What operations should you use?

4. What answer results from each operation you perform?

5. Does your answer make sense?

Building Confidence with Word Problems

Carefully read word problems A and B and do the exercises that follow.

A. Last weekend, Hamburger Heaven sold $1,843 worth of hamburgers, $1,257 worth of fries, and $1,385 worth of drinks. How much money did Hamburger Heaven take in on these three products last weekend?

B. Last weekend, Hamburger Heaven sold $50 worth of hamburgers, $20 worth of fries, and $30 worth of drinks. How much money did Hamburger Heaven take in on these three products last weekend?

For problems 6 and 7, check (✓) the one answer that most closely expresses your opinion.

6. Which problem above, A or B, seems more difficult?

   A _____   B _____   About the same _____

7. If you checked A or B above, why do you think that problem was more difficult than the other?

   _____ Different situations are described.

   _____ The harder problem contains larger numbers.

   _____ The harder problem is longer.

If you're like most students, you think problem A is more difficult. Why? Most likely because it contains larger numbers. By using a calculator, you can concentrate on solving the problem. All types of numbers—large and small—become easier to work with.

Estimating

Herald Gazette

Read All About It!
Math Common Sense Rescues Shopper
Lilly Sharp was sharper than a cash register yesterday when she was about to be charged $45.29 for some purchases. Saved by her common sense, Lilly insisted that the cashier ring up her total again. This time the total was $26.29. Sharp reported, "I bought things for $11.59, $9.95, and $4.75. I knew I spent less than 12 dollars plus 10 dollars plus 5 dollars. I can't afford not to be careful!"

Lilly may be fictional, but her story illustrates an important fact.

• Being able to spot an incorrect answer is a very valuable skill.

Sometimes you can spot a wrong answer by using **math intuition** or **common sense.** You can **estimate** or **approximate** a value to check a calculator or cash register result.

• Math intuition comes from thinking about what an answer should be. Estimation told Lilly that her purchases cost less than $27.

• To estimate, you use rounded numbers. Rounded numbers are easier to work with than exact values.

EXAMPLE 1   On another occasion, Lilly paid for a $28.63 purchase with a $50 bill. Is $12.37 a reasonable amount of change?

Lilly expected to get about $20 in change. Lilly thought, "$28.63 is about $30, and $50 − $30 is $20. My change should be about $20. So $12.37 is not enough change!"

As Lilly discovered, the best protection against calculator error is the ability to spot a wrong answer. And estimating is your most helpful tool.

Throughout the rest of this book, you'll use estimation to check calculator answers. By using estimation to catch keying errors, you'll learn to use a calculator accurately and confidently.

Estimating with Whole Numbers

To estimate, replace each number in a problem with a **rounded number.** A rounded number has zeros to the right of a chosen place value, such as the tens place, the hundreds place, the thousands place, and so on.

For example, $28.63 rounded to the nearest ten dollars is $30.00.

<u>EXAMPLE 2</u> Estimate an answer for the addition problem at the right.

To do this, round each number to the nearest hundred. Then add.

Problem	Estimate
912	900
786	800
+ 328	+ 300
2,026 ← close → 2,000	

....

Estimate an answer to each problem by rounding. Round each number to the nearest ten. The first one is done for you.

		Estimate		Estimate		Estimate
1.	89	90	48		92	
	+72	+ 70	+ 33		− 41	
		160				

Round each number to the nearest hundred.

		Estimate		Estimate		Estimate
2.	488	500	897		$724	
	− 213	− 200	+108		− 336	
		300				

Round each number to the nearest thousand.

		Estimate		Estimate		Estimate
3.	4,927	5,000	7,849		12,193	
	+ 2,083	+ 2,000	+ 4,906		− 7,826	
		7,000				

Find the best estimate for the answer to each problem below.

Computation Problems

_____ **4.** 38 + 54 =

_____ **5.** 92 − 33 =

_____ **6.** 22 + 19 + 9 =

_____ **7.** 189 − 93 =

_____ **8.** 234 + 512 =

Estimates

a. 50

b. 100

c. 700

d. 90

e. 60

Problems 9 and 10 are based on the following diagram.

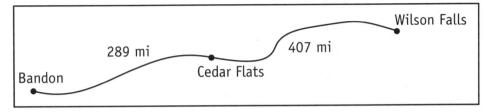

Bandon — 289 mi — Cedar Flats — 407 mi — Wilson Falls

9. What is the distance between Bandon and Wilson Falls?

_____
estimate

_____
exact

10. How much farther is the distance from Cedar Flats to Wilson Falls than the distance from Cedar Flats to Bandon?

_____
estimate

_____
exact

11. At a yard sale on Sunday, Jesse bought tools for $23.88 and an electric motor for $19.95. He also bought a small vise. After writing a check for $60.00, Jesse received $3.89 in change. How much did Jesse spend in all? (**Hint:** Necessary information: $3.89, $60.00; Extra information: $23.88, $19.95)

_____
estimate

_____
exact

12. Of the 91 people entered in the Senior Jog-A-Thon, 19 are over 65 years of age and only 29 are under 50 years of age. More than half, 49 to be exact, are women. Given these figures, determine the number of men entered in this year's Senior Jog-A-Thon.

_____
estimate

_____
exact

13. On the invoice shown at the right, what is the total cost of the three newly purchased items, not counting the cost of the insurance, shipping, and C.O.D. service charges?

_____
estimate

_____
exact

Anderson Manufacturing Company

Item #	Description	Quantity	Amount
28474B	Brass Table Lamp	1	$89.96
10277C	Oval Wall Mirror	1	$38.75
03278E	4-Shelf Bookcase	1	$48.89
	Insurance		$4.75
	Shipping		$23.85
	C.O.D. Service Charge		$8.00
		TOTAL COST	$176.31

Application: Balancing a Checkbook

Balancing a checkbook involves keeping a careful record of all the transactions: writing checks, making deposits, and paying bank service charges. A calculator can save you lots of time, especially if you need to recheck your work when your checkbook and bank statements don't match.

Recording Transactions

Below is a sample **check register,** a page in a checkbook. The account holder, Leona Jenson, is not charged a fee for the checks that she writes or for the deposits that she makes.

Number	Date	Description of Transaction	Payment/ Debit (−)	✓ T	Fee (−)	Deposit/ Credit (+)	Balance $1568 43	
202	6/1	North Street Apartments	$ 825 00		$	$	743	43
203	6/4	Amy's Market	39 74					
204	6/8	Import Auto Repair	109 66					
	6/15	Payroll Deposit				1442 45		
205	6/19	Value Pharmacy	13 29					
206	6/21	Gazette Times	18 75					

1. Use your calculator to determine each daily balance in Leona's checking account. Record your answers in the BALANCE column.

   • Subtract each check (PAYMENT/DEBIT column) from the BALANCE column.

   • Add each deposit (DEPOSIT/CREDIT column) to the BALANCE column.

2. Record the following new transactions in the register. Then compute Leona's daily balance up through June 30 and enter it on each line in the BALANCE column.

   Check 207, written to Nelsen's on June 23 for $39.83
   Check 208, written to Hi-Ho Foods on June 24 for $63.79
   Check reorder charge of $26.50 on June 26
   Payroll deposit of $1442.45 on June 30

Multiplying Numbers

The ⊠ key is called the **multiply key** and is used to multiply two numbers. The answer to a multiplication problem is call the **product**. Multiplication is a quick way of adding.

> The word clues for multiplication are often the same as those for addition: *total*, *in all*, and *altogether*.

EXAMPLE 1 To multiply 235 times 54 on your calculator, press keys as shown.

Press Keys	Display Reads
[2] [3] [5]	235.
[×]	235.
[5] [4]	54.
[=]	12690.

ANSWER: 12,690

As shown in Example 2 below, more than two numbers can be multiplied by pressing ⊠ before each new multiplication. As in addition and subtraction, you press [=] only once, after entering the final number to be multiplied.

EXAMPLE 2 Oil is on sale for $2.19 per quart. How much do 7 cases of oil cost if each case contains 12 quarts?

To solve, multiply $2.19 by the total number of quarts—the number of quarts per case (12) times the number of cases (7).

$2.19 × 12 × 7 =

Press Keys	Display Reads
[2] [.] [1] [9]	2.19
[×]	2.19
[1] [2] *number of quarts per case*	12.
[×]	26.28
[7] *number of cases*	7.
[=]	183.96

ANSWER: $183.96

Fill in the numbers and the symbols to show how you would key in each problem. Do not write the solution.

1. the product of seventy-six and forty

   ☐ ☐ ☒ ☐ ☐ ☐=

2. one hundred six times eighty-eight

   ☐ ☐ ☐ ☐ ☐ ☐ ☐

3. multiply nine dollars and four cents by seven

   ☐ ☐ ☐ ☐ ☐ ☐ ☐

Compute both an exact answer and an estimate for each problem below. Remember that estimates can help you see if you have made keying errors.

- **Round numbers between 10 and 100 to the nearest ten.**

- **Round numbers greater than 100 to the nearest hundred.**

	Exact	Estimate		Exact	Estimate		Exact	Estimate
4.	48	50		67			88	
	× 32	× 30		× 59			× 19	
		1,500						

	Exact	Estimate		Exact	Estimate		Exact	Estimate
5.	192			289			207	
	× 57			× 32			× 74	

Use your calculator to solve each of the following problems. Remember to clear your calculator before each problem.

6. $7 \times 8 \times 5 =$ $19 \times 8 \times 6 =$ $23 \times 17 \times 5 =$

7. $74 \times 28 \times 3 =$ $143 \times 7 \times 2 =$ $258 \times 127 \times 3 =$

8. $\$23.45 \times 6 =$ $\$12.74 \times 20 =$ $\$52.09 \times 18 =$

9. At a Labor Day sale, how much will Brad pay for four cases of orange juice concentrate?

Labor Day Special
Orange Juice Concentrate
$0.89 per can

1 case

24 cans

Dividing Numbers

To divide is to see how many times one number (called the **divisor**) can go into a second number (called the **dividend**). The answer to a division problem is called the **quotient.**

> Divide when you have a total and need to find equal parts. Some word clues for division are *each* and *average.*

As a quick review, the three ways that division problems are usually written are shown below.

$$27\overline{)675}^{\,25}$$

$$675 \div 27 = 25$$
dividend ÷ divisor = quotient

$$\frac{675}{27} = 25$$

$$\text{divisor}\overline{)\text{dividend}}^{\,\text{quotient}}$$

$$\frac{\text{dividend}}{\text{divisor}} = \text{quotient}$$

To divide on your calculator, follow these steps.

STEP 1 Enter the dividend.

STEP 2 Press ⌈÷⌉, the divide key.

STEP 3 Enter the divisor.

STEP 4 Press ⌈=⌉.

EXAMPLE 1 $49\overline{)833}$

To solve, press keys as shown.

Press Keys	Display Reads
8 3 3	833.
÷	833.
4 9	49.
=	17.

ANSWER: 17

EXAMPLE 2 $\$39.76 \div 7 =$

Clear your calculator display. Then press keys as shown.

Press Keys	Display Reads
3 9 . 7 6	39.76
÷	39.76
7	7.
=	5.68

ANSWER: $5.68

Identify the dividend and divisor in each problem below. Then show how you would key in each problem. Do not write the answers.

1. $19\overline{)152}$ dividend _____
   divisor _____

   ☐ ☐ ☐ ☐ ☐ ☐ ☐

2. $\$19.68 \div 8$ dividend _____
   divisor _____

   ☐ ☐ ☐ ☐ ☐ ☐ ☐

3. $\dfrac{361.56}{23}$ dividend _____
   divisor _____

   ☐ ☐ ☐ ☐ ☐ ☐ ☐ ☐

4. $27\overline{)576}$ dividend _____
   divisor _____

   ☐ ☐ ☐ ☐ ☐ ☐ ☐

Estimate each quotient. Then use your calculator to compute an exact answer.

5.

Problem	Estimate	Exact Quotient
$418 \div 19$		
$693 \div 21$		
$288 \div 18$		

Use your calculator to solve each of the following problems. (Hint: Some problems may require multiplication.)

6. $11\overline{)495}$ $364 \div 14$ $19\overline{)\$912}$ $\dfrac{1,708}{28}$

7. Two hundred fifty-six people plan to attend this year's church picnic. If one table can seat eight people, how many tables will be needed in all?

> **Discovery:** On some word problems, you may not know whether to multiply or divide. Do both on your calculator! Only one of the two answers will make sense.

8. Mrs. Owens gives 21 music lessons each week for a total of $735. How much does she charge for each lesson?

9. Last week Joni worked a total of 39 hours. If her hourly pay rate is $8.75, how much were Joni's earnings last week before taxes?

10. The Oregon state lottery prize of $19,972,800 is to be divided equally among 9 winners. Determine each winner's share.

11. West Side Tool Manufacturing makes and ships 4,392 wrenches each day. If a full shipping box contains 18 wrenches, how many boxes are needed each day by West Side Tool?

12. The professional wrestling match between the Slippery Savage and Pretty Boy MacDougal attracted 7,090 fans. Each paid $4.75 for a ticket. What amount of money was brought in from ticket sales for this match?

Problems 13–16 refer to the following story. Each question requires its own specific information. This information may be entirely in the story, or it may be partly in the question itself. Choose information carefully as you answer each question.

Maria works as a secretary at Jackson Bookkeeping Services. For her work she receives $330 each week. Only one year ago, though, Maria worked as a receptionist at an office and earned $268 each week.

Maria's husband, Mel, earns $34,580 each year as a lab technician at Lewis Electronic Fabricators.

13. When Maria worked as a receptionist, how much could she earn in one year if she worked all 52 weeks?

14. In her job as a secretary, how much does Maria now earn each year if she is paid for 52 weeks of work?

15. Assuming she works 40 hours each week, what is Maria paid hourly as a secretary?

16. Determine Mel's average weekly pay. Assume he is paid for 52 weeks.

Multistep Word Problems

Solving some problems involves more than one step.

EXAMPLE 1 Ellen is buying 6 bottles of hair conditioner on sale. Each bottle costs $2.89. How much change will Ellen receive if she pays the clerk with a $20 bill?

Solving this problem takes two steps: multiplication and subtraction.

STEP 1 Multiply to find the cost of the conditioner.

$2.89 × 6 = $17.34

STEP 2 Subtract to find Ellen's change from $20.

$20.00 − $17.34 = $2.66

There are two methods for using a calculator to solve a multistep problem.

- **Method I:** Use pencil and paper to record and use the results from each step.

  STEP 1 Multiply to find the cost of the conditioner. Then write the cost, $17.34, on paper so you don't forget it.

  STEP 2 Clear the display and enter $20.00. Subtract $17.34 from $20.00 to get the answer $2.66.

- **Method II:** Use the **memory keys** to save and use the results of each step. Pencil and paper are not needed.

Exploring Your Calculator's Memory

The calculator's memory can help you solve problems that involve more than one step.

Uses of Memory Keys

- Pressing [M+] adds the displayed number to the memory. You will see M appear in the display when a number is entered into the memory.

- Pressing [SHIFT] [M−] subtracts the displayed number from the memory.

- Pressing [MR] Memory Recall displays the total currently stored in memory.

- Pressing [ON] clears the memory and the display.

- Pressing [0] [SHIFT] [X ↔ M] (over the [C] key) clears the memory, but NOT the display.

- Pressing [C] clears the display but not the memory.

EXAMPLE 2 Jake teaches music at the elementary and middle schools. On Monday, Wednesday, and Friday, he drives 8 miles round trip from his home to the elementary school. On Tuesday and Thursday he drives 5 miles round trip to the middle school. How many miles does he drive to and from school in a week?

	Press Keys	Display Reads
In the sequence shown at the right, pressing M+ does three things:	8 × 3	
• It completes the multiplication of 8 and 3.	M+	24.
• It displays the answer 24.	5 × 2	
• It stores the number 24 in the memory.	M+	10.
MR displays the total (34) that is stored in memory.	MR	34.

ANSWER: 34 MILES

EXAMPLE 3 Ellen is buying 6 bottles of hair conditioner on sale. Each bottle costs $2.89. How much change will Ellen receive if she pays the clerk with a $20 bill?

Press Keys	Display Reads
6 × 2.89	
M+	17.34
20 − MR =	2.66

ANSWER: $2.66

Discovery: When adding a list of numbers, you may make a mistake on one entry. If you do, press the clear key C to clear the display. Then reenter the number correctly and continue adding. In this way, **you do not need to redo the whole problem.** You may also use the backspace key ▶ to correct an error in the entry.

Use the calculator memory keys to solve each problem. Remember to clear the calculator before each problem.

1. In the *News Tribune*, a weekend classified ad costs $15.75 for the first 16 words. Additional words are charged at the rate of $0.95 per word. At this rate, how much will Randi pay for a 24-word ad?

2. The brochure at the right lists the child-care charges at the Little Bunnies Center. Li leaves her daughter at the center three full days each week and two half days. What amount is Li charged each week for child care?

    Little Bunnies Center

    Child-Care Rates

Full Day	$28.75
Half Day	$17.75
Hourly	$5.50

3. At Twin Pines Hardware Store, Denise bought 6 gallons of white paint at $12.48 per gallon and 3 quarts of blue paint at $4.29 per quart. What was her bill before taxes?

4. As assistant manager of Burger Supreme, Adah keeps track of weekly sales figures. The figures for the week of March 3 are shown at the right. By how much is this week's total below Burger Supreme's weekly average of $85,283.28?

    Sales Figures Starting 3/3

Monday	$11,472.25
Tuesday	$11,784.04
Wednesday	$11,800.34
Thursday	$12,028.50
Friday	$12,135.79
Saturday	$12,465.93
Sunday	$12,233.34
Total:	

Application: Depositing Money in a Checking Account

Retail businesses (those which sell directly to the public) take in money and checks every day. Accurately counting these receipts and depositing them in the company checking account is an important employee responsibility. Needless to say, a calculator can be a big help in a job like this.

The following definitions are used on a **checking account deposit slip.**
- **Currency:** paper money such as five-dollar bills
- **Coin:** pennies, nickels, dimes, and so on
- **Cash Received:** money that you request the bank to give back to you from your deposit
- **Net Deposit:** the amount you actually deposit, which is the TOTAL minus CASH RECEIVED

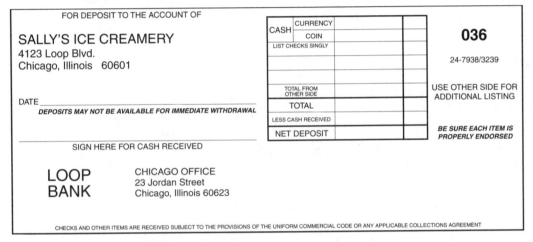

Each Tuesday morning, Brett deposits the business receipts of Sally's Ice Creamery. Today's deposit consists of the money indicated below.

Coins	Currency	Checks	
150 pennies	1,168 one-dollar bills	#24-72	$44.89
80 nickels	137 five-dollar bills	#31-29	$39.85
250 dimes	29 ten-dollar bills	#42-16	$120.00
160 quarters	33 twenty-dollar bills		

Use your calculator and write each of the following on the deposit slip.

1. the total amount of CURRENCY
2. the total amount of COIN
3. the amount of each CHECK
4. the TOTAL (CURRENCY, COIN, and CHECKS). The amount of CASH RECEIVED is zero, so write the TOTAL in the space labeled NET DEPOSIT.

Calculator Division and Remainders

Remainders in Division

Many division problems contain a remainder as part of the answer. For example, if you divide 17 sheets of drawing paper among 5 students, each student gets 3 sheets. Since 5×3 is 15, 2 sheets are left over. Dividing 17 by 5 gives an answer of 3 with a remainder of 2.

There are three ways to write a remainder.

1. as a whole number following r

$$\begin{array}{r} 3\,r\,2 \\ 5\overline{)17} \\ \underline{15} \\ 2 \end{array}$$

2. as the numerator of a fraction

$$\begin{array}{r} 3\frac{2}{5} \\ 5\overline{)17} \\ \underline{15} \\ 2 \end{array}$$

3. as a decimal fraction

$$\begin{array}{r} 3.4 \\ 5\overline{)17.0} \\ \underline{15} \\ 2\;0 \\ \underline{2\;0} \end{array}$$

Calculator Division

When dividing whole numbers with your calculator, the calculator displays a remainder as a decimal fraction. When you work with dollars, a decimal fraction represents cents.

For some problems, if the calculator shows a decimal remainder, you need to round to the next whole number.

EXAMPLE 1 Lena is packing 16 books in each box. How many boxes will she need for 189 books?

To solve, divide 189 by 16. The whole number part of the answer tells us that 11 boxes will be filled with books ($11 \times 16 = 176$). There is a remainder, so one more box will be needed. (That box will have $189 - 176 = 13$ books.)

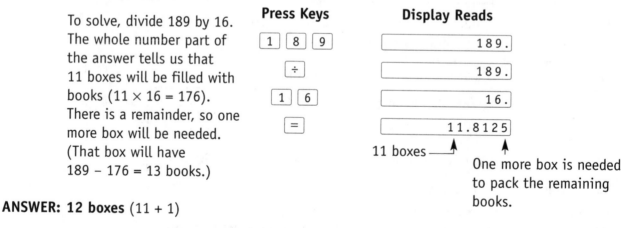

ANSWER: 12 boxes (11 + 1)

Use your calculator to solve each problem.

1. A schoolbus can transport 80 students. How many buses are needed to transport 475 students?

2. A computer disk can hold electronic files for 35 photographs. How many computer disks are needed to hold electronic files for 450 photographs?

Finding the Value of a Remainder

In some problems, you want to know the value of a remainder.

EXAMPLE 1 Jason needs to haul 94 cubic yards of dirt by the end of the day. His truck can carry a maximum of 12 cubic yards. Assuming he fills his truck when possible, how much dirt will Jason carry on his final load?

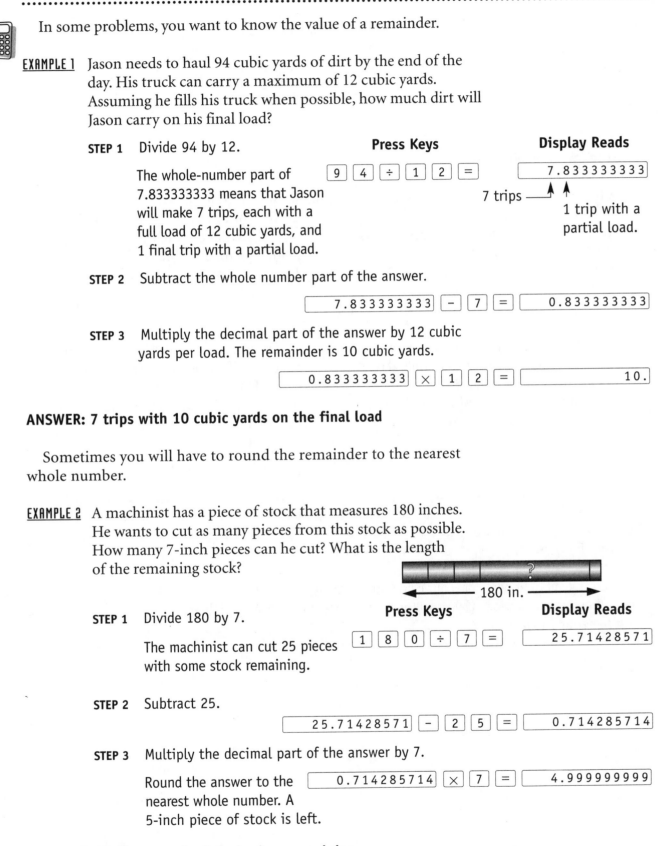

STEP 1 Divide 94 by 12.

Press Keys   **Display Reads**

The whole-number part of 7.833333333 means that Jason will make 7 trips, each with a full load of 12 cubic yards, and 1 final trip with a partial load.

$\boxed{9}\ \boxed{4}\ \boxed{\div}\ \boxed{1}\ \boxed{2}\ \boxed{=}$ $\boxed{7.833333333}$

7 trips ⟶   1 trip with a partial load.

STEP 2 Subtract the whole number part of the answer.

$\boxed{7.833333333}\ \boxed{-}\ \boxed{7}\ \boxed{=}\ \boxed{0.833333333}$

STEP 3 Multiply the decimal part of the answer by 12 cubic yards per load. The remainder is 10 cubic yards.

$\boxed{0.833333333}\ \boxed{\times}\ \boxed{1}\ \boxed{2}\ \boxed{=}\ \boxed{10.}$

ANSWER: 7 trips with 10 cubic yards on the final load

Sometimes you will have to round the remainder to the nearest whole number.

EXAMPLE 2 A machinist has a piece of stock that measures 180 inches. He wants to cut as many pieces from this stock as possible. How many 7-inch pieces can he cut? What is the length of the remaining stock?

⟵ 180 in. ⟶

STEP 1 Divide 180 by 7.

Press Keys   **Display Reads**

The machinist can cut 25 pieces with some stock remaining.

$\boxed{1}\ \boxed{8}\ \boxed{0}\ \boxed{\div}\ \boxed{7}\ \boxed{=}\ \boxed{25.71428571}$

STEP 2 Subtract 25.

$\boxed{25.71428571}\ \boxed{-}\ \boxed{2}\ \boxed{5}\ \boxed{=}\ \boxed{0.714285714}$

STEP 3 Multiply the decimal part of the answer by 7.

Round the answer to the nearest whole number. A 5-inch piece of stock is left.

$\boxed{0.714285714}\ \boxed{\times}\ \boxed{7}\ \boxed{=}\ \boxed{4.999999999}$

ANSWER: 25 pieces and a 5-inch piece remaining

Use your calculator. Write each answer as a whole number and a remainder.

1. $258 \div 17 =$ _____ r _____

2. $494 \div 53 =$ _____ r _____

3. $749 \div 41 =$ _____ r _____

4. $980 \div 25 =$ _____ r _____

5. $1{,}260 \div 81 =$ _____ r _____

6. $45{,}620 \div 200 =$ _____ r _____

Solve each word problem below.

7. A bolt of yard goods has 47 yards of fabric on it. Sue is making dance costumes. Each costume requires 3 yards of fabric. How many costumes can she make? How much fabric will be left?

8. Jason agreed to remove 114 cubic yards of gravel from a building site. Assuming he again carries 12 cubic yards each full load, how many cubic yards of gravel will Jason carry on his final load?

9. On a cross-country trip, Shari drove 350 miles each day except her final day. If she drove a total of 3,185 miles, determine the number of miles Shari drove the final day of the trip.

10. A worker has produced 1,497 parts in his 8-hour shift. The parts are shipped 75 in a box. How many boxes will he fill and how many parts are left over to start a new box?

Discovery: Once in a while, you may accidentally try to do a calculation that your calculator is unable to do. The calculator will then display an **error symbol**—an E. Here is an example.
Division by 0 error: Trying to divide by 0. You cannot divide by 0.
Example: $45 \div 0$

	- E -

If an error symbol appears on your calculator display, press [AC] or [ON] and redo your calculation. If you still get an error symbol, do the problem with paper and pencil.

Whole Numbers and Money Review

This review covers the material you have just studied. When you finish, check your answers at the back of the book.

Use your calculator to solve each problem.

1. Write the number nine hundred fifty.

2. What is 431 subtracted from 807?

3. Find the quotient and remainder for $45,622 \div 300$.

4. Complete the following check register by calculating the cash balance after each transaction.

Number	Date	Description of Transaction	Payment/ Debit (−)		✓ T	Fee (−)		Deposit/ Credit (+)		Balance $ 186 40	
110	5/6	Dr. William Tuff	$	45 43							
	5/10	Deposit						$	220 15		
111	5/15	Allen's Hardware	$	83 56							
112	5/16	Amberst Insurance	$	176 45							

5. A plumbing contractor bought a new van for $26,020. It is estimated that the van will decrease in value $4,500 the first year; $2,900 the second year; $2,500 the third year; and $1,000 for each of the fourth and fifth years. What will be the estimated value of the van after five years?

6. Paul Hale is paid for each acceptable part he makes at work. During the week, he made the following: Monday 413; Tuesday 305; Wednesday 540; Thursday 298; Friday 397. Forty-eight parts were rejected for quality issues. How many parts was he paid for?

7. Bill purchased a stereo for $498. He put $120 down and will pay the balance in 12 monthly installments. How much will each monthly payment be?

8. **a.** An assembly requires 6 bolts. Chuck has 98 bolts. How many assemblies can he complete?

   b. How many more bolts does he need to complete another assembly?

9. Complete the calculations on the invoice below to find the total invoice amount. Use the memory on your calculator.

DICH'S SPORTING GOODS

Sold to: R. J. Cleary
32 Maplewood
Cottonwood, NY 13111

Invoice no. 3361
Date: March 15, 20____

Quantity	Description	Unit Price	Total Amount
50	Jump Ropes	$2.49	
1	Shuffleboard Set	$49.98	
10	Pkg. Golf Balls	$11.95	
5	Basketballs	$15.95	
2	Jump Suits #N-395	$31.75	
	Total:		

Whole Numbers and Money Review Chart

Circle the number of any problem that you missed and review the appropriate pages. A passing score is 7 correct answers. If you miss more than two questions, you should review this chapter.

PROBLEM NUMBERS	SHILL AREA	PRACTICE PAGES
1	place value	5–6
2	subtraction	13–14
3	division with remainder	30
4, 5, 9	applications	20, 29
6, 7	multistep word problems	26–28
8	finding the value of a remainder	31–32

DECIMALS

Working with decimals comes easily on a calculator. You have already used the decimal point key ⌈·⌉, tenths, and hundredths when you solved problems involving money.

Introducing Decimals

What's the most common use of decimals? You're correct if you answer, "Money!"

- Cents are the **decimal** part of a dollar.

If you enter keystrokes such as ⌈1⌉ ⌈1⌉ ⌈÷⌉ ⌈8⌉ ⌈=⌉, your calculator displays ⌈ 1.375⌉, which shows the second most common use of decimals.

- The remainder is often written as a decimal.

Reading Decimals

To get yourself ready to work with decimal-place values, review the meaning of each simple decimal below.

Decimal	Value	Meaning
0.1	one tenth	1 part out of 10 parts
0.01	one hundredth	1 part out of 100 parts
0.001	one thousandth	1 part out of 1,000 parts
0.0001	one ten-thousandth	1 part out of 10,000 parts
0.00001	one hundred-thousandth	1 part out of 100,000 parts
0.000001	one millionth	1 part out of 1,000,000 parts

EXAMPLE		Read the name of a decimal.	Decimal 1 0.042 ↑	Decimal 2 0.0070 ↑
	STEP 1	Identify the place value of the digit farthest to the right.	thousandths	ten-thousandths
	STEP 2	Read the number to the right of the decimal point. Ignore zeros at the left.	forty-two	seventy
	STEP 3	Read the number and the place value together.	**forty-two thousandths**	**seventy ten-thousandths**

Mixed Decimals

A **mixed decimal** is a whole number plus a decimal. The number 7.18 is a mixed decimal. The amount $3.99 is also a mixed decimal.

mixed decimal = whole number + decimal

When reading a mixed decimal, read the decimal point as the word *and*. Do not say *and* in any other part of the number. For example, 107.18 is read "one hundred seven *and* 18 hundredths." The money amount $1,075.99 is read "one thousand seventy-five dollars *and* 99 cents."

· ·

Write words to express the value of each decimal below.

1. 0.05 _____

2. 0.5 _____

3. 0.000005 _____

4. 0.005 _____

5. 0.00005 _____

6. 0.0005 _____

Determine the value of each displayed number below. Choose each answer from the choices given.

7. | 0.206 |
   a. 26 hundredths
   b. 206 hundredths
   c. 206 thousandths

8. | 0.047 |
   a. 47 tenths
   b. 47 hundredths
   c. 47 thousandths

9. | 0.7 |
   a. 7 tenths
   b. 7 hundredths
   c. 7 thousandths

10. | 0.15 |
    a. 15 hundredths
    b. 15 thousandths
    c. 150 ten-thousandths

Use your calculator to solve each of the following division problems. Choose the correct way to say the answer to the problem.

11. [1] [÷] [8] [=]
    a. 1 and 25 tenths
    b. 125 thousandths
    c. 1 and 25 hundredths

12. [9] [÷] [1] [0] [0] [=]
    a. 9 tenths
    b. 9 hundredths
    c. 9 thousandths

13. [3] [0] [÷] [8] [=]
    a. 375 hundredths
    b. 3 and 75 hundredths
    c. 3 and 75 thousandths

14. [5] [÷] [1] [6] [=]
    a. 3,125 hundredths
    b. 3,125 thousandths
    c. 3,125 ten-thousandths

Rounding Decimals

For most problems, you will only need one or two decimal places.

EXAMPLE 1 Gasoline prices are always given to three decimal places. If the price per gallon is $1.489, how much do 16 gallons of gas cost?

$1.489 × 16 = $23.824

This answer rounds to $23.82.

In many cases, a rounded answer will do. You can use the sign ≈ to mean "is approximately equal to."

$1.489 × 16 = $23.824 ≈ **$23.82**

Rounding a Decimal

Steps for rounding decimals:

STEP 1 Find the digit you wish to round to, and underline that digit.

STEP 2 Look at the digit to the right of the underlined digit.

- If the digit to the right is greater than or equal to 5, add 1 to the underlined digit.

- If the digit to the right is less than 5, leave the underlined digit as it is.

- Discard all digits to the right of the underlined digit.

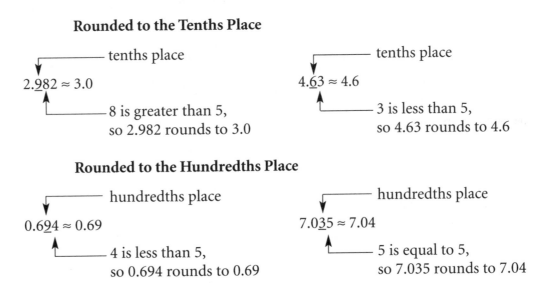

Rounded to the Tenths Place

tenths place

2.9̲82 ≈ 3.0

8 is greater than 5, so 2.982 rounds to 3.0

tenths place

4.6̲3 ≈ 4.6

3 is less than 5, so 4.63 rounds to 4.6

Rounded to the Hundredths Place

hundredths place

0.69̲4 ≈ 0.69

4 is less than 5, so 0.694 rounds to 0.69

hundredths place

7.03̲5 ≈ 7.04

5 is equal to 5, so 7.035 rounds to 7.04

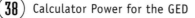

Using Your Calculator to Round Decimals

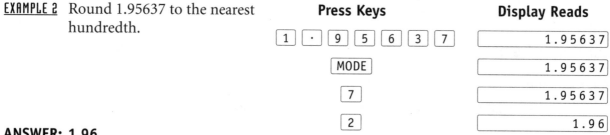

STEP 1 Enter the decimal number to be rounded or the problem to be solved.

STEP 2 Press MODE.

STEP 3 Press 7.

STEP 4 Press the digit on the calculator of the number of decimal places you want to round to. (Press 1 for tenths, 2 for hundredths, and so on.)

STEP 5 Press =. (FIX will appear in the display.)

EXAMPLE 2 Round 1.95637 to the nearest hundredth.

Press Keys	Display Reads
1 · 9 5 6 3 7	1.95637
MODE	1.95637
7	1.95637
2	1.96

ANSWER: 1.96

EXAMPLE 3 Premium gas is selling for $1.879 per gallon. How much will 21.4 gallons cost?

Press Keys	Display Reads
1 · 8 7 9	1.879
×	1.879
2 1 · 4	21.4
=	40.2106
MODE	40.2106
7	40.2106
2	40.21

ANSWER: $40.21

**Round each amount below to the nearest ten cents. Circle one of the
two answer choices.**

Mental Math

1. $0.27: $0.20   or   ($0.30)

3. $7.93: $7.90   or $8.00

Use Your Calculator

2. $0.95: $0.90   or $1.00

4. $0.62: $0.60   or $0.70

Round each number below to the place value indicated.

Mental Math

Use Your Calculator

	Tenths	Hundredths		Hundredths	Thousandths
5. 3.457	3.5	3.46	**6.** 8.0073	_____	_____
7. 14.382	_____	_____	**8.** 24.0049	_____	_____

**Use your calculator to divide. Write both the displayed answer and the
rounded answer.**

Round each answer to the tenths place. (Press [MODE] [7] [1] on your calculator.)

9. $16 \div 13 = 1.2307692 \approx 1.2$ $11 \div 8 =$ $24 \div 7 =$

└─ less than 5   ≈ _____   ≈ _____

Round each answer to the hundredths place. (Press [MODE] [7] [2] on your calculator.)

10. $31 \div 16 = 1.9375 \approx 1.94 $15 \div 8 =$ $17 \div 9 =$

└─ greater than 5   ≈ _____   ≈ _____

Round each answer to the thousandths place. (Press [MODE] [7] [3] on your calculator.)

11. $23 \div 16 = 1.4375 \approx 1.438$ $45 \div 22 =$ $16 \div 7 =$

└─ equal to 5   ≈ _____   ≈ _____

Solve each word problem below.

12. A jeweler wishes to cut a 33-inch long
gold wire into 7 equal pieces. To the
nearest hundredth of an inch, how long
should each of the 7 pieces be?

13. One inch equals 2.54 centimeters. How
many centimeters are equal to the length
of 1 yard (36 inches)? Express your answer
to the nearest tenth of a centimeter.

Adding Decimals

When you use paper and pencil to add, the first step is to line up the decimal points. Your calculator does that step automatically. To catch keying errors, keep your eye on the number of decimal places in the answer.

EXAMPLE 1 $12.047 + 9.36 =$

To add 12.047 and 9.36 on your calculator, press the keys as shown.

Press Keys	Display Reads
1 2 . 0 4 7	12.047
+	12.047
9 . 3 6	9.36
=	21.407

ANSWER: 21.407

Discovery: When you use paper and pencil to add or subtract decimal numbers, you may add a placeholding zero.
 When you use a calculator, you do not have to enter placeholding zeros.

Pencil and Paper
```
   12.047
+   9.360   ←  placeholding 0
   21.407
```

EXAMPLE 2 $\$5.60 + \$9 + \$7.82 =$

To add $5.60, $9, and $7.82, press the keys as shown.

Press Keys	Display Reads
5 . 6 0	5.60
+	5.6
9	9.
+	14.6
7 . 8 2	7.82
=	22.42

ANSWER: $22.42

Discovery: When you add a whole number to a decimal, you do not need to enter a decimal point to the right of the whole number. The calculator does this for you.

Practice keeping your eye on the number of decimal places so you can catch keying errors. Complete each problem below by placing a decimal point in the answer. If you find it helpful, rewrite each problem with one number above the other, lining up the decimal points.

1. $0.56 + 0.8 = 1\ 3\ 6$ $0.7 + 0.29 = 9\ 9$ $2.4 + 0.75 + 0.8 = 3\ 9\ 5$

2. $0.07 + 0.09 = 1\ 6$ $1.6 + 0.9 = 2\ 5$ $3.06 + 8 + 0.59 = 1\ 1\ 6\ 5$

Estimate an answer to each problem below. Follow these guidelines:
- **Round numbers less than 10 to the nearest whole number.**
- **Round numbers between 10 and 99 to the nearest ten.**
- **Round numbers of 100 or more to the nearest hundred. Then compute an exact answer.**

	Estimate	Exact	Estimate	Exact	Estimate	Exact
3.	8	8.3		6.3		9.7
	+ 6	+ 5.6		+ 7.1		+ 6.5
	14	13.9				
4.		25.8		27.85		75.60
		+ 13.6		+ 12.4		+ 24.83
5.		328.65		900		547.69
		211.06		375.8		243.63
		+ 123		+ 245.18		+ 181.8

Calculate the exact answer to each problem. Use your calculator to round each answer to the nearest whole number (or dollar).

6. $21.8 + 14.7 =$ $57.14 + 37.5 =$ $\$154.85 + \$49.50 =$

7. $250 + 136.8 =$ $231.8 + 85.95 =$ $\$34.54 + \$23.50 =$

Use your calculator to solve the problem below.

8. Find the combined length in inches of the three spacers pictured at the right.

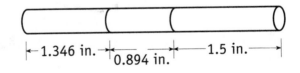

←—1.346 in.—→ ←—→ ←—1.5 in.—→
0.894 in.

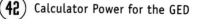

Subtracting Decimals

You subtract decimals in the same way you subtract whole numbers. Be sure to enter the numbers in the correct order! In decimal subtraction, as in decimal addition, the calculator lines up the decimal points for you.

EXAMPLE 1 $9.1 - 4.76 =$

To subtract 4.76 from 9.1 on your calculator, press the keys as shown.

Press Keys	Display Reads
9 · 1	9.1
−	9.1
4 · 7 6	4.76
=	4.34

ANSWER: 4.34

EXAMPLE 2 $15 - 3.5 - 8.375 =$

To subtract 3.5 and 8.375 from 15, press the keys as shown.

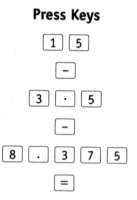

Press Keys	Display Reads
1 5	15.
−	15.
3 · 5	3.5
−	11.5
8 · 3 7 5	8.375
=	3.125

ANSWER: 3.125

EXAMPLE 3 Fran must cut a dowel so that its finished length is 8.765 inches. If she starts with a 10-inch-long dowel, how much will Fran need to remove?

To solve, subtract 8.765 from 10.

Press Keys	Display Reads
1 0	10.
−	10.
8 · 7 6 5	8.765
=	1.235

ANSWER: 1.235 inches

When you subtract decimals, read the problem carefully to decide which number to enter first.

EXAMPLE 4 Sam Rogers is 1.46 meters tall, and his brother Ken is 1.7 meters tall. Which brother is taller and by how much?

	1.7	1.46

STEP 1 Compare the number of decimal places. If there are not the same number of places, add placeholder zeros to give them the same number of places.

1.70   1.46
larger

STEP 2 Subtract the smaller number from the larger.

1.70 – 1.46 = 0.24

ANSWER: Ken Rogers is 0.24 meters taller.

....

Circle the greater decimal in each pair below.

1. 0.81 or 0.79   **2.** 0.102 or 0.11   **3.** 0.035 or 0.0093

Find the difference between each pair of decimals below.

4. 0.36 and 0.59   0.93 and 0.755   0.405 and 0.386

5. 0.09 and 0.134   0.8 and 0.79   0.354 and 0.38

Calculate the answer to each problem.

6.   0.298
    − 0.145

7. $13.45
    −   8.80

8. $25 – $12.45 – $11.85 =

9. When Shannon had the flu, her temperature rose as shown below. How much higher is her fever temperature than normal?

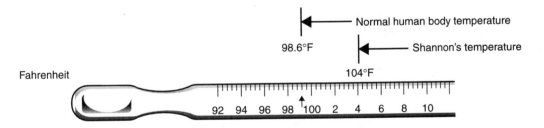

Normal human body temperature

Shannon's temperature

98.6°F

104°F

Fahrenheit

92 94 96 98 100 2 4 6 8 10

Decimal Addition and Subtraction Problems

When you read a word problem, remember to look for **key words** as you did using whole numbers.

> ## Review of Some Key Words
>
> | | |
> |---|---|
> | **Addition** | *sum, and, more, in all* |
> | **Subtraction** | *less than, difference, lost* |
> | **Multiplication** | *times, total, per* |
> | **Division** | *equal, each, average* |

In each problem below, circle the symbol standing for the key word that you recognize. Then use your calculator to solve the problem. Remember to clear your calculator before each problem.

1. Angie wants to save $510 to buy a new stereo. How much must she save each month if she plans to buy the stereo on one year's time? (one year = 12 months)

   $+$ $-$ $\times$ $\div$ Answer: _____

2. At a picnic, two tables were placed end to end. If the first table is 2.89 meters long and the second is 1.94 meters long, what is the combined length in meters of the two tables?

   $+$ $-$ $\times$ $\div$ Answer: _____

3. Ming is trying to decide which of two pork roasts to buy. One weighs 4.79 pounds, and the other weighs 6.2 pounds. How much heavier is the larger roast than the smaller one?

   $+$ $-$ $\times$ $\div$ Answer: _____

4. Hanna's car gets 22.5 miles per gallon in city driving and 28.4 miles per gallon on the highway. How many miles of city driving can Hanna get per 16 gallons of gas?

   $+$ $-$ $\times$ $\div$ Answer: _____

5. George and four friends are going camping. They've agreed that each of them should carry the same amount of weight while hiking. If the gear weighs 142 pounds, what weight should each of them carry?

   $+$ $-$ $\times$ $\div$ Answer: _____

For problems 6–8, estimate your answer first. Then use your calculator to compute the answer.

6. With his football uniform on, Rocky can run the 100-yard dash in 14.26 seconds. Wearing only running clothes, he can run the same distance in 11.89 seconds. How much faster can Rocky run the 100-yard dash when he's not wearing football gear?

     _____
           estimate

     _____
           exact

7. Following the weekend sale, The Gift Shoppe raised the prices of all vases by $2.29. What would be the new price of a vase that had been priced at $11.88 during the sale?

     _____
           estimate

     _____
           exact

For problems 8–10, look at the list or drawing to the right of each problem to find necessary information.

8. As shown on the map at the right, Leslie lives almost halfway between the theater and the swimming pool. By how many miles is Leslie closer to one than the other?

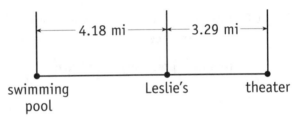

9. Gloria keeps a record of her gasoline purchases. Part of that record is shown at the right. How many more gallons of gas did Gloria purchase on February 28 than on January 24?

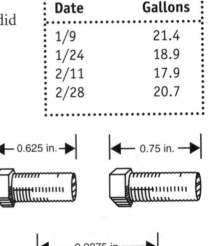

Date	Gallons
1/9	21.4
1/24	18.9
2/11	17.9
2/28	20.7

10. Expressing your answer as a decimal, how much longer is the total length of the two shorter bolts than the length of the longest bolt?

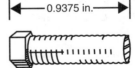

Multiplying Decimals

 You can use your calculator to multiply a decimal times a whole number or to multiply two or more decimals.

As in whole number multiplication, enter each number into the calculator and press $\times$. Press $=$ only once, after the final number is multiplied.

EXAMPLE 1 $6.84 \times 3.7 =$

To multiply 6.84 times 3.7 on your calculator, press the keys as shown.

Press Keys	Display Reads
6 · 8 4	6.84
×	6.84
3 · 7	3.7
=	25.308

ANSWER: 25.308

EXAMPLE 2 Multiply $5.06 \times 4 \times 0.088$. Round the answer to the nearest cent.

To solve, press keys as shown.

Press Keys	Display Reads
5 · 0 6	5.06
×	5.06
4	4.
×	20.24
· 0 8 8	0.088
=	1.78112
MODE	1.78112
7	1.78112
2	1.78

ANSWER: $1.78

Discovery: When you compute with paper and pencil, you total the number of decimal places in the problem to place the decimal point in the answer.

The calculator correctly places the decimal point for you.

Pencil and Paper

6.84	two decimal places
× 3.7	+ one decimal place
25.308	three decimal places

Complete the following problems by correctly placing a decimal point in each answer. You will be able to catch keying errors on your calculator if you have a sense of where decimal points should be placed.

1.
7.8	25.7	8.04	13.1	12.4
× 6	× 0.3	× 0.7	× 5.5	× 0.062
4 6 8	7 7 1	5 6 2 8	7 2 0 5	7 6 8 8

Use your calculator to solve each of the following problems. Round each answer to the tenths place.

2. $7.5 \times 3.2 \times 6 =$

3. $21.4 \times 3.1 \times 5.2 =$

Round each answer to the nearest cent.

4. $\$2.75 \times \$8.80 \times \$4.60 =$

5. $\$15.45 \times \$3.50 \times \$5.25 =$

Use your calculator to solve problems 6–13.

6. To the nearest cent, what will Beth pay for 16.4 gallons of gas bought at the Gas City pump price shown at the right?

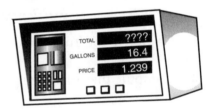

7. According to a weight reduction group, a good way to approximate your ideal weight is to

    - measure your height

    - multiply the number of inches over 5 feet (60 inches) by 5.5

    - add 110 to this number

    Juanita is 66 inches tall. What is her ideal weight?

8. If the average heart weights 0.5 kilograms, how many pounds does it weight? (1 kilogram ≅ 2.2 pounds)

A **purchase order** is a form that a company fills out when it orders products from another company. Tina Vinson orders items for a hardware store as supplies run low. Her partially completed purchase order to Western Industrial Supply is shown below.

WESTERN INDUSTRIAL SUPPLY

Item #	Description	Quantity	Cost/Per	Total Amount
29-75A	Cordless Drill	12	$32.45	$389.40
34-08V	3-Drawer Tool Chest	5	$39.99	
03-14A	Star Claw Hammer	9	$12.95	
07-24C	Deluxe Square Shovel	17	$18.88	
47-83B	Bench-Grip Vise	8	$15.49	
62-80B	10-Foot Ladder	6	$56.29	
09-12A	#6 Screwdriver Set	16	$9.65	
Purchaser: _Tina Vinson_			**Total Purchase**	

9. Complete the Total Amount column.

10. Compute the Total Purchase amount.

11. When the order arrived, there was a note saying that Western Industrial no longer carried Star Claw Hammers. Since these hammers weren't shipped, what is the new Total Purchase amount?

Sheri and Roberto Robertson need child care for their daughter Ashley for three months in the summer—June, July, and August. The costs of the two centers in their community are shown below. Ashley would be using transportation at either center.

	Super Kids Care	Huggy Bear Center
Registration Fee (one-time fee, paid the first month)	$35.00	$65.00
Child care	$255.50/month	$15.85/day*
Transportation (only charged for days of attendance)	$6.75/day*	$4.50/day*

*Figure that every month has 20 working days.

12. Find the total costs for 3-month summer attendance for Super Kids Care and for Huggy Bear Center.

13. What is the difference in the 3-month costs between the two choices?

Dividing Decimals

As the following examples show, you can use your calculator to divide a decimal by a whole number or to divide one decimal number by another.

As in whole number division, your first step is to correctly identify the dividend (the number *being divided*) and the divisor (the number you are *dividing by*).

EXAMPLE 1 Divide 7.894 ÷ 4.

To solve, press the keys as shown.

Press Keys	Display Reads
7 · 8 9 4	7.894
÷	7.894
4	4.
=	1.9735

ANSWER: 1.9735

> **Discovery:** A calculator carries out division until there is no remainder—or until the display is full. For this reason, the answer may contain more decimal places than the dividend (the number being divided). See Examples 1 and 2.

EXAMPLE 2 One foot (12 inches) is the same as 30.48 centimeters. How many centimeters are in 1 inch?

To solve, divide 30.48 by 12, as shown.

Press Keys	Display Reads
3 0 · 4 8	30.48
÷	30.48
1 2	12.
=	2.54

ANSWER: There are 2.54 centimeters in 1 inch.

In the following problems, identify the dividend (the number *being divided*) and the divisor (the number you are *dividing by*). Circle the number you enter into your calculator first. Then solve.

1. 6.54 ÷ 3.1 =

dividend _____

divisor _____

quotient _____

2. 8 divided by 2.7

dividend _____

divisor _____

quotient _____

3. $12\overline{)604.86}$ dividend _____   **4.** $130.41 \div 13.8 =$ dividend _____

divisor _____   divisor _____

quotient _____   quotient _____

Round each answer to the tenths place.

5. $363.2 \div 8.1 =$ $76.26 \div 3.14 =$ $8.01\overline{)57.75}$ $4.1\overline{)33.7}$

Round each answer to the hundredths place.

6. $78 \div 2.3 =$ $\$24.71 \div 8 =$ $6\overline{)\$142.88}$ $3.7\overline{)8.93}$

Use your calculator to solve each problem.

7. Sherry bought a roast and weighed it on a scale. Fill in the $ PER LB amount to show how much Sherry is paying per pound. Write your answer to the nearest cent.

Scale	
Total Price	$33.17
5.87 LB	$ __.__ __
Weight	$ PER LB

Fill in
← this
amount.

8. At Big Bear Foods, Vicki paid $3.13 for a sack of bananas. If the sack weighed 2.9 pounds, how much did Vicki pay per pound? Write your answer to the nearest cent.

9. Yoshi's Import Foods received a box weighing 59.8 pounds that was filled with jars of pickled vegetables. If the box contains 22 jars, what is the weight of each jar to the nearest tenth of a pound? (Ignore the weight of the box itself.)

Decimals Review

This review covers the material that you have just studied. When you finish, check your answers at the back of the book.

Use your calculator to compute the answer to each of the following questions.

1. Heather is buying the following items at the mini-mart: a dozen eggs for $0.99, a two-liter bottle of soda for $1.69, a can of cat food for $0.45, and a candy bar for $0.55. If she does not have to pay tax on these items, how much will her bill be?

2. If Heather gives the cashier at the mini-mart a $20 bill to pay for her purchases in problem 1, how much change will she receive?

3. Water weighs approximately 8.3 pounds per gallon. Determine the weight of water in a hot water heater that contains 48 gallons when filled.

4. Riley has a 36-inch metal pipe that he is cutting into sections, each 6.5 inches long. How many whole pieces of pipe will Riley have?

5. To the nearest hundredth of an inch, how much leftover pipe will Riley have after he has cut it into 6.5-inch sections?

Problems 6–8 refer to the following information.

Anna has been offered a job at Data Systems. She'll be paid $9.44 an hour and work a standard 40-hour shift. However, a friend who works there has told Anna that Data Systems almost always offers 5 hours of overtime work each week to each employee. Data Systems pays an overtime pay rate of 1.5 times normal hourly wage.

6. Not counting overtime, how much would Anna's weekly salary be at Data Systems?

7. Determine how much Anna would make for each hour of overtime at Data Systems.

8. Working 5 hours of overtime each week, how much total pay could Anna earn weekly at Data Systems?

Use your calculator to solve each problem.

9. A jeweler wishes to cut a 33-inch long gold wire into 7 equal pieces. To the nearest hundredth of an inch, how long should each of the 7 pieces be?

10. Jason Sports is advertising that ski jacket prices have been drastically reduced from $61.89 to $39.99. How much of a savings is this advertised price reduction?

11. Bill and two friends agreed to divide the $13.95 rental cost of a VCR and two movies, each movie renting for $1.99. To the nearest cent, what is Bill's share of the total cost?

12. After writing a check for $124.62 and making a deposit of $79.98, Bridget's checking balance is $957.99. What was Bridget's balance *before* these transactions?

Decimals Review Chart

Circle the number of any problem that you missed and review the appropriate pages. A passing score is 10 correct answers. If you miss more than two questions, you should review this chapter.

PROBLEM NUMBERS	SHILL AREA	PRACTICE PAGES
5	rounding decimals	37–39
1, 11, 12	adding decimals	40–41
2, 10, 12	subtracting decimals	42–43
3, 6, 7, 8	multiplying decimals	46–48
4, 9, 11	dividing decimals	49–50

FRACTIONS

Using the Casio *fx*-260 calculator can make working with fractions easier. This chapter will show you how to use the calculator to change fractions to decimals, to reduce fractions, and to add, subtract, multiply, and divide fractions.

Understanding Fractions

A **fraction** is a value that shows equal parts taken of a whole. A fraction is written as one number over the other. The symbol used to indicate a fraction is the slash (/) or the bar (—). The slash or bar means the same thing as the ÷ sign.

$\frac{3}{4}$ numerator   The numerator tells how many parts you have.

denominator   The denominator tells how equal parts the whole is divided into.

On the ruler below, the line measures $\frac{11}{16}$ inch. The inch is divided into 16 equal parts and the length of the line measures to 11 of those equal parts.

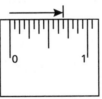

A fraction can also be thought of as a division problem. The fraction line (/) means "divided by".

You read the fraction $\frac{3}{4}$ as "three fourths" or as "3 divided by 4."

3 divided by 4 = 0.75, so you can say $\frac{3}{4}$ = 0.75

Types of Fractions

Fractions are written in one of three ways:

- As a **proper fraction** in which the top number is always less than the bottom number

  EXAMPLE $\frac{1}{3}, \frac{2}{3}$

$\frac{1}{3}$ is missing.

$\frac{2}{3}$ of a pie is shown.

- As an **improper fraction** in which the top number is the same as or greater than the bottom number

  EXAMPLE $\frac{5}{3}$

$\frac{5}{3}$ is $\frac{2}{3}$ greater than 1 whole $\left(\frac{3}{3}\right)$.

$\frac{5}{3}$ pies are shown.

- As part of a **mixed number,** which is the sum of a whole number and a proper fraction

  EXAMPLE $1\frac{3}{4}$

$1 + \frac{3}{4} = 1\frac{3}{4}$

$1\frac{3}{4}$ pies are shown.

You read this mixed number as one and three fourths.

....

Write the following in fractional form.

1. five sixths

2. two and three eighths

3. twelve fifths

4. thirteen and one third

5. twenty-five tenths

6. fifteen sixteenths

7. four hundredths

8. two hundred halves

9. one and eight ninths

10. ten tenths

Tell whether each of the following is a proper fraction (P), an improper fraction (I), or a mixed number (M).

11. $\frac{18}{16}$ $4\frac{1}{2}$ $\frac{110}{75}$ $\frac{35}{50}$

12. $8\frac{3}{4}$ $\frac{23}{5}$ $\frac{6}{48}$ $\frac{99}{100}$

Write the length of the line in fractional form.

13.

14.

15.

16.

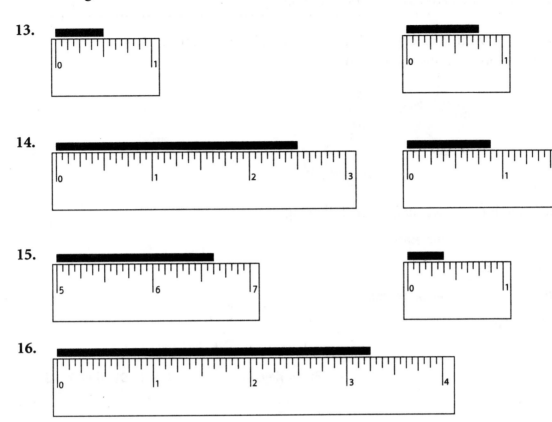

Write the fractional part that is shaded.

17.   18.

19.   20.

21.   22.

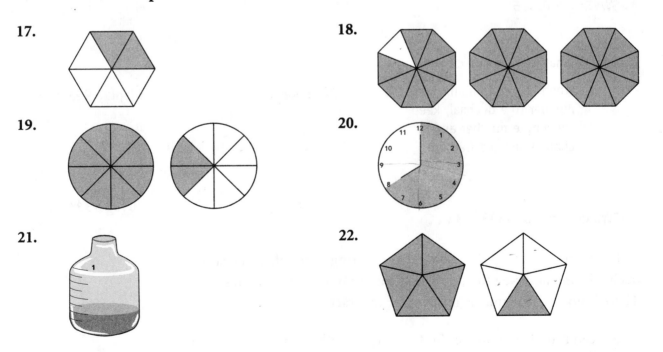

Decimal and Fractional Equivalents

You can write any fraction as a decimal. You saw that $\frac{3}{4}$ is equal to 0.75. If you think about money, $\frac{3}{4}$ of a dollar is $0.75.

 To change a fraction to a decimal, do the following:

STEP 1 Enter the numerator.

STEP 2 Press ÷ .

STEP 3 Enter the denominator.

STEP 4 Press = .

EXAMPLE 1 Change $\frac{7}{8}$ to a decimal.

Press Keys	Display Reads
7	7.
÷	7.
8	8.
=	0.875

ANSWER: $\frac{7}{8}$ = 0.875

EXAMPLE 2 Change $4\frac{1}{3}$ to a decimal.

When changing a mixed number to a decimal, keep the whole number and change just the fraction.

Press Keys	Display Reads
1	1.
÷	1.
3	3.
=	0.333333333

ANSWER: $4\frac{1}{3}$ = 4.333333333 . . .

The decimal 0.333333333 is called a **repeating decimal**. A repeating decimal has a never-ending, repeating pattern of one or more digits. There is no exact decimal equivalent for the fraction $\frac{1}{3}$.

You can round your answer. To the nearest tenth, 4.333333333 equals 4.3; to the nearest hundredth, 4.33; and so on.

To tell which is greater, a fraction or a decimal, change the fraction to a decimal and then compare the decimals.

EXAMPLE 3 Which is greater, $\frac{11}{16}$ or 0.65?

		Press Keys	**Display Reads**
STEP 1	Change $\frac{11}{16}$ to a decimal.		
STEP 2	To compare 0.6875 with 0.65, give each decimal the same number of decimal places. Do this by adding two placeholder zeros to 0.65.	11	1 1.
		÷	1 1.
		16	1 6.
		=	0 . 6 8 7 5

$$0.65 = 0.6500 \qquad \frac{11}{16} = 0.6875$$

ANSWER: $\frac{11}{16}$ **is greater** than 0.65 because 0.6875 is greater than 0.6500.

· ·

Use your calculator to change each fraction to a decimal.

1. $\frac{3}{8} =$

2. $\frac{9}{10} =$

3. $25\frac{4}{5} =$

4. $\frac{1}{16} =$

5. $\frac{4}{15} =$

6. $3\frac{7}{8} =$

Use your calculator to change each fraction to a decimal. Then circle the greater number in each pair.

7. $\frac{3}{4}$ or 0.76 $\frac{5}{8}$ or 0.616   0.4 or $\frac{4}{15}$ 0.865 or $\frac{5}{7}$

Change both fractions to decimals and then compare. Circle the greater fraction.

8. $\frac{2}{3}$ or $\frac{3}{5}$ $\frac{9}{17}$ or $\frac{6}{13}$ $\frac{21}{32}$ or $\frac{2}{3}$ $\frac{8}{10}$ or $\frac{51}{64}$

9. Put the following size screws in order from least to greatest. Change the fractions to decimals and compare.

$\frac{3}{4}$ in. $\frac{7}{8}$ in. $\frac{3}{16}$ in. $\frac{19}{32}$ in.

least _____   _____   _____   _____ greatest

Reducing Fractions

When writing fractions, most of the time you should write them in **reduced form**. The reduced form is sometimes referred to as **simplest form** or **lowest terms**. Simplest form is the form of the fraction that has the least possible denominator. For example, a woodworker would call $\frac{6}{12}$ of a foot, $\frac{1}{2}$ foot.

When a fraction is reduced, the *value* of the fraction does not change, only the way the fraction appears.

To reduce fractions to lowest terms, divide the numerator and denominator by the same number. This number is called a **factor**. Ask yourself, "What number will go evenly into both the numerator and denominator of this fraction?"

EXAMPLE 1 Write $\frac{9}{12}$ in lowest terms.

STEP 1 Determine the number that will divide evenly into 9 and 12. 3 will divide evenly into both 9 and 12.

$$\frac{9 \div 3}{12 \div 3} = \frac{3}{4}$$

STEP 2 If the fraction is still not in lowest terms, repeat this process. When you can no longer find a number that will divide evenly into both numerator and denominator, the fraction is in lowest terms.

ANSWER: $\frac{9}{12}$ in lowest terms is $\frac{3}{4}$.

Using Your Calculator to Reduce Fractions

Reducing a fraction to lowest terms using your calculator is as easy as entering the fraction and pressing the $\boxed{=}$ key. Your calculator will automatically find the greatest factor of the numerator and denominator, perform the division, and show in the display the reduced form of the fraction.

To enter a fraction into the calculator, do the following:

STEP 1 Enter the numerator of the fraction.

STEP 2 Press $\boxed{\text{a b/c}}$.

STEP 3 Enter the denominator of the fraction.
Fractions look different on a calculator. The numerator and denominator are divided by a separator $\rfloor$.

STEP 4 Press $\boxed{=}$ and the fraction will reduce if it is not already in lowest terms.

EXAMPLE 2 Reduce $\frac{6}{8}$ to lowest terms with the calculator.

Press Keys	Display Reads
6	6.
a b/c	6⌐.
8	6⌐8.
=	3⌐4.

ANSWER: $\frac{6}{8}$ **reduced to lowest terms is** $\frac{3}{4}$**.**

To enter mixed numbers into the calculator, do the following:

STEP 1 Enter the whole number.

STEP 2 Press a b/c .

STEP 3 Enter the numerator.

STEP 4 Press a b/c .

STEP 5 Enter the denominator.

EXAMPLE 3 Reduce $2\frac{6}{16}$ to lowest terms with the calculator.

Press Keys	Display Reads
2	2.
a b/c	2⌐.
6	2⌐6.
a b/c	2⌐6.
16	2⌐6⌐16.
=	2⌐3⌐8.

ANSWER: $2\frac{6}{16} = 2\frac{3}{8}$

....

Use your calculator to reduce each fraction or mixed number to lowest terms.

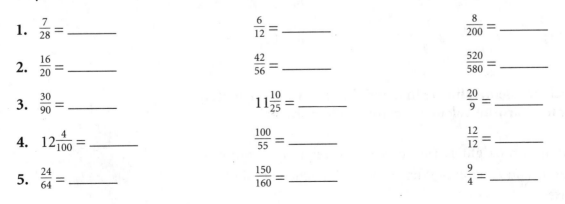

1. $\frac{7}{28} =$ _____ $\frac{6}{12} =$ _____ $\frac{8}{200} =$ _____

2. $\frac{16}{20} =$ _____ $\frac{42}{56} =$ _____ $\frac{520}{580} =$ _____

3. $\frac{30}{90} =$ _____ $11\frac{10}{25} =$ _____ $\frac{20}{9} =$ _____

4. $12\frac{4}{100} =$ _____ $\frac{100}{55} =$ _____ $\frac{12}{12} =$ _____

5. $\frac{24}{64} =$ _____ $\frac{150}{160} =$ _____ $\frac{9}{4} =$ _____

Adding Fractions and Mixed Numbers

Sometimes you need to add two or more fractions together. Your calculator makes this easy.

STEP 1 Enter the fraction or mixed number on your calculator.

STEP 2 Press $\boxed{+}$.

STEP 3 Enter the second fraction or mixed number.

STEP 4 Press $\boxed{=}$.

EXAMPLE Find the sum of $\frac{1}{6} + \frac{2}{3}$ using your calculator.

Press Keys	Display Reads
$\boxed{1}$	1.
$\boxed{\text{a b/c}}$	1 ⌐.
$\boxed{6}$	1 ⌐ 6.
$\boxed{+}$	1 ⌐ 6.
$\boxed{2}$	2.
$\boxed{\text{a b/c}}$	2 ⌐.
$\boxed{3}$	2 ⌐ 3.
$\boxed{=}$	5 ⌐ 6.

ANSWER: $\frac{5}{6}$

Add. Remember to clear your calculator before you start a new problem.

1. $\frac{3}{4} + \frac{5}{16} =$

2. $\frac{2}{3} + \frac{5}{8} =$

3. $\frac{2}{5} + \frac{1}{4} + \frac{5}{12} =$

4. $\frac{7}{10} + \frac{1}{3} + \frac{1}{6} =$

5. $8\frac{5}{6} + \frac{1}{8} =$

6. $\frac{4}{5} + 20\frac{2}{3} =$

7. $6\frac{1}{16} + 2\frac{3}{32} + \frac{5}{8} =$

8. $12\frac{3}{4} + 9\frac{5}{6} + \frac{2}{3} =$

To solve each problem, estimate first and then use your calculator. Remember to clear your calculator before each problem.

9. The dolly at the right carries three boxes weighing $5\frac{1}{2}$ pounds, $4\frac{3}{4}$ pounds, and $7\frac{3}{8}$ pounds. What is the total weight, in pounds, of the boxes?

10. John, Jim, and Al are doing part-time carpentry work. They work for a customer who wants them to build an extra bath and bedroom in his basement. Use the chart below to discover which of the three men worked more hours on the basement.

Hours Worked						
	Mon.	**Tue.**	**Wed.**	**Thu.**	**Fri.**	**Sat.**
John	3	$2\frac{1}{4}$	$3\frac{1}{2}$	$4\frac{3}{4}$	$4\frac{1}{4}$	$7\frac{1}{2}$
Al	$8\frac{1}{2}$	0	4	$3\frac{1}{3}$	$4\frac{3}{4}$	$2\frac{1}{2}$
Jim	$4\frac{3}{4}$	4	$5\frac{1}{4}$	$2\frac{1}{2}$	$1\frac{3}{4}$	$6\frac{1}{2}$

11. In the construction of a foundation, the following loads of cement were used to pour the foundation: $20\frac{1}{4}$ yards, $19\frac{1}{2}$ yards, $15\frac{1}{8}$ yards, $25\frac{5}{6}$ yards, and $22\frac{3}{4}$ yards. Find the total number of yards of cement used for the foundation.

12. What is the distance between the holes in the bracket?

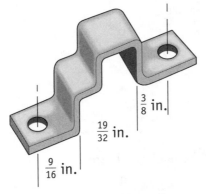

13. What is the perimeter (distance around) of this piece of property?

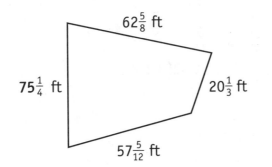

Subtracting Fractions and Mixed Numbers

 When you subtract fractions, you are finding the **difference** between the two numbers. You can use your Casio *fx*-260 to subtract fractions and mixed numbers.

STEP 1 Enter the first fraction or mixed number.

STEP 2 Press $\boxed{-}$.

STEP 3 Enter the second fraction or mixed number.

STEP 4 Press $\boxed{=}$.

EXAMPLE Find the difference of $\frac{9}{16} - \frac{3}{8}$ using your calculator.

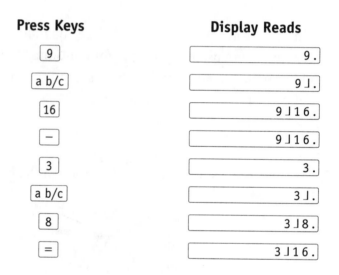

Press Keys	Display Reads
9	9.
a b/c	9⌐.
16	9⌐16.
−	9⌐16.
3	3.
a b/c	3⌐.
8	3⌐8.
=	3⌐16.

ANSWER: $\frac{3}{16}$

Subtract. Remember to clear your calculator before each problem.

1. $\frac{3}{4} - \frac{3}{8} =$

2. $\frac{4}{5} - \frac{13}{20} =$

3. $\frac{7}{10} - \frac{9}{16} =$

4. $8 - 2\frac{15}{32} =$

5. $15\frac{1}{2} - \frac{7}{8} =$

6. $9\frac{3}{21} - 8\frac{19}{20} =$

7. $101\frac{5}{16} - 87\frac{7}{8} =$

8. $2\frac{3}{8} - 1 =$

To solve each problem, estimate first and then use your calculator. Remember to clear your calculator before each problem.

9. Find the length of y in inches.

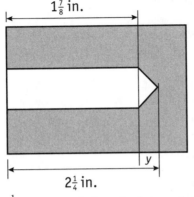

10. A tank consists of $4\frac{1}{8}$ gallons of chemical A and $10\frac{5}{8}$ gallons of chemical B. The rest of the mixture is water. If the tank is full and holds 17 gallons, how much water is in the tank?

11. A plumber estimated a job would take 30 hours. After he completed the job he added his logged time at $8\frac{3}{4}$ hours, $4\frac{5}{6}$ hours, $5\frac{1}{4}$ hours, $8\frac{1}{2}$ hours, $3\frac{2}{3}$ hours. Did the plumber over- or underestimate the time for the job? By how much?

12. You cut two pieces of wire from a 20-foot wire. The pieces are $10\frac{2}{3}$ feet and $5\frac{1}{6}$ feet. How much wire is left?

13. Your ceiling is 94 inches. If your curtains are $83\frac{1}{2}$ inches long and you want to allow $\frac{3}{4}$-inch clearance from the floor, how far should the curtain rod be placed from the ceiling?

14. What is the width of x?

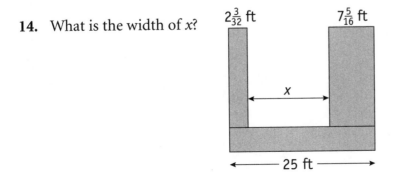

Multiplying Fractions and Mixed Numbers

Multiplication of fractions and whole numbers is a shortcut for adding equal amounts. For example, $4 \times \frac{3}{8}$ means $\frac{3}{8} + \frac{3}{8} + \frac{3}{8} + \frac{3}{8}$.

When multiplying two fractions together like $\frac{1}{2}$ and $\frac{3}{5}$, divide $\frac{3}{5}$ into 2 equal parts and then take 1 of the 2 equal parts.

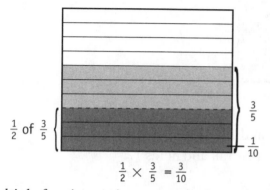

$$\frac{1}{2} \times \frac{3}{5} = \frac{3}{10}$$

To multiply fractions using your calculator, do the following:

STEP 1 Enter the first fraction, mixed number, or whole number.

STEP 2 Press $\boxed{\times}$.

STEP 3 Enter the second fraction, mixed number, or whole number.

STEP 4 Press $\boxed{=}$.

EXAMPLE Find the product of $\frac{3}{4} \times \frac{1}{3}$ using your calculator.

Press Keys	Display Reads
$\boxed{3}$	3.
$\boxed{\text{a b/c}}$	3⌐.
$\boxed{4}$	3⌐4.
$\boxed{\times}$	3⌐4.
$\boxed{1}$	1.
$\boxed{\text{a b/c}}$	1⌐.
$\boxed{3}$	1⌐3.
$\boxed{=}$	1⌐4.

ANSWER: $\frac{1}{4}$

Multiply. Remember to clear your calculator before each problem.

1. $4 \times \frac{3}{8} =$

2. $\frac{1}{2} \times \frac{1}{2} =$

3. $\frac{4}{7} \times \frac{7}{15} =$

4. $\frac{3}{4} \times \frac{5}{6} \times \frac{1}{10} =$

5. $\frac{9}{16} \times 3\frac{5}{9} =$

6. $4\frac{5}{8} \times 2\frac{2}{3} =$

7. $8 \times 4\frac{1}{16} =$

8. $4\frac{4}{5} \times 2\frac{2}{3} \times 3 =$

To solve each problem, estimate first and then use your calculator. Remember to clear your calculator before each problem.

9. A dressmaker needs $4\frac{5}{6}$ yards of fabric to make a bridesmaid's dress. She is making 6 dresses. How much fabric should she buy?

10. An 8 × 10 inch ($w \times l$) picture is scanned so that each dimension is $\frac{3}{5}$ its original size. What is the measurement of each side?

$$w = \qquad l =$$

11. A nail is pounded into a piece of wood that is $\frac{15}{16}$-inch thick. The nail is $\frac{3}{4}$ of the way through the thickness of the wood. How long is the nail?

12. What is the length of the part shown below?

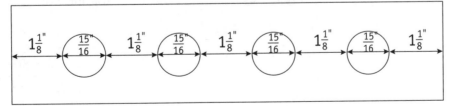

13. A gas tank holds $18\frac{1}{3}$ gallons. You have a plastic gas can that holds $4\frac{3}{4}$ gallons. You fill the gas can 3 times to fill the tank. Will the tank hold another full can of gas?

14. How many minutes are in $\frac{2}{3}$ of an hour?

Dividing Fractions and Mixed Numbers

Division of fractions is a shortcut for subtracting equal amounts. For example, $\frac{1}{2} \div \frac{1}{8}$ means how many times is $\frac{1}{8}$ contained in $\frac{1}{2}$.

$$\frac{1}{2} - \frac{1}{8} = \frac{3}{8}$$

$$\frac{3}{8} - \frac{1}{8} = \frac{2}{8}$$

$$\frac{2}{8} - \frac{1}{8} = \frac{1}{8}$$

$$\frac{1}{8} - \frac{1}{8} = 0$$

Since $\frac{1}{8}$ can be subtracted from $\frac{1}{2}$ four times, then $\frac{1}{8}$ is contained in $\frac{1}{2}$ four times, or $\frac{1}{2} \div \frac{1}{8} = 4$.

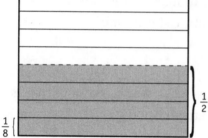

$\frac{1}{8}$ is contained in $\frac{1}{2}$ four times

To divide fractions using your calculator, do the following:

STEP 1 Enter the dividend (number to be divided).

STEP 2 Press ÷ .

STEP 3 Enter the divisor (number you are dividing by).

STEP 4 Press = .

EXAMPLE   Find the quotient of $\frac{2}{3} \div \frac{4}{5}$ using your calculator.

Press Keys	Display Reads
2	2.
a b/c	2⌐.
3	2⌐3.
÷	2⌐3.
4	4.
a b/c	4⌐.
5	4⌐5.
=	5⌐6.

ANSWER: $\frac{5}{6}$

Divide. Remember to clear your calculator before each problem.

1. $\frac{2}{5} \div 2\frac{1}{4} =$

2. $12 \div \frac{1}{2} =$

3. $\frac{8}{15} \div \frac{7}{12} =$

4. $3\frac{1}{3} \div 5\frac{5}{9} =$

5. $\frac{15}{16} \div 16 =$

6. $\frac{1}{2} \div \frac{1}{3} =$

7. $100 \div \frac{1}{4} =$

8. $6\frac{7}{8} \div 1\frac{4}{5} =$

To solve each problem, estimate first and then use your calculator. Remember to clear your calculator before each problem.

9. Linda paid \$17.75 for $12\frac{3}{4}$ pounds of peaches. To the nearest cent, how much is Linda paying per pound?

10. A 2 by 4 is a board that is actually $1\frac{1}{2}$ inches by $3\frac{1}{2}$ inches. How many 2 by 4's lying flat side by side would it take to make a picnic tabletop that is 42 inches wide?

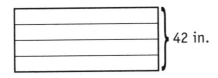

42 in.

11. A truck travels 432 miles in $6\frac{3}{4}$ hours. In miles per hour, how fast is the truck going?

12. You cut a board measuring 30 inches into three equal lengths. An additional $\frac{1}{16}$ inch is lost with each cut. How long are the finished pieces?

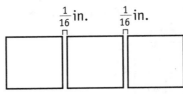

$\frac{1}{16}$ in. $\frac{1}{16}$ in.

13. Bob is building a garage. If it takes Bob $\frac{1}{3}$ of an hour to measure, cut, and nail one stud in place, how many studs will he have completed in $5\frac{1}{2}$ hours?

Fractions Review

This review covers the material you have just studied. When you finish, check your answers at the back of the book.

Solve each problem.

1. A round metal rod with a diameter of $1\frac{1}{16}$ inches is machined down $\frac{3}{32}$ inch. What is the new diameter of the rod after being machined?

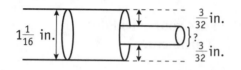

2. To find material requirements for a production run of chairs, an estimator finds the length of wood required for the chair leg below. How many inches of wood are required to make a chair leg?

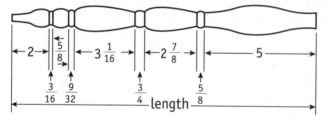

3. A recipe for chicken salad makes 12 servings. It calls for $\frac{1}{8}$ teaspoon paprika and $\frac{1}{3}$ cup mayonnaise. If Joan is making the chicken salad for 6 people, how much paprika and how much mayonnaise will she need?

4. How much ribbon is needed to wrap the box below? Allow 8 inches for the bow.

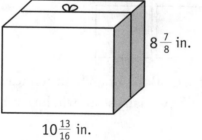

5. Ed earns \$16.50 an hour working overtime. Of his pay, $\frac{3}{8}$ is taken out for taxes. How much will Ed take home after taxes when he works 4 hours overtime?

6. A blueprint of a part has an overall length measuring $3\frac{1}{4}$ inches. If the tolerance is $\pm\frac{3}{16}$ inch, what is the maximum measurement the part can be? (**Hint:** Add the tolerance to get the maximum measurement.)

7. An upholsterer purchases 150 yards of fabric. Each chair needs $3\frac{7}{8}$ yards of fabric. How many chairs can be upholstered from the 150 yards of fabric?

8. Noreen is buying $3\frac{3}{4}$ gallons of punch for a party. At \$2.95 a gallon, how much will she pay to the nearest cent?

Fractions Review Chart

Circle the number of any problem that you missed and review the appropriate pages. A passing score is 6 correct. If you miss more than two questions, you should review this chapter.

PROBLEM NUMBERS	SKILL AREA	PRACTICE PAGES
5, 8	multiplication of mixed numbers and proper fractions	64–65
1	subtraction of proper fractions from mixed numbers	62–63
2, 4, 6	addition of proper fractions and mixed numbers	60–61
3, 7	division of proper fractions and mixed numbers	66–67

PERCENT

People use percent as part of daily life. We use percent when we calculate sales taxes, interest amounts, costs of sale items, and many other things. Two tools can make it easier to calculate with percent—your calculator and a memory device called the **percent circle.** In this part of the book, you will use these two tools.

Find the percent sign on your calculator. Notice it is above the = key and is written in yellow. On the Casio *fx*-260 calculator, percent is a "second function." Each of the keys on your calculator has two functions—the main function and the second function written in yellow above the key. To use a "second function," press the SHIFT key in the upper-left corner of the calculator and then press the key of the function you want. This is much like using the SHIFT key on a computer keyboard. Each time you want to use a second function, press the SHIFT key first.

Overview for Percent

The three main types of percent problems are listed below. They are based on the statement

25% of $300 is $75.

Some **percent** of a **whole amount** is a **part** of that amount.

1. Finding **part** of a whole
   What is 25% of $300?
   $75

2. Finding what **percent** a part is of a whole
   What percent of $300 is $75?
   25%

3. Finding a **whole** when a part of it is given
   If 25% of the price is $75, what is the total price?
   $300

In a percent problem, you are given two of these factors (*part, percent* or *whole*), and you must find the third.

The Percent Circle

On the pages ahead, we'll show you how a calculator can simplify solving each type of percent problem. On those pages we'll refer to a memory device shown below called the **percent circle.**

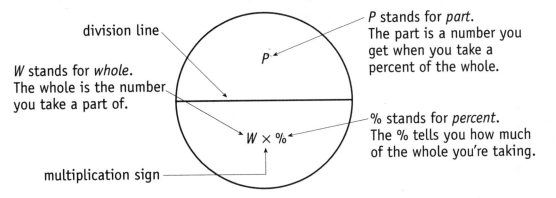

division line

P stands for *part*.
The part is a number you get when you take a percent of the whole.

W stands for *whole*.
The whole is the number you take a part of.

% stands for *percent*.
The % tells you how much of the whole you're taking.

multiplication sign

To use the percent circle, do the following:

1. If you are finding the part, cover *P* (Part) on the percent circle. The circle tells you to multiply the *W* (whole) times % (percent).

2. If you are finding the percent, cover the % sign on the percent circle. The circle tells you to divide *P* (part) by *W* (whole).

3. If you are finding the whole, cover *W* (whole) on the percent circle. The circle tells you to divide *P* (part) by % (percent).

···

In each problem, use the percent circle to determine what it is you're asked to find, *P*, %, or *W* in the percent circle. Then place a check to indicate whether the problem is solved by multiplication or division.

1. Jimi had to pay a $0.42 sales tax when he bought lunch for $7.00. What tax rate did Jimi pay?

   _____ multiplication _____ division

2. Each month, Arnie's net pay is $1,845 and he saves 9% of it. How much does Arnie save each month?

   _____ multiplication _____ division

3. To pass her math test, Francine needs to answer 42 questions correctly. If 42 questions is 70% of the test, how many questions are on the test?

   _____ multiplication _____ division

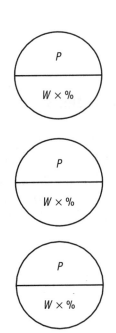

Finding Part of a Whole

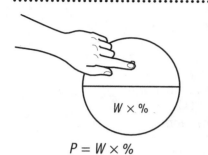

$P = W \times \%$

 Here are the steps for using a calculator to find part of a whole.

> **How to Find the Part**
> To find part of a whole, multiply the whole by the percent.

STEP 1 Enter the number representing the whole.

STEP 2 Press ☒.

STEP 3 Enter the percent number.

STEP 4 Press ⎣SHIFT⎦ ⎣%⎦.

EXAMPLE 1 Of your $300 check, 17% is withheld for taxes. How much is withheld? $P = W \times \%$.

Using a Calculator	**Compare with Pencil-and-Paper Solution**

Using a Calculator

STEP 1 Identify W and %.
$W = 300$, % $= 17$

STEP 2 Multiply $300 \times 17\%$ on your calculator.

Press Keys	**Display Reads**
③ ⓪ ⓪	300.
☒	300.
① ⑦	17.
SHIFT %	51.

ANSWER: 51

Compare with Pencil-and-Paper Solution

STEP 1 Identify W and %.
$W = 300$, % $= 17\%$

STEP 2 Change 17% to a decimal by moving the decimal point two places to the left.
$17\% = 0.17$

STEP 3 Multiply 300 by 0.17.

$$\begin{array}{r} 300 \\ \times\ 0.17 \\ \hline 2100 \\ 300 \\ \hline 51.00 \end{array}$$

ANSWER: 51

Discovery: Try pressing keys in this order: ① ⑦ % ☒ ③ ⓪ ⓪ ⎣=⎦
What happens? Be sure to enter whole numbers first when you solve percent problems on the Casio *fx*-260 calculator.

EXAMPLE 2 At a rate of $5\frac{1}{2}\%$, how much sales tax, to the nearest cent, will be charged on a $14.80 purchase?

		Press Keys	Display Reads
STEP 1	Identify W and %. $W = \$14.80$, $\% = 5\frac{1}{2}\%$	1 4 · 8 0	14.80
STEP 2	To solve on your calculator, multiply $14.80 by $5\frac{1}{2}\%$.	×	14.8
		5	5.
		a b/c	5⌐.
		1	5⌐1.
		a b/c	5⌐1⌐.
		2	5⌐1⌐2.
		SHIFT %	0.814

ANSWER: $0.81 $0.814 to the nearest cent is $0.81.

....

Use your calculator to find each number indicated below. The correct keying order is shown for the first problem in each row. Remember when using the percent key, enter the whole (W) or the part (P) first.

Percents Between 1% and 100%

1. 20% of 90   35% of 240   8% of $25.50   75% of 88

   9 0 × 2 0 SHIFT %

Decimal Percents

2. 0.5% of $4   0.7% of 85   · 5.5% of $30   3.4% of 62

   4 × · 5 SHIFT %

Fraction Percents

3. $\frac{3}{4}\%$ of 10 $5\frac{3}{8}\%$ of $200 $10\frac{1}{3}\%$ of 1,000 $25\frac{1}{9}\%$ of 90

   1 0 × 3 a b/c 4 SHIFT %

Percents Greater than 100%

4. 250% of 18   300% of $58   150% of 90   100% of $56

   1 8 × 2 5 0 SHIFT %

5. Each week Kyle saves 15% of the $243.60 paycheck from his part-time job. What amount is Kyle able to save each week?

6. When his $460 property tax bill goes up by 2.5%, how much additional property tax will Kiwon have to pay?

Finding the Percent

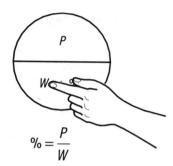

$$\% = \frac{P}{W}$$

> **How to Find the Percent**
> To find what percent a part is of a whole, divide the part by the whole.

 Here are the steps for using a calculator to find the percent.

STEP 1 Enter the number representing the part.

STEP 2 Press ÷ .

STEP 3 Enter the whole.

STEP 4 Press SHIFT % .

EXAMPLE 1 In just over 3 months, Amy lost 40 pounds. If she originally weighed 200 pounds, what percent of her weight did Amy lose?

Using a Calculator

STEP 1 Identify P and W.
$P = 40$, $W = 200$

STEP 2 Divide 40 by 200. Press SHIFT % to tell the calculator to display the answer as a percent.

Press Keys	Display Reads
4 0	40.
÷	40.
2 0 0	200.
SHIFT %	20.

ANSWER: 20%

Compare with Pencil-and-Paper Solution

STEP 1 Identify P and W.
$P = 40$, $W = 200$

STEP 2 Divide 40 by 200.

$$200\overline{)40.00} \quad \frac{0.20}{}$$

STEP 3 Change 0.20 to a percent by moving the decimal point two places to the right and adding a percent sign.

$0.2 = 0.20 = \textbf{20\%}$

ANSWER: 20%

> **Discovery:** Although your calculator has a % key, no % symbol appears on the display.

<u>EXAMPLE 2</u> Change $\frac{3}{4}$ to an equivalent percent.

To change $\frac{3}{4}$ to a percent, you are asking, "3 is what percent of 4?" So 3 is the part and 4 is the whole. Looking at the percent circle, you see to divide the part (3) by the whole (4).

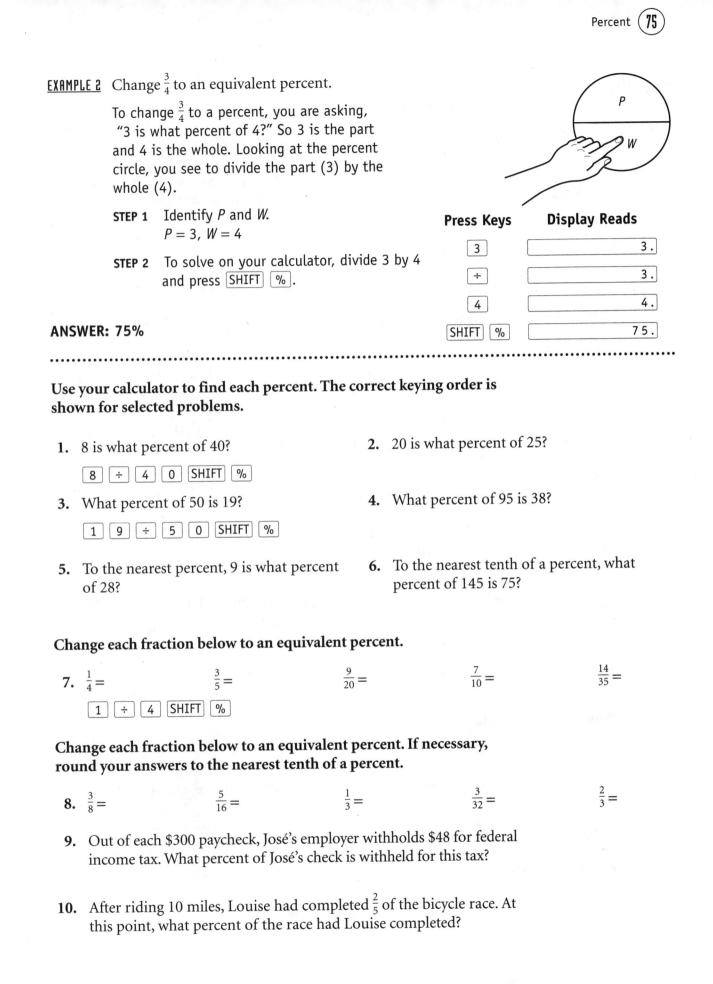

STEP 1 Identify P and W.
$P = 3, W = 4$

Press Keys	Display Reads
3	3.

STEP 2 To solve on your calculator, divide 3 by 4 and press [SHIFT] [%].

÷	3.
4	4.

ANSWER: 75%

[SHIFT] [%]	75.

....

Use your calculator to find each percent. The correct keying order is shown for selected problems.

1. 8 is what percent of 40?

    [8] [÷] [4] [0] [SHIFT] [%]

2. 20 is what percent of 25?

3. What percent of 50 is 19?

    [1] [9] [÷] [5] [0] [SHIFT] [%]

4. What percent of 95 is 38?

5. To the nearest percent, 9 is what percent of 28?

6. To the nearest tenth of a percent, what percent of 145 is 75?

Change each fraction below to an equivalent percent.

7. $\frac{1}{4} =$ $\frac{3}{5} =$ $\frac{9}{20} =$ $\frac{7}{10} =$ $\frac{14}{35} =$

    [1] [÷] [4] [SHIFT] [%]

Change each fraction below to an equivalent percent. If necessary, round your answers to the nearest tenth of a percent.

8. $\frac{3}{8} =$ $\frac{5}{16} =$ $\frac{1}{3} =$ $\frac{3}{32} =$ $\frac{2}{3} =$

9. Out of each $300 paycheck, José's employer withholds $48 for federal income tax. What percent of José's check is withheld for this tax?

10. After riding 10 miles, Louise had completed $\frac{2}{5}$ of the bicycle race. At this point, what percent of the race had Louise completed?

Finding the Whole

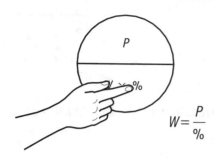

$$W = \frac{P}{\%}$$

 When using a calculator to find the whole, follow these steps.

STEP 1 Enter the number representing the part.

STEP 2 Press $\div$.

STEP 3 Enter the number of the percent.

STEP 4 Press SHIFT %.

When the percent is less than 100%, then the whole will be *greater* than the part. However, if the percent is greater than 100%, then the whole will be *less* than the part.

Discovery: You may notice that the order of keying used to find the *whole* is the same as that used to find the *percent* (discussed on page 74). Be aware of this—but not confused by it! Think of it as simplifying your work.

EXAMPLE 1 When he bought a piano, Willis paid $270 as a down payment. If the down payment is 15% of the price of the piano, what was the original price of the piano?

Using a Calculator

STEP 1 Identify P and %.
$P = 270$, % = 15%

STEP 2 Divide 270 by 15% on your calculator.

Press Keys	Display Reads
2 7 0	270.
$\div$	270.
1 5	15.
SHIFT %	1800.

ANSWER: $1,800

Compare with Pencil-and-Paper Solution

STEP 1 Identify P and %.
$P = 270$, % = 15%

STEP 2 Change 15% to a decimal by moving the decimal point two places to the left.

15% = 0.15

STEP 3 Divide 270 by 0.15.

$$0.15\overline{)270.00} = 1800.$$

ANSWER: $1,800

EXAMPLE 2 The sale price of a TV is $289. If $289 is 80% of the original price, what did the TV cost before the sale?

		Press Keys	**Display Reads**
STEP 1	Identify P and %. $P = \$289$, % = 80%	2 8 9	289.
		÷	289.
STEP 2	To solve on your calculator, divide 289 by 80%.	8 0	80.
		SHIFT %	361.25

ANSWER: $361.25

....

Use your calculator to solve each problem below. The correct keying order is shown for problems 2, 3, and 6.

1. 25% of what number is 67?

2. 5.7% of what number is 57?
   5 7 ÷ 5 · 7 SHIFT %

3. 52.5 is 35% of what number?
   5 2 · 5 ÷ 3 5 SHIFT %

4. 12% of what number is 30?

5. 7.5% of what amount is $150?

6. $\frac{3}{4}$% of what number is 3?
   3 ÷ 3 a b/c 4 SHIFT %

7. $90 is 3.6% of what amount?

8. 32 is $5\frac{1}{3}$% of what amount?

9. During May, Raymond lost 6 pounds, which is 30% of the weight he hopes to lose on his diet. How many pounds does Raymond hope to lose in all?

10. For the month of January, Guy paid $9.90 in interest charges on his Visa card. Guy pays 1.5% interest charges each month on any unpaid balance. Given these figures, determine the amount of Guy's unpaid balance for the month of January.

11. Shirley is a real estate agent. She earns $1\frac{2}{3}$% commission on each sale. Last month her commission for selling a house was $2,145. How much was the cost of the house?

Increasing or Decreasing a Whole by a Part

Many percent problems involve increasing or decreasing a whole by a part. For example, suppose you want to find the purchase price of a sweater in a state where there is a 5% sales tax. Without a calculator, this can take two steps.

- First, you find the amount of the sales tax (the part).

- Second, you add the sales tax to the original selling price (the whole).

As the example below shows, the % key on your calculator combines these two steps into a single step. This single step is much easier and faster.

EXAMPLE 1 In a state with a 5% sales tax, what is the purchase price of a sweater vest selling for $29.60?

Using a Calculator

STEP 1 Identify % and *W*.
% = 5%, *W* = $29.60

STEP 2 On your calculator, you add $29.60 and 5% of $29.60. The complete calculation is done by pressing the keys shown below.

Press Keys	Display Reads
2 9 . 6 0	29.60
×	29.6
5	5.
SHIFT %	1.48
+	31.08

ANSWER: $31.08

Compare with Pencil-and-Paper Solution

STEP 1 Identify % and *W*.
% = 5%
W = $29.60

STEP 2 Change 5% to a decimal.
5% = 0.05

STEP 3 To find the sales tax, multiply $29.60 by 0.05.
$29.60
× 0.05
1.48 00 = $1.48

STEP 4 To find the purchase price, add the sales tax ($1.48) to the selling price ($29.60).
$29.60
+ 1.48
$31.08

ANSWER: $31.08

Discovery: To **subtract** 5%, press 2 9 . 6 0 × 5 SHIFT % − . Your calculator will automatically subtract 1.48 (5% of 29.60) from 29.60.

Below are several types of problems in which you can use your calculator to increase or decrease a whole by a percent. Remember:

- **To solve an increase problem, add the percent.**
- **To solve a decrease problem, subtract the percent.**

RATE INCREASE: New amount = original amount + amount of increase

1. In 1980 the population of North Oswego was 48,600. By 1990 the population had risen 24%. In 1990, what was the population?

2. Property taxes are going up to $2\frac{1}{5}$% next year. Bill paid $1,950 in property taxes this year. What will his property taxes be next year?

RATE DECREASE: New amount = original amount − amount of decrease

3. Due to an unusually warm winter, the Thurmans' heating bill was 30% lower this year than last year. If last year's heating bill was $184.60, how much did they pay this year?

4. Van had a part-time job that paid her $13,432 per year. She changed jobs, and her new salary is 8.5% lower than her old salary. Find her yearly income at her new part-time job.

MARKUP: Selling price = store's cost + markup

5. Lucky Saver Stores places a 15% markup on every item they sell. Knowing this, determine the price Lucky Saver will charge for a pair of work boots that cost Lucky Saver $54.60.

6. At Fran's Clothes Closet, Fran pays $56.00 for the Paris Nights evening gowns that she sells. If Fran adds a 30% markup to her cost, what price does she ask for these gowns?

DISCOUNT: Sale price = original price − amount of discount

7. At a Saturday Only sale, Special Electronics is offering a discount of 25% on all store merchandise. There is also a 10% coupon on car stereos. What will be the final price of a car stereo that normally sells for $149.80?

8. In problem 7 above, would the price be the same if the discount were 35%? If not, what would the price be?

Percent and a Family Budget

To keep track of expenses, many families prepare a household budget. Using a calculator makes it much easier to check and recheck numbers.

Last year the Corwin family had a take-home income of $44,624. At the end of the year, they prepared a record of their yearly expenses. Using this budget, the Corwins are better able to decide how to save money during the coming year.

The two circle graphs below show the Corwins' yearly expenses broken down into various expense categories.

- The graph at the left shows the *dollar amounts* spent.
- The graph at the right (partially completed) shows the *percent* of take-home income spent in each category.

The example shows how the percent for housing (32%) is calculated.

EXAMPLE   What percent of their take-home income do the Corwins spend on housing?

> **STEP 1**   On the graph at the left, find the dollar amount for housing. $14,280
>
> **STEP 2**   Calculate what percent $14,280 is of $44,624.

Press Keys	Display Reads
1 4 2 8 0 ÷ 4 4 6 2 4 SHIFT %	32.0007171

ANSWER: 32%

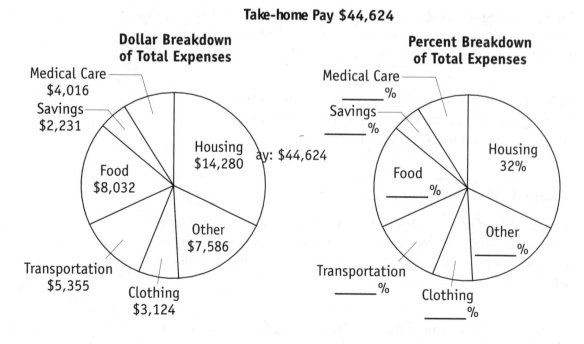

Take-home Pay $44,624

Dollar Breakdown of Total Expenses

Medical Care $4,016
Savings $2,231
Food $8,032
Transportation $5,355
Housing $14,280
Other $7,586
Clothing $3,124

Percent Breakdown of Total Expenses

Medical Care _____ %
Savings _____ %
Food _____ %
Transportation _____ %
Housing 32%
Other _____ %
Clothing _____ %

Use your calculator and the information on page 80 to do each problem below. Remember to use the percent circle (page 71) to help you decide whether to multiply or divide.

1. Fill in the *Percent Breakdown of Total Expenses* graph on page 80. The percent value for housing is completed as an example. Express each answer to the nearest percent.

2. Last year Mrs. Corwin worked part-time and earned 16% of the family take-home income. What dollar amount of take-home income did Mrs. Corwin earn?

3. Each month last year, the Corwins made a $194.50 car payment. To the nearest percent, what percent of their yearly transportation costs was spent on car payments? (**Hint:** Don't forget to multiply their monthly payment by the number of months in a year.)

4. The Corwins made monthly rent payments of $870.25 during last year. To the nearest percent, what percent of their total take-home pay was spent last year for rent?

5. If the Corwins spent $878.45 last year on prescription drugs, what percent of their medical care expenses was spent for these medicines? Express your answer to the nearest percent.

6. Last year the Corwins donated 1.25% of their total take-home income to charities. To the nearest dollar, what amount did they give to charities?

7. To save money this year, the Corwins have decided to cut back on transportation costs. By taking the bus to work, Mr. Corwin figures he can save 15% on family transportation expenses. If he's right, how much money can Mr. Corwin actually save by riding the bus?

8. The Corwin family has set a goal of putting 25% more money into savings this year than they did last year. To achieve this goal, how much will they need to place in savings this year?

Finding Percent of Increase or Decrease

One type of multistep problem involves finding percent of increase or percent of decrease. These problems combine your percent skills with your skills of evaluating arithmetic expressions.

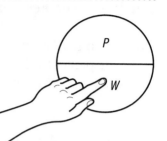

$$\% = \frac{P}{W} = \frac{\text{part (amount of increase)}}{\text{original amount}}$$

EXAMPLE When she changed part-time jobs, Lee's monthly income rose from $720 to $864. What percent of increase is this?

		Press Keys	Display Reads
STEP 1	Subtract to find the **amount of increase**— the part (*P*). $P = \$864 - \$720$	8 6 4	864.
		−	864.
STEP 2	Divide *P* by *W* (the original amount $720) to find the **percent of increase** (%).	7 2 0	720.
		=	144.
		÷	144.
		7 2 0	720.
		SHIFT %	20.

ANSWER: 20%

Calculate each percent of increase or percent of decrease. Round your answers to the nearest percent.

$$\% = \frac{P}{W} \quad \bigg| \quad \% \text{ of increase or decrease} = \frac{\text{amount of increase or decrease}}{\text{original amount}}$$

1. Last month, Cybil's salary was raised from $8.60 per hour to $9.30 per hour. What percent raise did Cybil receive?

2. Nora's Woolens reduced the price of a sweater from $38.50 to $27.95. What percent of price reduction is this?

3. Between 1990 and 2000, the value of Will's condominium increased from $48,600 to $62,800. What percent of value increase is this?

4. In the past 10 years, the population of Oak Grove decreased from 72,600 to 61,710. What percent of population decrease does this change represent?

5. Between September 1 and June 1, the average weekly rainfall in Newton increased from 1.2 inches to 1.5 inches. What percent of increase in rainfall does this change represent?

6. For the weekend, Jerry's lowered the price of its single-scoop ice cream cones from $2.25 to $1.75. What percent of price decrease is this price reduction?

Percent Review

This review covers the material you have just studied. When you finish, check your answers at the back of the book.

Solve each problem.

1. The Mullens are moving to a new house. Their bedroom area is 600 square feet. This is 30% of the total square footage of the house. How many square feet is the house?

2. Taxes are going up 6.5% this year. The increase is $130. What were the taxes last year?

3. A nautical mile is a unit of length used to measure distance at sea. A nautical mile is 6,076 feet. In standard units, a mile is 5,280 feet. What percent of a standard mile is a nautical mile? Round your answer to the nearest whole percent.

4. Last year mortgage rates were $8\frac{1}{2}$%. This year they are $7\frac{1}{8}$%. To the nearest tenth, what is the percent of decrease in mortgage rates?

5. The Smith family had the following consumption of electricity.

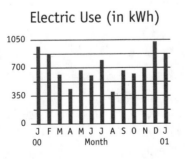

Electric Use (in kWh)

What was the percent of increase from the lowest month of consumption to the highest?

6. How many ounces of butterfat are in 64 ounces of cream that is 32% butterfat?

7. The Elston Company is offering production jobs at a starting salary of $24,250. In the first 2 years, there will be a $3\frac{1}{8}\%$ increase each year. What would be the wages in the third year of work?

8. Renee and Bridget went shopping. They each bought boots. Renee bought a pair for $49.48 marked down from $78.98. Bridget bought a pair for $65.00 marked down from $110.00. Who received the greater discount?

9. Acklin Appliances is marking down its appliances by 20%. What will be the sale price of a washer that normally sells for $289?

Percent Review Chart

Circle the number of any problem that you missed and review the appropriate pages. A passing score is 7 correct answers. If you missed more than two questions, you should review this chapter.

PROBLEM NUMBERS	SKILL AREA	PRACTICE PAGES
1	finding the whole	76–77
2, 5, 7	percent of increase	82
3, 8	finding the percent	74–75
4	percent of decrease	82
6	finding the part	72–73
9	decreasing a whole by a part	78–79

GED PRACTICE

The GED has a newly designed format and answer sheet. Some of the questions are multiple choice, and some are alternate format. The alternate format questions will be answered on a number grid as shown below. In order to prepare you for the new format, the GED Practice sections in *Calculator Power for the GED* have multiple choice answers as well as number grids.

Alternate Format Items

For alternate format problems you will write your answer in a number grid as shown. Fill in the top row with your answer and then fill in the ovals underneath to indicate your desired answer. The answers can be set to the right, to the left, or in the center. Unused columns should be left blank.

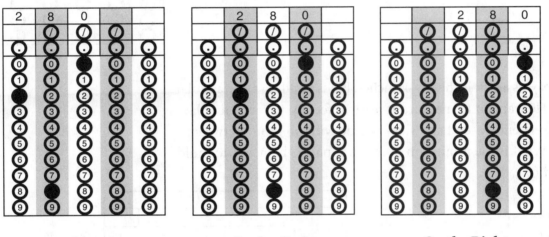

On the Left   **In the Center**   **On the Right**

The grid can also be used for fractional answers as well as decimal answers. Mixed numbers cannot be entered on the number grid.

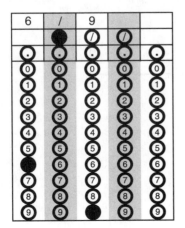
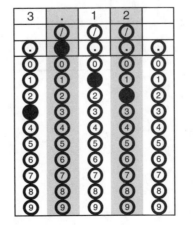

1. A nickel measures $\frac{1}{16}$ inch in thickness. What is the value of a stack of nickels $2\frac{1}{2}$ inches high?

   (1) $ 0.025
   (2) $ 1.56
   (3) $ 2.00
   (4) $ 2.50
   (5) $40.00

2. Yogurt is sold in three different types of packages.
   - a 6-pack of 4-ounce containers for $2.89
   - an 8-ounce container for $0.85
   - a 16-ounce container for $1.80

   Jane is buying yogurt to serve at a luncheon for 8 people. Each serving will be 4 ounces. What is the least she can spend to serve her guests? Mark your answer on the number grid.

3. Patio pavers are $8\frac{1}{2}$ inches by $4\frac{1}{2}$ inches. Bill is building a rectangular patio. He wants it to measure at least 10 feet by 12 feet. He is laying the pavers end-to-end and side-by-side with no grout between them. What is the minimum number of pavers he needs to build the patio?

   (1) 120
   (2) 416
   (3) 451
   (4) 459
   (5) 480

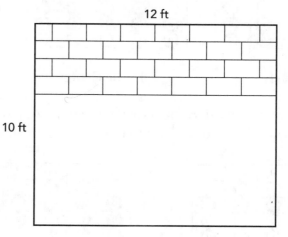

4. The Northern Company manufactures cartridges for printers. They are packaged 30 to a carton. The company produced 8925 cartridges last week. Of the cartridges produced, 123 were rejected for defects. How many cartons were filled last week?

   (1) 72
   (2) 73
   (3) 293
   (4) 294
   (5) Not enough information is given.

5. How many more cartridges need to be produced to fill the next carton? Mark your answer on the number grid.

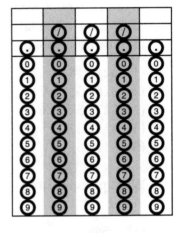

6. To find the average of numbers, add the numbers and divide the sum by the number of numbers you added. The high temperature for the day was 37.5° C. The low temperature for the day was 17.2° C. What was the average temperature for the day in degress Celsius?

   (1)   10.15°
   (2)   20.3°
   (3)   27.35°
   (4)   54.7°
   (5) 109.4°

7. Each area of a plant is keeping attendance records. On a specific day, the following information was recorded:
   Area A had 16% of its people absent.
   Area B had 20 out of 23 people at work.
   Area C had 0.15 of its people absent.

   Which area had the best attendance for the day?

   (1) A
   (2) B
   (3) C
   (4) A and C
   (5) Not enough information is given.

Questions 8 and 9 refer to the table below which shows costs associated with purchasing a term life insurance policy.

Cost Per Thousand Per Year		
	Smokers	**Non-Smokers**
Under 50	$4.15	$3.45
50 and over	$4.45	$3.62

8. Juanita's date of birth is February 15, 1946. She has never smoked. According to the table, how much will she pay for a $75,000 term life insurance policy for one year?

    (1) $217.18
    (2) $262.50
    (3) $271.50
    (4) $311.25
    (5) $315.61

9. What percent more does a smoker under 50 pay than a non-smoker under 50?

    (1) 5%
    (2) 7%
    (3) 8%
    (4) 17%
    (5) 20%

10. A riveted metal plate is shown. What fractional part of the rivets are in rows 2 and 3? Mark your answer on the number grid.

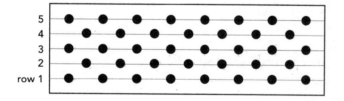

Algebra

SIGNED NUMBERS

Locating Points on a Number Line

A **number line** has positive and negative numbers. The numbers to the left of 0 are negative and have a value less than 0. The numbers to the right of 0 are positive and have a value greater than 0. Zero is neither positive nor negative.

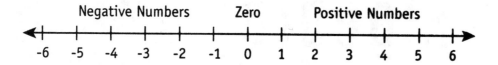

When writing a number with a value less than 0, or a negative number, write a minus sign (−) in front of the number. A positive number is written with no sign or a + sign. Positive and negative numbers are sometimes referred to as **signed numbers**. A number line can be vertical or horizontal. A thermometer is an example of a vertical number line.

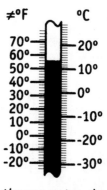

A thermometer shows both positive and negative temperatures.

- The numbers above 0° are positive.

- The numbers below 0° are negative.

- A temperature of −4°F is read 4 degrees below 0. The minus sign indicates the temperature is less than zero.

- A temperature of 4°F is read as 4 degrees. This temperature could also be written as +4°.

Graph each of the following numbers on the number line. Label the point by writing the number below the point.

1. -1 3 4.5 $\frac{5}{2}$ $-\frac{5}{2}$

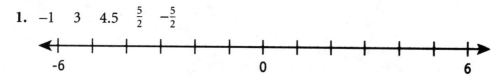

Write the number that corresponds to the letter of the point.

2.

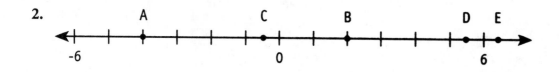

Adding Signed Numbers

Patterns and rules can help you solve problems involving positive and negative numbers. Look at the pattern below.

$$4 + (-2) = 2$$
$$4 + (-3) = 1$$
$$4 + (-4) = 0$$
$$4 + (-5) = -1$$
$$4 + (-6) = -2$$
$$4 + (-7) = -3$$

As you add smaller numbers, the sum gets smaller.
To add signed numbers, do the following:

- If the numbers have the same sign, add the numbers. Keep the sign of the numbers.

EXAMPLE 1 $5 + 2 =$

The signs are alike. Add the numbers and give the sum a positive sign. $5 + 2 = 7$

EXAMPLE 2 $(-3) + (-2) =$

The signs are alike. Add the numbers and give the sum a negative sign. $(-3) + (-2) = -5$

- If the numbers have different signs, subtract the numbers. Give the sum the sign of the greater number.

EXAMPLE 3 $-7 + 4 =$

The signs are different. Subtract the numbers. Give the sum a negative sign. (7 is greater than 4.) $-7 + 4 = -3$

Predict whether the sum will be positive or negative. Write + or −.

1. $1 + (-3) =$ $-2 + (-1) =$ $18 + (-2) =$

2. $\frac{6}{7} + \frac{5}{8} =$ $-2.1 + (-0.5) =$ $-\frac{1}{4} + \frac{1}{2} =$

3. $20.25 + (-24.5) =$ $-135 + 129 =$ $(-7.8) + (-\frac{1}{2}) =$

Subtracting Signed Numbers

Look at the pattern of the subtraction problems.

$$4 - 4 = 0$$
$$4 - 3 = 1$$
$$4 - 2 = 2$$
$$4 - 1 = 3$$
$$4 - 0 = 4$$
$$4 - (-1) = 5$$
$$4 - (-2) = -6$$
$$4 - (-3) = -7$$

As you subtract smaller numbers, the difference becomes greater.
To subtract signed numbers, do the following:

STEP 1 Change the sign of the number that is being subtracted.

STEP 2 Change the subtraction sign to addition.

STEP 3 Follow the rules for addition.

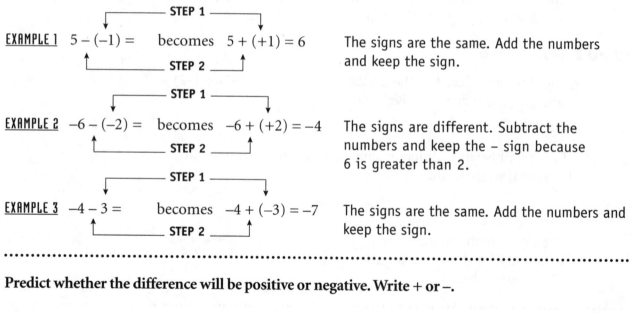

EXAMPLE 1 $5 - (-1) =$ becomes $5 + (+1) = 6$ The signs are the same. Add the numbers and keep the sign.

EXAMPLE 2 $-6 - (-2) =$ becomes $-6 + (+2) = -4$ The signs are different. Subtract the numbers and keep the – sign because 6 is greater than 2.

EXAMPLE 3 $-4 - 3 =$ becomes $-4 + (-3) = -7$ The signs are the same. Add the numbers and keep the sign.

Predict whether the difference will be positive or negative. Write + or –.

1. $-2 - (-4) =$ $-2 - 6 =$ $8 - (+9) =$

2. $5 - (-8) =$ $-3 - (-9) =$ $4.5 - (+6) =$

3. $\frac{1}{2} - 1 =$ $-11 - 5 =$ $-10\frac{1}{2} - (+5) =$

Using Your Calculator to Add and Subtract Signed Numbers

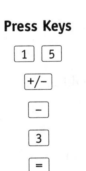

You can use your calculator to add and subtract signed numbers. On the Casio *fx*-260 the key for positive and negative numbers [+/−] is the key above the [7] key. When you enter a negative number, enter the number first, then press the [+/−] key to make the number negative. A − sign will appear in the display. This will work for decimals and fractions as well.

−2 on your display looks like this:

| − 2. |

EXAMPLE 1 $10 + (-4) =$

Press Keys	Display Reads
[1] [0]	10.
[+]	10.
[4]	4.
[+/−]	− 4.
[=]	6.

ANSWER: 6

EXAMPLE 2 $-15 - 3 =$

Press Keys	Display Reads
[1] [5]	15.
[+/−]	− 15.
[−]	− 15.
[3]	3.
[=]	− 18.

ANSWER: −18

Use your calculator to find the sum or difference.

1. $12 + (-2) =$

2. $-10 - (-5) =$

3. $-78 + (22) =$

4. $-1.35 - 0.4 =$

5. $6 + (-6) =$

$0.25 + (-1) =$

$-\frac{1}{2} + (-\frac{1}{6}) =$

$(-9.1) + 7.5 =$

$3\frac{3}{4} + (-1\frac{1}{3}) =$

$25 + 16 - 6 =$

$\frac{3}{8} + (-\frac{5}{8}) + (-\frac{1}{2}) =$

$-10.25 + 1.1 - 6.4 =$

$8 - 9 =$

$-4 + (-6) + 3 =$

$7 - (-6) =$

Multiplying Signed Numbers

In algebra, as well as arithmetic, multiplication can be shown in three ways:

- by a times sign: -8×-7
- by parentheses: $(-8)(-7)$
- by a raised dot: $-8 \cdot -7$

Rules for multiplying signed numbers:
- If the signs of the numbers are alike, multiply the numbers and give the product a positive sign.

  positive × positive = positive   negative × negative = positive

- If the signs of the numbers are different, multiply the numbers and give the product a negative sign.

  positive × negative = negative   negative × positive = negative

EXAMPLE 1 $-8 \times -4 =$

    STEP 1   Multiply the numbers. $-8 \times -4 = +32$

    STEP 2   Because the signs are both negative, the product is positive.

EXAMPLE 2 $(-3)(7) =$

    STEP 1   Multiply the numbers. $(-3)(7) = -21$

    STEP 2   Because the signs are different, the product is negative.

Predict whether the product will be positive or negative. Write + or −.

1. $4 \times (-6) =$ $-3(1.01) =$ $(-5)(-5) =$

2. $(-6)(-2) =$ $-\frac{7}{8} \times 10 =$ $(-3)(-3)(-3) =$

3. $23(4) =$ $(2.25)(-0.1) =$ $(-\frac{3}{4})(-\frac{1}{2}) =$

Dividing Signed Numbers

The division problem $2\overline{)10}$ can be shown in three other ways:

- by a division sign: $10 \div 2$
- by a slash: $10/2$
- by a fraction bar: $\frac{10}{2}$

Rules for dividing signed numbers:
- If the signs of the numbers are alike, divide the numbers and give the quotient a positive sign.

  positive ÷ positive = positive   negative ÷ negative = positive

- If the signs of the numbers are different, divide the numbers and give the quotient a negative sign.

  positive ÷ negative = negative   negative ÷ positive = negative

EXAMPLE 1 $-6 \div -2 =$

STEP 1   Divide the numbers. $-6 \div -2 = +3$

STEP 2   Because the signs are both
negative, the quotient is positive.

EXAMPLE 2 $\frac{20}{-4} =$

STEP 1   Divide the numbers. $\frac{20}{-4} = -5$

STEP 2   Because the signs are different,
the quotient is negative.

Predict whether the quotient will be positive or negative. Write + or −.

1. $\frac{12}{-12} =$ $\frac{-35}{7} =$ $(-6) \div (-2) =$

2. $6 \div 2 =$ $\frac{18}{-6} =$ $\frac{2}{3} \div \frac{1}{2} =$

3. $24 \div -4 =$ $\frac{-25}{-5} =$ $-3.5 \div 0.7 =$

Using Your Calculator to Multiply and Divide Signed Numbers

Like addition and subtraction, you can use your calculator to multiply and divide signed numbers. When you enter a negative number, enter the number first, then press the $\boxed{+/-}$ key to make the number negative. A – sign will appear in the display. You can enter negative decimals and fractions using the same steps.

EXAMPLE 1 $(-28)(-\frac{3}{4}) =$

	Press Keys	Display Reads
	$\boxed{2}$ $\boxed{8}$	28.
	$\boxed{+/-}$	-28.
	$\boxed{\times}$	-28.
	$\boxed{3}$ $\boxed{\text{a b/c}}$ $\boxed{4}$	3⌐4.
	$\boxed{+/-}$	-3⌐4.
	$\boxed{=}$	21.

ANSWER: 21

EXAMPLE 2 $-50 \div (-\frac{1}{2}) =$

	Press Keys	Display Reads
	$\boxed{5}$ $\boxed{0}$	50.
	$\boxed{+/-}$	-50.
	$\boxed{\div}$	-50.
	$\boxed{1}$ $\boxed{\text{a b/c}}$ $\boxed{2}$	1⌐2.
	$\boxed{+/-}$	-1⌐2.
	$\boxed{=}$	100.

ANSWER: 100

Use your calculator to find the product or quotient.

1. $(-12)2 =$ $18 \div (-\frac{2}{3}) =$ $-\frac{5}{12} \div 6 =$

2. $\frac{150}{-25} =$ $12 \div (-\frac{3}{4}) =$ $(-5)(-5) =$

3. $-0.25 \times 80 =$ $(-15)(\frac{3}{5}) =$ $(8)(12)(-1) =$

4. $\frac{-12}{8} =$ $(-\frac{1}{2})(-\frac{1}{3}) =$ $(-3)(\frac{1}{3})(-7) =$

5. $(8)(-\frac{1}{2}) =$ $\frac{8.4}{-4} =$ $(5)(-5)(-2) =$

Signed Numbers Review

The review covers the material you have just studied. When you finish, check your answers at the back of the book.

Solve each problem.

1. Label the number line with these points: 1   –2   4   –4

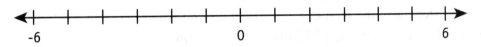

2. Which letter on the number line below corresponds to the number $-2\frac{1}{2}$?

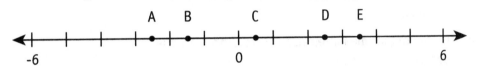

3. Which example, a, b, c, or d, is in correct numerical order?

   a. 8   –2   2   **c.** –8   1.1   6

   b. $1\frac{3}{4}$ 0   3   **d.** –10   –12   –4

Add, subtract, multiply, or divide.

4. $7 + (-5) =$ $-16 + (-6) =$ $-8 + 3 =$ $11 + (-9) =$

5. $-5 - (-9) =$ $-12 - 6 =$ $5 - 9 =$ $15 - 18 =$

6. $8(-4) =$ $(-9)(-6) =$ $(-1)(-4)(7) =$ $(-1)(0)(-3) =$

7. $24 \div -8 =$ $-48 \div -3 =$ $-27 \div 3 =$ $-14 \div -16 =$

Use your calculator to help you solve these problems.

8. In one hour the temperature rose 7°F then dropped 13°. If the temperature started at 34°F, what is the temperature now?

9. The closing price of a stock decreased $50 over one week. If the rate of decrease was the same over the five days, how much did the price of the stock decrease in one day?

10. A football player had a gain of 24 yards on the first play, a loss of 13 yards on the second, and a loss of 8 more yards on the third. What was the total net yardage gained or lost in the three plays?

11. Tolerance is the amount of variation permitted for a given measurement. Signed numbers are used to show tolerance. A measurement of 2 inches $\pm\frac{1}{2}$ inch is read "2 inches plus or minus one-half inch." The tolerance for this measurement is $\frac{1}{2}$ inch. The target measurement is 2 inches. To be within the tolerance, the measurement must be between $1\frac{1}{2}$ inches and $2\frac{1}{2}$ inches.

   STEP 1 To find minimum measure, subtract the tolerance from the target measure.

   STEP 2 To find the maximum measure, add the tolerance to the target measure.

   Find the minimum and maximum measure for this part.

   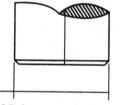

   35.8 mm ±0.01 mm

12. Mt. McKinley is the highest peak in the U.S., measuring approximately 20,300 feet above sea level. Death Valley is the lowest land point in the U.S., measuring approximately 1,290 feet below sea level. What is the difference, in feet, between the highest and lowest points in the U.S.?

13. If a temperature is falling at a constant rate of 3°F per hour, how much higher was the temperature 6 hours ago?

14. Find two signed numbers with a sum of −13 and a product of 40.

15. In a game, Mike was *down* 20 points. If the winning score is 50 points, how many points does Mike need to gain to win the game?

Signed Numbers Review Chart

Circle the number of any problem that you missed and review the appropriate pages. A passing score is 13 correct. If you missed more than two questions, you should review this chapter.

PROBLEM NUMBERS	SKILL AREA	PRACTICE PAGES
1, 2, 3	number line	90
4, 8, 10, 11	adding signed numbers	91, 93
5, 8, 11, 12, 15	subtracting signed numbers	92, 93
6, 13, 14	multiplying signed numbers	94, 96
7, 9	dividing signed numbers	95, 96

POWERS AND ROOTS

What Is a Power?

A **power** is the product of a number multiplied by itself one or more times. A power is commonly written as a **base** and an **exponent**.

power or exponent

4^2 is read 4 to the second power or 4 squared and means 4×4

base

The number you are multiplying is called the *base*.
The *exponent* tells how many times the number is being multiplied.

Look at these examples.

Product	As a base and exponent	In words
4×4	4^2	4 to the second power or 4 squared
$(-2)(-2)$	$(-2)^2$	−2 to the second power or −2 squared
$5 \times 5 \times 5$	5^3	5 to the third power or 5 cubed
$\frac{1}{2} \times \frac{1}{2} \times \frac{1}{2} \times \frac{1}{2}$	$(\frac{1}{2})^4$	$\frac{1}{2}$ to the fourth power
$10 \cdot 10 \cdot 10 \cdot 10 \cdot 10$	10^5	10 to the fifth power

When writing a decimal or fractional number with a power, it will often be written with parentheses around it.

EXAMPLES 12.5^2 is often written $(12.5)^2$
           $\frac{1}{3}^2$ is often written $(\frac{1}{3})^2$

When you find powers of numbers less than 1, the value decreases. Finding powers of a fraction or decimal means multiplying that fraction or decimal by itself. You saw in the decimal and fraction units that the product is less than the multipliers.

$$(\tfrac{1}{4})^2 = \tfrac{1}{4} \times \tfrac{1}{4} = \tfrac{1}{16}$$
$$(0.5)^3 = 0.5 \times 0.5 \times 0.5 = 0.125$$

> • Any number raised to the 0 power is 1. $8^0 = 1$
>
> • Any number raised to the first power is the number itself. $8^1 = 8$

Use exponents to rewrite the following multiplication problems.

1. $7 \times 7 \times 7 \times 7 \times 7 =$ $1 \times 1 \times 1 =$

2. $\frac{1}{4} \times \frac{1}{4} \times \frac{1}{4} =$ $0.3 \times 0.3 \times 0.3 \times 0.3 =$

3. $10 \times 10 =$ $-5 \times -5 =$

4. $2 \times 2 \times 2 \times 2 =$ inch × inch × inch =

5. feet × feet × feet =   meter × meter =

Write the following as multiplication.

6. $3^2 =$ $5^3 =$ $1^4 =$

7. $2^3 =$ $(7.5)^2 =$ $2^5 =$

8. $20^1 =$ $(-6)^2 =$ $\left(\frac{1}{2}\right)^3 =$

Rewrite as a power.

9. 100 cubed   30 to the first power

10. 15 to the third power   10 cubed

11. 5 squared -3 to the fifth power

12. $\frac{2}{10}$ to the fourth power $\frac{2}{100}$ to the second power

13. $\frac{3}{8}$ to the fifth power   8 to the zero power

Finding Squares

You can use your calculator to square a number. Find the $\boxed{x^2}$ key on the top row of keys on the Casio *fx*-260. Enter the number to be squared and then press the $\boxed{x^2}$ key. You do not need to press the $\boxed{=}$ key.

EXAMPLE 1 Find the area of a room that measures 12.5 feet on each side.

$A = s^2$

$A = (12.5)^2$

	Press Keys	Display Reads
	$\boxed{1}\ \boxed{2}\ \boxed{\cdot}\ \boxed{5}$	12.5
	$\boxed{x^2}$	156.25

ANSWER: 156.25 sq ft

When you enter a fraction on your calculator and use the $\boxed{x^2}$ key, the answer will NOT be in fractional form. Rather it will be in decimal form. To get a fractional answer, square the numerator and denominator on your calculator separately.

EXAMPLE 2 $(\frac{2}{3})^2 = \frac{2}{3} \times \frac{2}{3}$

To Get a Decimal Answer:

Press Keys	Display Reads
$\boxed{2}$	2.
$\boxed{a\ b/c}$	2⌐.
$\boxed{3}$	2⌐3.
$\boxed{x^2}$	0.444444444

ANSWER: 0.444444444 . . .

To Get a Fractional Answer:

Press Keys	Display Reads
$\boxed{2}$	2.
$\boxed{x^2}$	4.
$\boxed{3}$	3.
$\boxed{x^2}$	9.

ANSWER: $\frac{4}{9}$

Use your calculator to find the value of each power.

1. $100^2 =$ $(-5)^2 =$ $(12)^2 =$

2. $(0.1)^2 =$ $13^2 =$ $(\frac{2}{3})^2 =$

3. $(2.5)^2 =$ $(-13)^2 =$ $(-\frac{1}{3})^2 =$

Find the value of each power.

                 decimal value   fractional value

4. $(\frac{3}{8})^2$

5. $(-\frac{5}{6})^2$

Finding Cubes and Other Powers

You have seen that a number raised to the third power or cubed means multiplying the number by itself three times.

$$4^3 = 4 \times 4 \times 4$$

You can use your calculator to cube a number. The $\boxed{x^3}$ function on the Casio *fx-260* is above the $\boxed{\blacktriangleright}$ key. To find the cube of a number, press the $\boxed{\text{SHIFT}}$ key first and then $\boxed{x^3}$.

EXAMPLE 1 Find the value of 6^3.

Press Keys	Display Reads
$\boxed{6}$	6.
$\boxed{\text{SHIFT}}$ $\boxed{x^3}$	216.

ANSWER: 216

You have seen that numbers can be raised to powers higher than three. You can find other powers on your calculator by using the $\boxed{x^y}$ key. This key is above the $\boxed{C}$ and $\boxed{AC}$ keys on the Casio *fx-260*.

$$x^y \longleftarrow \text{exponent}$$
$$\uparrow$$
$$\text{base}$$

EXAMPLE 2 What is the value of 4^6?

Press Keys	Display Reads
$\boxed{4}$	4.
$\boxed{x^y}$	4.
$\boxed{6}$	6.
$\boxed{=}$	4096.

ANSWER: 4,096

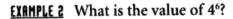

Use your calculator to find the value of each power.

1. $3^3 =$ $(-2)^3 =$ $(0.3)^2 =$

2. $(\frac{1}{2})^3 =$ $(-15)^3 =$ $2^{10} =$

3. $0.2^2 =$ $6^7 =$ $(-8)^4 =$

4. $100^3 =$ $100^4 =$ $100^1 =$

5. $5^5 =$ $3^4 =$ $4^3 =$

What Is a Root?

The **root** of a number is a quantity taken two or more times as an equal factor of the number. Finding a root is the opposite operation of finding a power. The radical symbol ($\sqrt{}$) is used to indicate the root of a number. The **index** indicates the amount of times that a root is to be taken as an equal factor to produce the given number.

$$\text{index} \longrightarrow \sqrt[3]{8} \longleftarrow \text{radical symbol}$$

The index is the small number written above and to the left of the radical symbol. The index 2 is usually omitted. It is understood. For example, to find $\sqrt{9}$, ask yourself, "What number times itself equals 9?"

$$3 \times 3 = 9, \text{ therefore } \sqrt{9} \text{ is 3.}$$

In the expression $\sqrt[3]{8}$, ask yourself, "What number times itself three times equals 8?"

$$2 \times 2 \times 2 = 8, \text{ therefore } \sqrt[3]{8} \text{ is 2.}$$

Look at these examples.

Notation	In Words
$\sqrt{4}$	square root of 4
$\sqrt[3]{8}$	cube root of 8
$\sqrt[4]{0.0016}$	fourth root of 0.0016
$\sqrt[5]{243}$	fifth root of 243
$\sqrt[10]{1,024}$	tenth root of 1,024

Write each sentence below in symbols. The first one is done as an example.

1. The square root of 25 is 5. $\sqrt{25} = 5$ The cube root of 1,728 is 12.

2. The fifth root of 32 is 2.   The tenth root of 59,049 is 3.

3. The cube root of 15.625 is 2.5.   The square root of $\frac{1}{4}$ is $\frac{1}{2}$.

Complete the statements below.

4. $1.5 \times 1.5 = 2.25$, so $\sqrt{2.25} =$ $1 \times 1 \times 1 \times 1 = 1$, so $\sqrt[4]{1} =$

5. $0.3 \times 0.3 \times 0.3 = 0.027$, so $\sqrt[3]{0.027} =$ $4 \times 4 \times 4 \times 4 \times 4 = 1024$, so $\sqrt[5]{1,024} =$

Square Roots

Numbers that have whole-number square roots are called **perfect squares**. The first 12 perfect squares are shown in the table below.

Table of Perfect Squares			
$1^2 = 1$	$4^2 = 16$	$7^2 = 49$	$10^2 = 100$
$2^2 = 4$	$5^2 = 25$	$8^2 = 64$	$11^2 = 121$
$3^2 = 9$	$6^2 = 36$	$9^2 = 81$	$12^2 = 144$

Square roots do not always come out evenly. To estimate the square root of a number, try a few numbers that have a perfect square root.

EXAMPLE 1 Find $\sqrt{75}$.

STEP 1 Find which numbers the square root value falls between.

$\sqrt{64} = 8$
$\sqrt{75} = ?$
$\sqrt{81} = 9$

STEP 2 The square root of the value is between their square roots. Because 75 is close to halfway between 64 and 81, the $\sqrt{75}$ is about 8.5.

$\sqrt{75}$ is between 8 and 9

You can use your calculator to find the square root of a number. The $\boxed{\sqrt{}}$ function on the Casio *fx-260* is above the $\boxed{x^2}$ key. Therefore, press the $\boxed{\text{SHIFT}}$ key before pressing $\boxed{\sqrt{}}$. You do not need to press the $\boxed{=}$ key.

EXAMPLE 2 Use your calculator to find $\sqrt{75}$ to the nearest hundredth.

	Press Keys	Display Reads
	$\boxed{7}$ $\boxed{5}$	75.
	$\boxed{\text{SHIFT}}$ $\boxed{\sqrt{}}$	8.660254038
Round the answer to the nearest hundredth:	$\boxed{\text{MODE}}$ $\boxed{7}$ $\boxed{2}$	8.66

ANSWER: 8.66

Estimate the value of each square root.

1. $\sqrt{5}$ $\sqrt{20}$ $\sqrt{30}$

2. $\sqrt{145}$ $\sqrt{80}$ $\sqrt{105}$

3. $\sqrt{110}$ $\sqrt{55}$ $\sqrt{45}$

For each problem, estimate the square root. Then use your calculator to find a more precise answer. If the answer is not a whole number, round the answer to the nearest tenth.

	estimate	calculator
4. $\sqrt{50}$	_____	_____
5. $\sqrt{0.04}$	_____	_____
6. $\sqrt{99}$	_____	_____
7. $\sqrt{1}$	_____	_____
8. $\sqrt{0.01}$	_____	_____
9. $\sqrt{2,500}$	_____	_____
10. $\sqrt{20.25}$	_____	_____
11. $\sqrt{10,000}$	_____	_____

Cube Roots

When finding the cube root of a number, ask yourself what number times itself 3 times equals that number. You will see that cube roots are often used in finding measurements.

EXAMPLE 1   A cubic tank has a volume (capacity) of 125 cubic feet. What is the length of one side of the tank?

To find the length of one side of the tank, find the cube root of the volume.

$V = s^3$

$5 \times 5 \times 5 = 125$, therefore, $\sqrt[3]{125} = 5$

ANSWER: The length of the side of the tank is **5 feet.**

You can use your calculator to find the cube root of a number. The $\sqrt[3]{}$ function on the Casio *fx*-260 is above the $\boxed{+/-}$ key. Notice $\sqrt[3]{}$ is a second function. Therefore, press the $\boxed{\text{SHIFT}}$ key first and then press $\sqrt[3]{}$. You do not need to press the $\boxed{=}$ key.

EXAMPLE 2   Find $\sqrt[3]{512}$.

Press Keys	Display Reads
$\boxed{5}\ \boxed{1}\ \boxed{2}$	5 1 2.
$\boxed{\text{SHIFT}}\ \boxed{\sqrt[3]{}}$	8.

ANSWER: 8

Use your calculator to find the following roots. Round your answer to the nearest hundredth.

1. $\sqrt{600}$ $\qquad$ $\sqrt{0.36}$ $\qquad$ $\sqrt{1}$

2. $\sqrt[3]{5,400}$ $\qquad$ $\sqrt[3]{8,000}$ $\qquad$ $\sqrt[3]{1}$

3. $\sqrt[3]{100}$ $\qquad$ $\sqrt{256}$ $\qquad$ $\sqrt[3]{15,625}$

4. $\sqrt[3]{0.027}$ $\qquad$ $\sqrt[3]{0.008}$ $\qquad$ $\sqrt[3]{3,000}$

Solve.

5. To find the length of the side of a square, find the square root of the area. A square lot has an area of 11,025 square feet. How many feet is each side?

6. To find the length of the side of a cube, find the cube root of the volume. A square building block has a volume of 1,400 cubic inches. To the nearest tenth of an inch, what does the side measure?

Powers and Roots Review

This review covers the material you have just studied. When you finish, check your answers at the back of the book.

Write the multiplication expressions using powers. Then find the value of each expression.

1. $6 \times 6 =$ $\qquad$ $1.5 \times 1.5 \times 1.5 =$ $\qquad$ $100 \times 100 =$

2. $\frac{1}{2} \times \frac{1}{2} =$ $\qquad$ $-4 \times -4 \times -4 \times -4 \times -4 \times -4 =$ $\qquad$ $a \times a =$

Write an equivalent expression using exponents. The first one is done for you.

3. $\sqrt{81} = 9$ because $9^2 = 81$ $\qquad$ $\sqrt[3]{1,331} = 11$ because

4. $\sqrt{100} = 10$ because $\qquad$ $\sqrt{169} = 13$ because

Write each of the following expressions using a radical ($\sqrt{}$) and index, where necessary.

5. The square root of 1,000 $\qquad$ 6. The cube root of 512 $\qquad$ 7. The fourth root of 6,561

Find the value of each expression. Round your answer to the nearest hundredth when necessary.

8. $\sqrt[3]{0.125}$ $\qquad$ $\sqrt{75}$ $\qquad$ $\sqrt[3]{2,000}$

9. $\sqrt[3]{30}$ $\qquad$ $\sqrt{441}$ $\qquad$ $(21)^2$

10. $(2.1)^3$ $\qquad$ $\sqrt[3]{1,000,000}$ $\qquad$ $(100)^3$

Solve.

11. A plot of land consists of two square parcels. The area of parcel A is 2,500 square yards. The area of parcel B is 6,889 square yards. Find, in yards, length C.

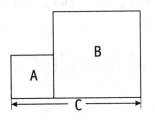

12. In the table below, volumes of cubes are given. Find the length of the side of each cube.

Volume	Length of Side(s)
27 cm³	cm
1,000 cu ft	ft
1 m³	m
216 cu ft	ft
8 cu yd	yd

Powers and Roots Review Chart

Circle the number of any problem that you missed and review the appropriate pages. A passing score is 10 correct. If you missed more than two questions, you should review this chapter.

PROBLEM NUMBERS	SKILL AREA	PRACTICE PAGES
1, 2, 3, 4	writing powers	100–101
5, 6, 7	writing roots	104–107
8, 9, 10	finding powers and roots	102–107
11, 12	finding roots	105–107

OPERATIONS WITH NUMBERS

Order of Operations

So far you have used only one operation at a time with numbers. When given a problem that involves more than one operation, the result that you get often depends upon which operation you do first. For example, in the expression

$$2 + 3 \times 4$$

if addition is done first	if multiplication is done first
$2 + 3 \times 4$	$2 + 3 \times 4$
5×4	$2 + 12$
20	14

Which answer is correct? 14 is the correct answer.

In order that we have a uniform number system and we all get the same answer to a mathematical problem, we follow the **order of operations**. The order of operations is as follows:

1. Do any operations in parentheses first.

2. Evaluate all powers and roots.

3. Do any multiplication or division, from left to right.

4. Do any addition or subtraction, from left to right.

The Casio *fx*-260 calculator is programmed to do the correct order of operations.

For each expression, write which operation would be performed first. Then use your calculator to find the answer. The first example is started for you.

	Operation	Answer
1. $9 + 25 \div 5$	*division*	_____
2. $16 \times \frac{1}{3} \div 4$	_____	_____
3. $-2 + 3 \times 6$	_____	_____
4. $2 - 8 \div 4$	_____	_____
5. $20 + 20 \div 5 + 5$	_____	_____

Expressions with Grouping Symbols

The customary order of operations that your scientific calculator performs automatically can be overridden by using the parentheses keys on your calculator.

When an expression with an operation is enclosed in parentheses, that operation is performed first, according to the order of operations. Parentheses can change the order in which operations are performed.

The following expressions are the same *except for the parentheses*. The addition of the parentheses changes the order of operations and thus changes the values of the expressions.

<u>EXAMPLE 1</u>

$4 + 6 \times 7$

$4 + 42$ multiplication before addition

ANSWER: 46

<u>EXAMPLE 2</u>

$(4 + 6) \times 7$

10×7 calculate the operation in ( ) first

ANSWER: 70

Find the parentheses keys $\boxed{[(...}$ $\boxed{...)]}$ in the center of the Casio *fx*-260. When you press the left parenthesis key $\boxed{[(...}$, notice that $\boxed{[01}$ appears in the display. This indicates that you have pressed the left parenthesis key for the first time. The Casio *fx*-260 will simplify expressions with more than one set of parentheses, and this helps keep track of how many times the parenthesis key has been pressed. When you "close" the parentheses by pressing the right parenthesis, nothing appears in the display.

Sometimes the multiplication sign is not written before an expression or number in parentheses. On the Casio *fx*-260 calculator, remember to press the $\boxed{\times}$ key, even though you do not see it written in the expression.

<u>EXAMPLE 3</u> $4(8 - 2) =$

Press Keys	Display Reads
$\boxed{4}$	4.
$\boxed{\times}$	4.
$\boxed{[(...}$	[0 1 0.
$\boxed{8}$	8.
$\boxed{-}$	8.
$\boxed{2}$	2.
$\boxed{...)]}$	6.
$\boxed{=}$	2 4.

ANSWER: 24

Sometimes an expression includes a fraction or a power along with parentheses keys. Key the expression into your calculator just as you read it, from left to right.

EXAMPLE 4 $4^2 - (6 \div \frac{2}{3}) =$

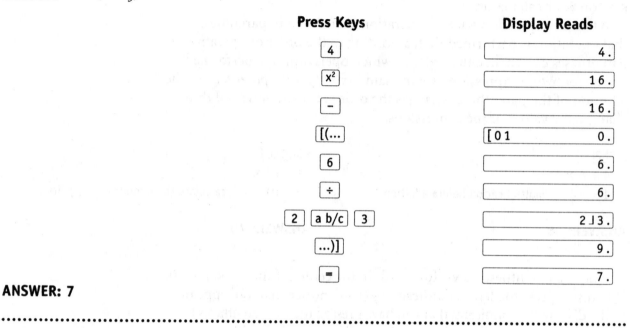

Press Keys	Display Reads
4	4.
x^2	16.
−	16.
[(...	[01 0.
6	6.
÷	6.
2 a b/c 3	2⌐3.
...)]	9.
=	7.

ANSWER: 7

Use your calculator to find the value of each expression.

1. $12(43 + 7) =$ $6(\frac{1}{2} + \frac{1}{3}) =$

2. $(56 - 28) \div 4 =$ $18.7 + (4.2 \times 3) =$

3. $(\$4.56 + \$2.31) \times 3 =$ $20 \div (7 + 3) =$

4. $(45 + 28 - 19) \div 9 =$ $12 - (3 \times \frac{2}{3}) =$

5. $14(63 - 35) =$ $2^2 + (6 \div 3) =$

As stated in the order of operations, the fraction bar is a grouping symbol. If a problem involves a fraction bar, do the calculations above and below the bar before you divide. On your calculator put parentheses around the numerator and denominator if they have an operation in them.

EXAMPLE 5 $\frac{20-5}{3} =$

	Press Keys	Display Reads
	[(...	[0 1 0.
	2 0	20.
	−	20.
	5	5.
	...)]	15.
	÷	15.
	3	3.
	=	5.

ANSWER: 5

Use your calculator to find the value of each expression.

6. $(84 + 3)(57 - 2) =$ $6(-4) + 2(-3 + 5) =$

7. $(8 - 4)^2 + (9 - 6)^2 =$ $(2 \times 14) \div (\frac{2}{5} \times 10) =$

8. $\$50.00 - (\$13.49 \times 2) - (\$5.88 \times 3) =$ $(16 + 10) + (15 \div 3)(4.5 + 2.5) =$

9. $\$25.00 - (\$5.25 \times 3) + (\$4.89 \times 2) =$ $\frac{120.25 + 20}{30 - 4.5} =$

10. $15 - (\frac{5}{8} \times 4) - (\frac{1}{2} \times 2) =$ $(1\frac{1}{2} \times 2) + (\frac{3}{4} \times 2) + 1 =$

11. $\frac{100}{25 + 15} =$ $\frac{1}{\frac{1}{4} + \frac{1}{4}} =$

12. $\frac{17 + 13}{25 - 10} =$ $\frac{25 - 5}{16 - 12} =$

Using Parentheses Keys to Solve Multistep Word Problems

You can use your calculator to solve multistep word problems. Read both examples carefully.

EXAMPLE 1   Lex brought 196 colored markers to school. He gave 84 markers to students in his morning class. He divided the rest equally among the 16 students in his afternoon class. How many markers did each student in the afternoon class get?

STEP 1   Write the expression. $(196 - 84) \div 16$

STEP 2   Evaluate the expression.

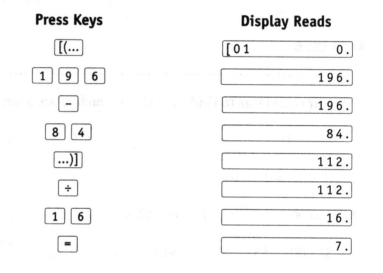

Press Keys	Display Reads
[(...	[01 0.
1 9 6	196.
–	196.
8 4	84.
...)]	112.
÷	112.
1 6	16.
=	7.

ANSWER: 7 markers per student

EXAMPLE 2   Kara bought three T–shirts at $18.99 each. If she pays with a $100 bill, how much change will she receive?

STEP 1   Write the expression. $100.00 - (\$18.99 \times 3)$

STEP 2   Evaluate the expression.

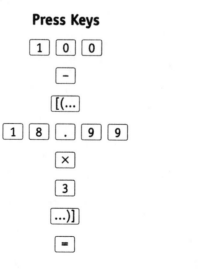

Press Keys	Display Reads
1 0 0	100.
–	100.
[(...	[01 0.
1 8 . 9 9	18.99
×	18.99
3	3.
...)]	56.97
=	43.03

ANSWER: $43.03

Write an expression that shows how to solve each problem. Then use your calculator to find the value of each expression.

1. A concert for a local band sold out. Three hundred tickets were sold at $21.00 each. One hundred fifty balcony tickets sold for $15.25 each. What were the total ticket receipts for the concert?

   expression:_____

   value:_____

2. Ron bought 5 quarts of motor oil for $1.79 and paid $0.67 tax. How much did he pay altogether for the oil?

   expression:_____

   value:_____

3. Vince walks to work and back each day, 5 days per week. He lives 1.9 miles from work. He also walks 0.2 miles each day to lunch and back. How many miles does Vince walk each week going to and from work and lunch?

   expression:_____

   value:_____

4. How much lighter than 20 pounds is a group of four packages if each package weighs 4.3 pounds?

   expression:_____

   value:_____

5. Cora bought a new clothes dryer for $329.99. She made a down payment of $44.99 and agreed to pay off the balance in three equal monthly payments. If she pays no interest, how much will Cora pay each month?

   expression:_____

   value:_____

6. For Christmas, Del bought 4.5 pounds of chicken priced at $3.08 per pound and 6.4 pounds of beef priced at $8.75 per pound. How much more did Del pay for the beef than he paid for the chicken?

   expression:_____

   value:_____

7. What is the total cost of a purchase of 50 pencils at $0.19 each and 10 workbooks at $13.95 each, with shipping costs of $7.25?

   expression:_____

   value:_____

Order of Operations with Powers and Roots

On your calculator, it is easy to simplify expressions with powers and roots by reading the expression from left to right and entering symbols and numbers as they occur in the expression. When you see a power or exponent, use the x^2, x^3, or x^y key. When you see a root, use the $\sqrt{}$ or the $\sqrt[y]{}$ key.

__EXAMPLE 1__ Evaluate $\sqrt{64} - 3^2$.

Press Keys	Display Reads
6 4	6 4 .
SHIFT $\sqrt{}$	8 .
−	8 .
3	3 .
x^2	9 .
=	− 1 .

__ANSWER: −1__

__EXAMPLE 2__ Find the value of $\sqrt{4^2 + 3^2}$.

Press Keys	Display Reads
4	4 .
x^2	1 6 .
+	1 6 .
3	3 .
x^2	9 .
=	2 5 .
SHIFT $\sqrt{}$	5 .

__ANSWER: 5__

Evaluate each expression.

1. $8^2 + 3^2 =$ $12^2 - 15^0 =$ $3^4 - 6^2 =$

2. $\sqrt{9} + \sqrt{16} =$ $0.5^2 + 1^2 =$ $(5 - 7)^3 =$

3. $2^3 - \sqrt{36} =$ $\sqrt{144} - \sqrt{169} =$ $\sqrt{625} - 4^2 =$

4. $(-4)^2(3)^2 =$ $\sqrt{100} - \sqrt{100} =$ $(-7)^2 + (-6)^2 =$

5. $10^2 - 4^2 =$ $13^2 - 12^2 =$ $8^2 + 15^2 =$

Operations with Numbers Review

This review covers the material you have just studied. When you finish, check your answers at the back of the book.

1. Find the value of $\frac{25 - 13 + 4}{2}$.

2. Evaluate $(1.5 \times 0.2)^2$.

Use your calculator to solve each problem.

3. John borrowed $3,800.00 from the bank for 24 months. According to the loan table, the interest charged for $3,000.00 is $25.00 per month. The interest charged for $800.00 is $5.30 per month. How much interest will he pay for the 24 months?

4. Lisa pays $\frac{1}{6}$ of her gross wages in payroll taxes. Of her gross income, $\frac{1}{12}$ is deducted for union dues and health insurance. If her gross wages for the month are $2,400, how much is Lisa paying for her payroll deductions?

5. On Friday 10,510 adults and 1,775 children attended the Erie County Fair. There were 15,898 adults and 3,065 children in attendance on Saturday, and 18,892 adults and 5,215 children on Sunday. Admission to the fair is $5.25 for adults and $2.00 for children. What were the receipts for admission for the three days?

Operations and Numbers Review Chart

Circle the number of any problem that you missed and review the appropriate pages. A passing score is 3 correct. If you missed more than two questions, you should review this chapter.

PROBLEM NUMBERS	SKILL AREA	PRACTICE PAGES
1, 2	order of operations	110–113
3, 4, 5	multistep word problems	114–115

FORMULAS IN ALGEBRA

Total Cost

Total cost is the cost of purchasing several units of an item. To find the total cost, multiply unit price by the number of items. The formula for total cost is

$$c = nr, \text{ where } c = \text{total cost, } n = \text{number of units, } r = \text{cost per unit}$$

EXAMPLE   When Smell Fresh detergent went on sale at several stores, Patrick decided to buy a case of 12 bottles. Which of the three stores below is offering the best buy?

Freddy's	**Home Foods**	**Value Foods**
Smell Fresh	Smell Fresh	Smell Fresh
$1.19 per bottle	$1.29 per bottle	$1.29 per bottle
(no case discount)	$1.50 rebate	$0.15 per bottle discount on
	each case	purchase of 12 or more

To find the best buy, compute the price of 12 bottles at each store. Use the formula $c = nr$.

Freddy's	**Home Foods**	**Value Foods**
$c = nr$	$c = (12 \times \$1.29) - \$1.50$	$c = \$1.29 - \$0.15 = \$1.14$
$c = 12 \times \$1.19$	$c = \$15.49 - \$1.50$	$c = 12 \times \$1.14$
$c = \$14.98$	$c = \$13.98$	$c = \$13.68$

ANSWER: Value Foods is offering the best buy for 12 bottles at $13.68.

Circle the store in each group that is offering the best buy.

1.   15 pounds of grapes

    Freddy's: $0.98 per pound

    Home Foods: $0.99 per pound, $0.50 discount on 15-lb bag

    Value Foods: $1.09 per pound, $1.50 rebate for purchases of $10.00 or more

2.   12 quarts of skim milk

    Save More: $1.04 per quart

    Buy Right: $1.19 per quart $1.00 discount on case of 12

    Marcy's: $1.13 per quart Buy 11 and get 1 free!

Unit Price

Unit price is the amount you pay per single unit of purchase.

- If you're buying tomatoes by the pound, the unit price is the price of each pound.

- If you're buying a dozen envelopes, the unit price is the price of each envelope.

When the brand name is not important, you can find the best buy by computing the lowest unit price.

- To compute unit price, divide the total price by the number of units purchased.

$r = \frac{c}{n}$, where c = total cost and n = number of units

EXAMPLE   Which of the following choices offers the best buy on peaches?

a. 6 pounds for $8.64
b. 5-pound bag for $6.90
c. 10-pound bag for $1.41 per pound

To find the price per pound (r), divide the total price (c) by the number of pounds (n).

a. $8.64 ÷ 6 = $1.44   **b.** $6.90 ÷ 5 = $1.38   **c.** given as $1.41 per pound

ANSWER: Choice b, at **$1.38 per pound** for a **5-pound bag**, is the best buy.

**Use your calculator to compute the unit price of each item below.
Circle the best buy in each group.**

1. rolls of film	**a.** 12-exposures for $5.76	**b.** 24-exposures for $11.76	**c.** 36-exposures for $16.92
2. multivitamins	**a.** 75 tablets for $14.25	**b.** 100 tablets for $20.00	**c.** 150 tablets for $31.50
3. margarine	**a.** two 8-ounce cups for $1.79	**b.** three 8-ounce cups for $2.49	**c.** 1 pound package for $1.59
4. navel oranges	**a.** 1 dozen for $3.40	**b.** 4 for $1.09	**c.** 6 for $1.78

Distance, Rate, and Time

Just think how often you've asked these questions:

How far is it? How fast are we going? How long will it take?

These three quantities—distance, rate, and time—are related by the **distance formula:** *distance* equals *rate* times *time.*

Distance (*d*)	=	Rate (*r*)	×	Time (*t*)
Usually expressed in miles		Speed—usually expressed in miles per hour (mph)		Usually expressed in hours

Written in short form as $d = rt$, the distance formula is used to find the distance when the rate and time are known. Once again, using a calculator carefully can be a big help.

EXAMPLE 1 The bus between Chicago and New York averages 45 miles per hour. How far can this bus travel in the first 8 hours of the trip?

> **STEP 1** Identify *r* and *t.*
> $r = 45$ miles per hour $t = 8$ hours

> **STEP 2** Substitute values into the distance formula: $d = rt$.
> $45 \times 8 = 360$

ANSWER: 360 miles

The distance formula can also be expressed as a **rate formula** (the speed) or **time formula.**

rate formula: $r = d \div t$ time formula: $t = d \div r$

EXAMPLE 2 On Sunday, Ann drove 336 miles in 8 hours. What was Ann's average speed?

> **STEP 1** Identify *d* and *t.*
> $d = 336$ miles $t = 8$ hours

> **STEP 2** Substitute values into the rate formula: $r = d \div t$.
> $336 \div 8 = 42$

ANSWER: 42 mph

EXAMPLE 3 How long will it take Alex to complete a 105-mile bicycle race if he averages 15 miles per hour?

> **STEP 1** Identify *d* and *r.*
> $d = 105$ miles $r = 15$ mph

> **STEP 2** Substitute values into the time formula: $t = d \div r$.
> $105 \div 15 = 7$

ANSWER: 7 hours

In each problem, decide whether you are trying to find the *distance*, *rate*, or *time*. Then use the correct formula to calculate your answer.

| distance formula: $d = rt$ | rate formula: $r = d \div t$ | time formula: $t = d \div r$ |

1. Over a 2-day period, Dale rode a total of 14 hours on a bike ride from Portland to Seattle. If he rode a total distance of 182 miles, what average speed did he ride?

2. On the first day of her trip to Canada, June averaged 59 miles per hour for seven straight hours. What distance did June drive during this time?

3. Averaging 620 miles per hour, how long will it take an airliner to travel across the United States, a distance of 3,255 miles?

4. If she stays within the highway speed limit of 65 miles per hour, what is the farthest that Shalinda can drive in 9 hours on that highway?

5. Last Saturday, Pam was travelling for a total of 13 hours. Except for the hour she stopped for lunch and the hour for dinner, she was driving. If she drove a total of 572 miles, what was Pam's average driving speed? (**Hint:** Ask yourself, "How many hours did Pam actually drive?")

6. Brandon left home at 8:00 A.M. Tuesday. If he drove at the speed limit of 55 mph all the way, at what time did he arrive in Chicago, a distance of 275 miles from his home? (**Hint:** First find how many hours Brandon drove.)

7. What speed must Erik average if he leaves home at 1:00 P.M. and hopes to reach San Francisco by 6:00 P.M., a distance of 265 miles? (**Hint:** How many hours does Erik want to drive?)

Simple Interest

Interest is money that is earned (or paid) for the use of money.

- If you deposit money in a savings account, interest is money that the bank pays you for using your money.

- If you borrow money or charge purchases on a credit card, interest is money that you pay the lender or charge-card company.

Simple interest is interest on a **principal** (the original amount borrowed or deposited). To compute simple interest, use the **simple interest formula.** In words: *interest* equals *principal* times *rate* times *time.* In symbols, the formula is $i = prt$.

Interest (*i*) =	**Principal (*p*)** ×	**Rate (*r*)** ×	**Time (*t*)**
Expressed in dollars	Expressed in dollars	Expressed as a percent	Expressed in years

EXAMPLE 1 Tani deposited $600 in a savings account that pays $6\frac{1}{8}$% simple interest. How much interest will Tani's account earn in 3 years?

		Press Keys	Display Reads
STEP 1	Identify *p, r,* and *t.* $p = \$600$, $r = 6\frac{1}{8}\%$, $t = 3$	6 0 0	600.
		×	600.
STEP 2	To find *i,* use $i = prt$. $i = 600 \times 6\frac{1}{8}\% \times 3$	6 a b/c 1 a b/c 8	6⌐1⌐8.
	When you press %, the display reads 36.75. This is the interest earned in one year.	SHIFT %	36.75
		×	36.75
		3	3.
		=	110.25

ANSWER: $110.25

Note: In actual practice, banks use a more complicated interest formula called the **compound interest formula.**

Although interest is earned (or paid) at a yearly rate, some deposits and loans are for part of a year. When using the simple interest formula, you change the part of a year to a decimal fraction. (**Remember:** 1 month $= \frac{1}{12}$ year)

EXAMPLE 2   4 months $= \frac{4}{12}$ year or $\frac{1}{3}$ yr   [4] [a b/c] [1] [2] [=] [_____ 1⌐3.]

ANSWER: $\frac{1}{3}$ year

EXAMPLE 3   1 year, 8 months $= 1\frac{8}{12}$ years   [1] [a b/c] [8] [a b/c] [1] [2] [=]

[_____ 1⌐2⌐3.]

ANSWER: $1\frac{2}{3}$ years

· ·

Express each time below as a reduced fraction.

1. 9 months

2. 3 years 1 month

3. 4 years 2 months

Use your calculator and the interest formula $i = prt$. Round each answer to the nearest cent.

4. How much interest would be earned on a deposit of $2,500 placed in a savings account for 3 years if the account pays $3\frac{1}{3}$% simple interest?

5. Larry borrowed $1,500 from his partner to buy stock. He agreed to repay the amount in 2 years, including $10\frac{1}{8}$% simple interest. At the end of 2 years, how much interest will he owe?

6. What amount of interest can Jules earn on $750 deposited for 2 years 2 months in an account that pays $4\frac{1}{4}$% simple interest?

Problems 7 and 8 refer to the chart at the right.

7. Doni deposited $375 in a new savings account at United Bank. How much will be in Doni's account at the end of 2 years 5 months? (**Hint:** Total saved = principal + interest)

8. Armand borrowed $650 from United Bank in order to buy a new TV set. Armand will repay the bank the entire amount at the end of 15 months. How much must Armand pay the bank at that time? (**Hint:** Total owed = principal + interest)

United Bank Simple Interest Accounts and Loans	
Savings Account	3.75%
Certificate of Deposit	5.82%
Car Loan	8.50%
Boat Loan	12.75%
Personal Loans	14.50%

Temperature

You substituted values in formulas for distance, total cost, and interest. When you substitute signed numbers in a formula or expression, the rules for adding, subtracting, multiplying, and dividing signed numbers apply, as well as the rules for the order of operations.

__EXAMPLE 1__ Find the value of a^2b, when $a = -4$ and $b = 5$.

Replace a with -4 and b with 5. (**Remember:** Two letters or a letter and a number next to each other mean to multiply.)

$$a^2b = (-4)^2 \times 5$$

Press Keys	Display Reads
4 [+/−]	− 4.
[x²]	1 6.
[×]	1 6.
5	5.
[=]	8 0.

ANSWER: 80

When you use formulas to solve problems, sometimes you may need to use both positive and negative numbers.

__EXAMPLE 2__ Convert 20°F to Celsius temperature.
The formula for this conversion is $C = \frac{5}{9}(F - 32)$.

STEP 1 Substitute the values into the formula. $\frac{5}{9} \times (20 - 32)$

STEP 2 Solve.

Press Keys	Display Reads
5 [a b/c] 9	5⌐9.
[×]	5⌐9.
[[(...]	[01 0.
2 0	2 0.
[−]	2 0.
3 2	3 2.
[...)]]	− 1 2.
[=]	− 6⌐2⌐3.

ANSWER: $-6\frac{2}{3}°C$

<u>EXAMPLE 3</u> The temperature on a bank sign reads –5°C.
To convert °C to °F, use the formula $F = \frac{9}{5}C + 32$.

STEP 1 Substitute the values into the formula. $F = \frac{9}{5} \times (-5) + 32$

STEP 2 Solve.

Press Keys	Display Reads
[9] [a b/c] [5]	9⌐5.
[×]	9⌐5.
[5] [+/–]	–5.
[+]	–9.
[3] [2]	32.
[=]	23.

ANSWER: 23°F

....

Find the value of these expressions when $a = -8, b = 4, d = \frac{1}{2}$, and $x = -0.1$.

1. $6a$ $-4x$ $\frac{1}{3}d$

2. $-5b$ a^2 $a + b$

3. ab $4d$ $\frac{1}{2}dx$

4. $(a + b)d$ $2x^2$ b^3

5. bd $\frac{b}{a}$ bdx

Use your calculator and the temperature formulas below to convert the temperatures.

$$C = \frac{5}{9}(F - 32)$$

$$F = \frac{9}{5}C + 32$$

6. $59°F = \underline{\hspace{1cm}}°C$ to the nearest degree

7. $0°C = \underline{\hspace{1cm}}°F$

8. A process requires a liquid to stay between 150°F and 180°F. State this range in °C. Express your answer to the nearest whole degree.

9. In Antarctica the temperature can reach as low as –72°F. What is this temperature in °C?

Formulas in Algebra Review

This review covers the material you have just studied. When you finish, check your answers at the back of the book.

Use the stated formulas for problems 1–3.

1. The value of an item that is depreciated each year is figured by the formula $V = C - Crt$, where $V =$ present value, $C =$ original cost, $r =$ rate of depreciation, $t =$ time in years.

   Find the present value of a copy machine that cost $2,000 when purchased 3 years ago. The rate of depreciation is 0.15.

2. The formula to determine a child's dose of medicine is Child's dose = age of child ÷ (age of child + 12) × average adult dosage.

   What dosage (number of milligrams) of a medicine should be given to a 4-year-old if the adult dosage is 250 milligrams?

3. To find the purchase price of an item, divide the sales tax by the sales tax rate. $P = T \div R$, where $P =$ purchase price, $T =$ sales tax, $R =$ sales tax rate

   If the sales tax rate is 8% in Erie County, what is the purchase price of a book that has a sales tax of $1.00?

Use the distance formula ($d = rt$), the total cost formula ($c = nr$), or the interest formula ($i = prt$) to solve problems 4–7.

4. The Sullivans paid $4,840 for $8\frac{4}{5}$ acres of land. How much did the land cost per acre?

5. James borrowed $1,500 from his father. James agreed to pay his father simple interest on the loan at a rate of 5% per year. When James repaid the loan 18 months later, how much interest did he pay his father?

6. The Palace Theater collected $3,596.25 in revenue for the holiday concert. If tickets cost $8.75 each, how many tickets were sold?

7. Cold weather fronts move on average 20 miles per hour. If a cold front starts in California, it takes 5 days (or 120 hours) to reach New York. Approximately how many miles is it from California to New York?

Use substitution to solve the following problems.

8. Eggs hatch at 104°F. Find this temperature in degrees Celsius. Use the formula $C = \frac{5}{9}(F - 32)$.

9. Find the value of $w - y$ when $w = -6$ and $y = 7$.

10. Find the value of $a^2 + b^2$ when $a = 5$ and $b = -12$.

Formulas in Algebra Review Chart

Circle the number of any problem that you missed and review the appropriate pages. A passing score is 8 correct. If you missed more than two questions, you should review this chapter.

PROBLEM NUMBERS	SKILL AREA	PRACTICE PAGES
1, 2, 3	using formulas	118–125
4, 6	total cost formula	118
5	interest formula	122–123
7	distance formula	120–121
8	temperature formula	124–125
9, 10	evaluating expressions	124–125

COORDINATE GRIDS

Becoming Familiar with a Coordinate Grid

A **coordinate grid** is formed by combining a vertical number line with a horizontal number line.

- The horizontal line is called the **x-axis**.

- The vertical line is called the **y-axis**.

- The point at which the two lines meet is called the **origin**.

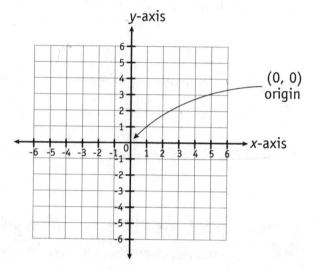

On a coordinate grid, every point is located by an ordered pair of numbers, (x, y).

- The first number in the pair is called the **x-coordinate**. The x-coordinate tells how far the point is from the y-axis.

- The second number in the pair is called the **y-coordinate**. The y-coordinate tells how far the point is from the x-axis.

- The coordinates of the origin are $(0, 0)$.

On the GED test you will see coordinate plane grids with small circles where you can mark the position of a point. In the grid at the right, the circle that is marked corresponds to the point $(5, -3)$.

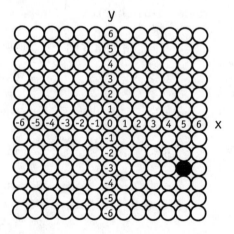

Write each pair of coordinates as an ordered pair. The first problem is done as an example.

1. $x = 4$
   $y = -2$
   $(4, -2)$

2. $x = -3$
   $y = 5$

3. $x = 2$
   $y = 6$

4. $x = -4$
   $y = -7$

Plotting Points on a Grid

To plot a point on a coordinate grid, follow these steps.

STEP 1 Locate the *x* value on the *x*-axis.

STEP 2 From the *x* value, move directly up (for a positive *y* value) or directly down (for a negative *y* value).

STEP 3 Label this point.

<u>**EXAMPLE 1**</u> Plot point $A = (5, -4)$ on the grid at the right.

STEP 1 Find the value $x = 5$ on the *x*–axis.

STEP 2 From the value 5 on the *x*-axis, move down to the *y* value −4.

STEP 3 Label point *A*.

<u>**EXAMPLE 2**</u> Plot point $B = (0, 5)$

STEP 1 Begin at $x = 0$, the *x* value. Move up to the *y* value 5.

STEP 2 Label point *B*.

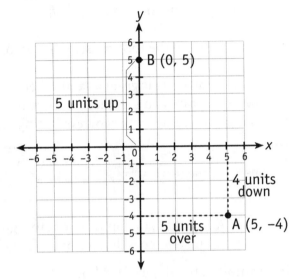

Plot and label each point.

1.

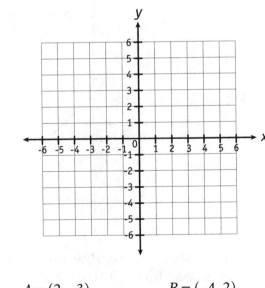

2.

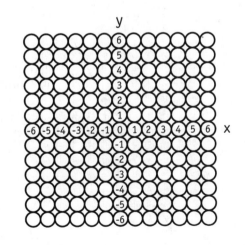

$A = (2, -3)$ $B = (-4, 2)$

$C = (0, 4)$ $D = (3, 5)$

$E = (4, 6)$ $F = (-1, -3)$

$G = (-5, 5)$ $H = (2, 0)$

Finding the Slope of a Line

The **slope** of the line is a ratio that tells how steep a line is. The ratio compares how far up or down the line goes to how far across it goes from left to right.

Think of the slope of a roof.

The roof *rises* 10 feet and *runs* 8 feet.
The slope of this roof line is $\frac{\text{rise}}{\text{run}} = \frac{10}{8}$ or $\frac{5}{4}$.

For every 5 feet the roof rises, it goes across 4 feet.

The slope of a line is given as a number. When you move between two points on the line, the slope is found by dividing the change in y value by the corresponding change in x value.

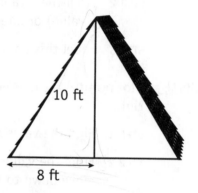

10 ft

8 ft

Slope of a line = $\dfrac{\text{Change in } y \text{ value (vertical change)}}{\text{Change in } x \text{ value (horizontal change)}}$

- A line that goes up from left to right has a *positive slope*.
- A line that goes down from left to right has a *negative slope*.

In Example 1, the slope of the line is 2.   In Example 2, the slope of the line is $-\left(\frac{2}{2}\right) = -1$.

EXAMPLE 1

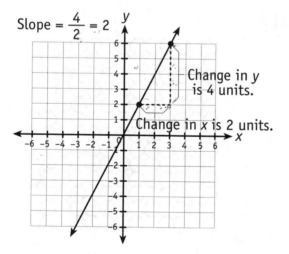

Slope $= \dfrac{4}{2} = 2$

Change in y is 4 units.

Change in x is 2 units.

The line above has *positive slope* because it goes *up* from left to right.

EXAMPLE 2

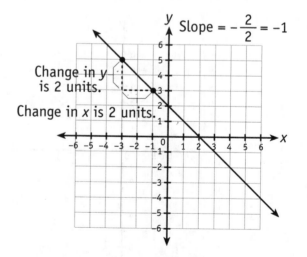

Slope $= -\dfrac{2}{2} = -1$

Change in y is 2 units.

Change in x is 2 units.

The line above has *negative slope* because it goes *down* from left to right.

Zero Slope and Undefined Slope

Two types of lines have neither positive nor negative slope.

- A horizontal line has *zero slope*. The *x*-axis (or any horizontal line) is a line with 0 slope.
- A vertical line has an *undefined slope*. The concept of slope does not apply to a vertical line. The *y*-axis (or any vertical line) is a line with undefined slope.

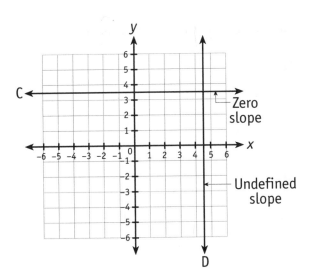

Slope Formula

You can find the slope of a line by using the slope formula. In algebra, the slope of a line is represented by the letter *m*.

To find the slope (*m*) of a line:

$$m = \frac{y_2 - y_1}{x_2 - x_1}, \text{ where } (x_1, y_1) \text{ and } (x_2, y_2) \text{ are two points in a plane.}$$

__EXAMPLE 3__ Find the slope of the line that passes through points $A(-3, 0)$ and $B(0, 2)$.

$$A(x_1, y_1) \text{ is } (-3, -2), \text{ so } x_1 = -3 \text{ and } y_1 = 0.$$
$$B(x_2, y_2) \text{ is } (0, 2), \text{ so } x_2 = 0 \text{ and } y_2 = 2.$$

To find the rise, subtract the *y* values of the points $(-3, \underline{0})$ and $(0, \underline{2})$.

To find the run, subtract the *x* values of the points $(\underline{-3}, 0)$ and $(\underline{0}, 2)$

Press Keys	Display Reads
2	2.
−	2.
0	0.
=	2.

ANSWER: The rise is 2.

Press Keys	Display Reads
0	0.
−	0.
3	3.
+/−	− 3.
=	3.

ANSWER: The run is 3.

Therefore, the slope of this line is $\frac{2}{3}$. The slope is positive. The line goes up 2 units for every 3 units it goes across from left to right.

Name the slope of each line as positive, negative, zero, or undefined.

1.

2.

3.

4.

5.

6.

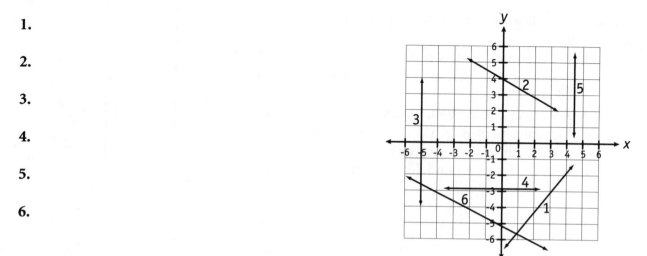

Plot the points, draw each line, and use your calculator to find the slope of each line.

7. (0, 0) and (3, −4)

    slope = _____

8. (−5, 4) and (3, −1)

    slope = _____

9. (−1, −4) and (3, 4)

    slope = _____

10. (0, 2) and (1, 4)

    slope = _____

11. (1, 2) and (−2, 5)

    slope = _____

12. (3, 1) and (4, 6)

    slope = _____

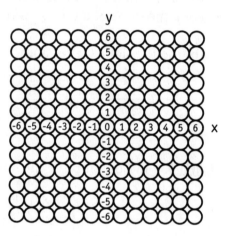

Finding the Distance Between Two Points

You may be asked to find the distance between two points on a grid. If you know the coordinates of two endpoints of a line segment, you can find the distance (d) between those points by using the distance formula.

$d = \sqrt{(x_2 - x_1)^2 + (y_2 - y_1)^2}$, where (x_1, y_1) and (x_2, y_2) are two points in a plane.

EXAMPLE Find the distance between point R and point S. Round your answer to the nearest tenth.

STEP 1 Find the coordinates of point $R(x_1, y_1)$ and point $S(x_2, y_2)$.
$R = (-4, -3)$ $S = (1, 1)$

STEP 2 Substitute the values of the coordinates in the distance formula.

$d = \sqrt{(x_2 - x_1)^2 + (y_2 - y_1)^2} =$

$\sqrt{(1-(-4))^2 + (1 - (-3))^2}$

STEP 3 Use your calculator to find the distance.

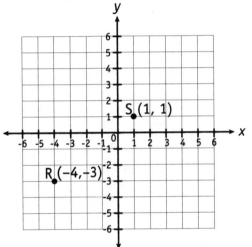

Press Keys	Display Reads
[(...	[0 1 0.
1 − 4	4.
+/−	− 4.
...)]	5.
x²	25.
+	25.
[(...	[0 1 0.
1 − 3	3.
+/−	− 3.
...)]	4.
x²	16.
=	41.
SHIFT √	6.403124237

ANSWER: 6.4

Find the distance between the points listed.

1. $A(-1, 6)$ and $E(-1, 1)$

2. $D(1, 1)$ and $C(4, 1)$

3. $B(4, 5)$ and $C(4, 1)$

4. $B(4, 5)$ and $D(1, 1)$

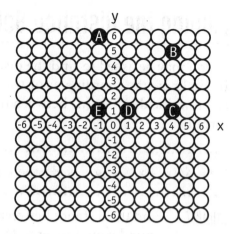

5. Find the distance between points I and J.

6. What is the distance between points G and H? Round your answer to the nearest tenth.

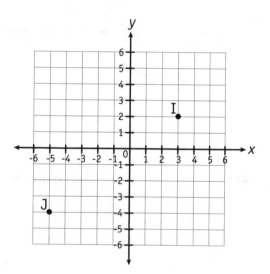

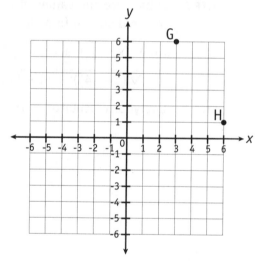

For problems 7 and 8, use the grid at the right.

7. Find the distance between points M and N. Round your answer to the nearest tenth.

8. Find the distance between points N and P. Round your answer to the nearest tenth.

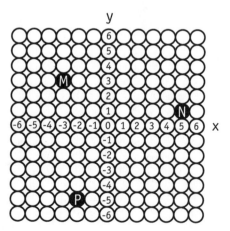

Coordinate Grids Review

This review covers the material you have just studied. When you finish, check your answers at the back of the book.

Use your calculator to solve these problems.

1. Plot and label each point.

   $A(5, 2)$
   $B(6, 0)$
   $C(0, 5)$
   $D(-3, -3)$
   $E(3, -4)$

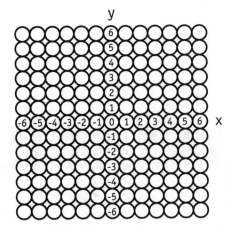

2. Find the slope of the line that passes through points $(0, 1)$ and $(6, -2)$. Round your answer to the nearest tenth.

3. Find the distance between the following points. Round your answer to the nearest tenth.

   point A and point B
   point A and point C
   point D and point E
   point C and point D
   point B and point E

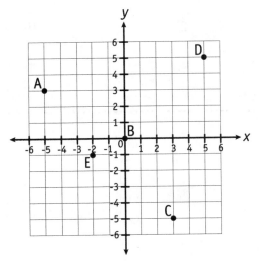

4. Plot triangle *RST*. To the nearest tenth, find the length of the shortest side of triangle *RST*.

$R(4, 3)$
$S(2, -3)$
$T(0, 0)$

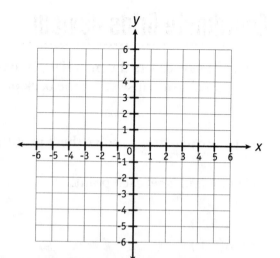

Coordinate Grids Review Chart

Circle the number of any problem that you missed and review the appropriate pages. A passing score is 3 correct. If you missed more than one questions, you should review this chapter.

PROBLEM NUMBERS	SKILL AREA	PRACTICE PAGES
1	plotting points	128–129
2	finding the slope of a line	130–132
3, 4	finding the distance between two points	133–134

GED Practice

Solve.

1. What is the value of point *B* on the number line below?

   (1) −3
   (2) −2
   (3) −$\frac{2}{3}$
   (4) $\frac{2}{3}$
   (5) 3

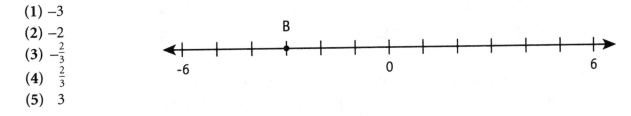

2. Point *C* is $\frac{3}{4}$ of the way from *A* to *B*. What is the value of point *C*?

   (1) −$\frac{3}{4}$
   (2) 0
   (3) $\frac{3}{4}$
   (4) 5
   (5) 9

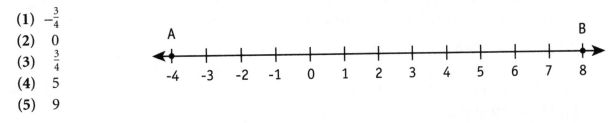

3. Each week Al drives his truck to Ridgeway, a distance of 1,320 miles. If he averages 60 mph for 8 hours a day, how many days of driving would be necessary to make the round trip? Mark your answer on the number grid.

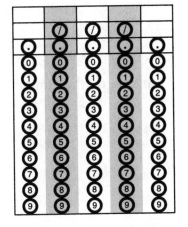

4. Bernie exercises at the gym. For each mile Bernie runs on the treadmill, he burns 50 calories. Bernie runs 5 miles on Monday, 3 miles on Wednesday, and 8 miles on Friday. Which expression could be used to find how many calories Bernie burns on the treadmill each week?

   (1) $(50 \times 5) \times (50 \times 3) \times (50 \times 8)$
   (2) $50 + 5 + 3 + 8$
   (3) $3 + 8 + (50 \times 5)$
   (4) $(5 + 8) + (50 \times 3)$
   (5) $50(5 + 3 + 8)$

5. A printer charges the following rates for color copies.

Color Copy Prices

	1—4	5—49	50—99	Over 100
$8\frac{1}{2} \times 11$	$1.25	$1.00	$0.80	Ask for Quote
11×17	$1.50	$1.25	$1.00	Ask for Quote

The Diversity Committee is holding a meeting. They need flyers, posters, and newsletters to advertise. They ordered 75 color $8\frac{1}{2}$ x 11 flyers, 40 color $8\frac{1}{2}$ x 11 posters, and 25 color 11 x 17 newsletters. Which expression could be used to find out how much the Diversity Committee will spend on advertising?

(1) 75($1.00 + $0.80) + 40 + 25
(2) $1.00(75 + 40 + 25)
(3) 40($1.00) + 75($0.80) + 25($1.25)
(4) 150($0.80 + $1.25)
(5) $0.80(75 + 40) + $1.25(25)

6. Evaluate $\sqrt{x^2 + y^2}$, where $x = 40$ and $y = 30$. Mark your answer on the number grid.

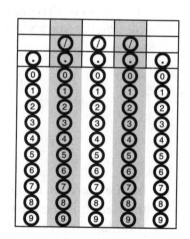

7. Joe worked 40 hours a week earning $10.50 an hour. He also worked 5 hours at time and a half. Which expression represents the amount of money he made this week?

(1) $40 \times \$10.50 \times 5$

(2) $(40 \times \$10.50)(50 \times \$10.50)$

(3) $\frac{40 \times \$10.50 \times 5}{1.5}$

(4) $(40 \times \$10.50) + (5 \times \$10.50 \times 1.5)$

(5) $\frac{40 \times \$10.50}{5 \times \$10.50 \times 1.5}$

8. What is the sum of 8, −11, −16, and 20?

   (1) −39
   (2)   1
   (3) 23
   (4) 33
   (5) 55

9. The Smith's electric meter reads 31,555 kilowatt-hours. Last month at this time, the meter read 30,950. If electricity costs $0.38 per kilowatt-hour, which expression tells how much the Smiths will pay this month for electricity?

   (1) $\frac{31,555 - 30,950}{0.38}$

   (2) $\frac{30,950 - 31,555}{0.38}$

   (3) $0.38(31,555 - 30,950)$

   (4) $0.38(30,950 - 31,555)$

   (5) $0.62(30,950 - 31,555)$

10. The formula for Body Mass Index is as follows:

    $BMI = \frac{W \times 705 \div H}{H}$, where W = weight in pounds, H = height in inches

    If the Body Mass Index is greater than 27 or less than 19, there is an increased risk for health problems. Sue measures 64 inches tall and weighs 140 pounds. What is her BMI to the nearest whole number?

    (1) 17
    (2) 21
    (3) 24
    (4) 29
    (5) Not enough information is given.

11. The net weight and price of five different kinds of orange juice concentrate are shown. Which is the best value for the money, assuming the quality is equal?

    (1) A
    (2) B
    (3) C
    (4) D
    (5) E

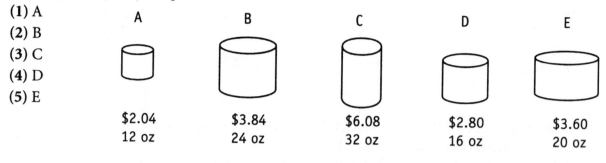

	A	B	C	D	E
	$2.04	$3.84	$6.08	$2.80	$3.60
	12 oz	24 oz	32 oz	16 oz	20 oz

12. Calculate the value of 90 + 15(26 − 17). Mark your answer on the number grid.

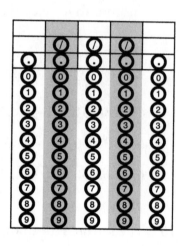

13. The high temperature for the day was 28°F. At night, the temperature dropped to a low of −9°F. Which of the following represents the change from the high temperature to the low temperature for the day?

    (1) −37°
    (2) −19°
    (3) +19°
    (4) +28°
    (5) +37°

14. During a 5-day week, a production line produces 1,250 quality parts. If the line runs Monday through Saturday at the same rate of production, which expression below represents how many quality parts will be produced?

    (1) 6(1,250)

    (2) 5(1,250) + 1

    (3) $\frac{5}{6}$(1,250)

    (4) $\frac{6}{5}$(1,250)

    (5) Not enough information is given.

15. A real estate saleswoman earns 1.5% commission on all sales. This month she sold three homes priced at $94,000, $84,500, and $79,900. How much commission will she receive? Mark your answer on the number grid.

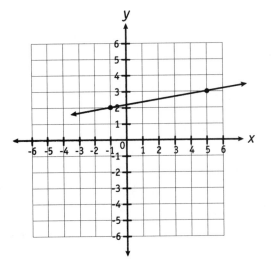

16. Which point has the coordinate (−4, 2)?

    (1) A
    (2) B
    (3) C
    (4) D
    (5) E

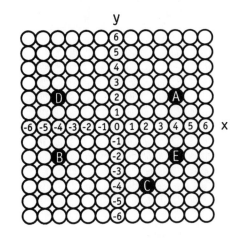

17. What is the slope of the line that passes through points (−1, 2) and (5, 3)?

    (1) $-\frac{1}{4}$
    (2) $\frac{1}{6}$
    (3) $\frac{5}{4}$
    (4) 6
    (5) −4

Geometry
and
Measurement

PLANE FIGURES

Identifying Geometric Figures

Geometry is the branch of mathematics that studies points, lines, plane (2-dimensional) and solid (3-dimensional) figures. Geometric applications are used in building houses, apartment buildings, roads, bridges, airplanes, automobiles, and practically everything used in modern living. Many occupations require a knowledge of geometry and the ability to apply this knowledge to practical on-the-job uses.

The following 2-dimensional shapes are used in plane geometry.

- A **triangle** is a three-sided figure with three sides and three angles.

- A **rectangle** is a four-sided figure with two pairs of parallel sides and four right angles. (*Parallel* means the lines will never meet or cross.)

- A **square** has four equal sides, two pairs of parallel sides, and four right angles.

- A **parallelogram** is a four-sided figure with two pairs of parallel sides and with opposite sides having equal length.

- A **trapezoid** is a four-sided figure with one pair of parallel sides.

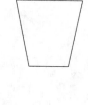

- A **circle** is a plane figure, each point of which is an equal distance from the center.

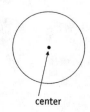

center

Perimeter

Perimeter (*P*) is the distance around a plane figure. Perimeter is measured in units of length, such as inches, feet, miles, or meters. To find the perimeter of a given figure, add the lengths of the sides or use a formula.

The following formulas may be used on the GED test.

The perimeter of a:

☐	square	$P = 4s$, where s = one side
▯	rectangle	$P = 2l + 2w$, where l = length and w = width
△	triangle	$P = a + b + c$, where a, b, and c are the sides

EXAMPLE   What is the perimeter of the square at the right?

1.5 m

STEP 1   Identify the figure and write the correct perimeter formula. $P = 4s$

STEP 2   Substitute known measures into the formula. $P = 4 \times 1.5$

STEP 3   Use your calculator to compute the perimeter.

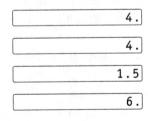

Press Keys	Display Reads
4	4.
×	4.
1 . 5	1.5
=	6.

ANSWER: 6 m

Use your calculator to find the perimeter for each figure.

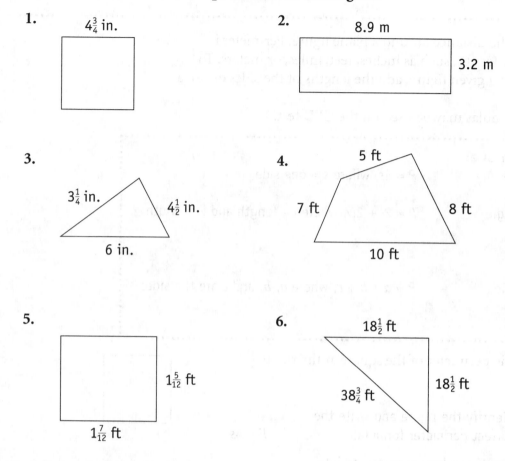

1.

$4\frac{3}{4}$ in.

2.

8.9 m

3.2 m

3.

$3\frac{1}{4}$ in. $4\frac{1}{2}$ in.

6 in.

4.

5 ft

7 ft   8 ft

10 ft

5.

$1\frac{5}{12}$ ft

$1\frac{7}{12}$ ft

6.

$18\frac{1}{2}$ ft

$38\frac{3}{4}$ ft $18\frac{1}{2}$ ft

Find the perimeter of each figure.

7. Square with sides of $1\frac{1}{2}$ feet

8. Rectangle with length of 1.25 m and width of 1 m

9. Triangle with sides of 11.6 cm, 9.7 cm, and 7.1 cm

10. Parallelogram with adjacent sides of 15 in. and 21 in.

11. Trapezoid with sides of 175 cm, 150 cm, 75 cm, and 80 cm

12. Square with sides of 4.5 cm

13. How much string is needed to tie up this package? Allow 8 inches extra for a bow.

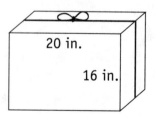

20 in.

16 in.

Circumference

The terms used to measure circular objects are different from those used to measure other figures. The distance around a circle is called the **circumference.** You can think of circumference as the perimeter of a circle.

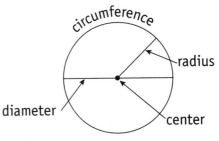

- The **radius** (r) is the distance from the center to any point on the circle's edge.

- The **diameter** (d) is the distance across the center of a circle. The diameter is equal to twice the radius. $d = 2r$

EXAMPLE 1 Find the diameter of a circle that has a radius of $2\frac{1}{4}$ inches.

STEP 1 Identify the formula to use.	$d = 2r$
STEP 2 Substitute the measure of the radius.	$d = 2 \times 2\frac{1}{4}$
STEP 3 Use your calculator to compute the diameter.	$d = 4\frac{1}{2}$ inches

ANSWER: $4\frac{1}{2}$ **inches**

The circumference (C), or distance around the circle, can be found by using a formula.

> **The circumference of a:**
>
> circle $C = \pi d$, where C = circumference, π = 3.14 or $\frac{22}{7}$, and d = diameter

Pi (π) is the ratio of circumference to diameter for any given circle. The number π is a nonrepeating, non-terminating decimal that is approximately equal to 3.14. On your calculator find the π function. Notice it is a second function over the [EXP] key.

To use the number π, press [SHIFT] and then [EXP]. When you press these keys, you should see the following decimal:

> 3.141592654

The formula $C = \pi d$ means the same as $C = \pi 2r$, because $d = 2r$.

EXAMPLE 2 To the nearest foot, find the circumference of a circle that has a diameter of 5 feet.

STEP 1 Identify the formula. $C = \pi d$

STEP 2 Substitute the diameter. $C = \pi(5)$

Press Keys	Display Reads
SHIFT π	3.141592654
×	3.141592654
5	5.
=	15.70796327

To round to the nearest whole:

Press Keys	Display Reads
MODE	15.70796327
7	15.70796327
0	16.

ANSWER: 16 ft

Use your calculator to solve each problem.

1. Kelly Reservoir is in the shape of a circle. If the distance across the reservoir is 4 miles, what is its circumference to the nearest tenth of a mile?

2. Janine built a new circular garden. The diameter is $6\frac{3}{8}$ feet. She wants to put a plastic edge around the garden. To the nearest foot, how much edging will she need to purchase?

3. A circular playground was built in a neighborhood park. Half the distance across the playground is 150 feet. If the neighbors decide to build a fence around the playground, approximately how many *yards* of fencing will they need?

4. Liam is striping the edge of the center circle on a basketball court. If the circle has a diameter of 3.1 meters, what is the distance around the circle? Round your answer to the nearest tenth of a meter.

5. A circular wading pool has a radius of 4.8 meters. To the nearest tenth of a meter, what is the distance around the pool?

Area of Squares and Rectangles

Area (*A*) is a measure of the amount of space inside a plane figure. Area is measured in square units such as square inches, square feet, square meters, or square kilometers. You may see the units abbreviated with an exponent.

> square inches = sq in. = in.²
>
> square feet = sq ft = ft²
>
> square meters = sq m = m²
>
> square kilometers = sq km = km²

Area is the total number of square units that cover the surface of the flat figure. The rectangle at the right has a length of 5 inches, a width of 3 inches, and an area of 15 square inches.

The following are formulas for finding area.

The area of a:

□	square	$A = s^2$, where s = a side
▭	rectangle	$A = lw$, where l = length and w = width

EXAMPLE 1 Use your calculator to find the area of a square with sides of 1.5 meters.

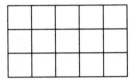

1.5 m

STEP 1	Identify the formula.	$A = s^2$
STEP 2	Substitute measures.	$A = 1.5^2$

Press Keys	Display Reads
1 . 5	1.5
x²	2.25

ANSWER: 2.25 m²

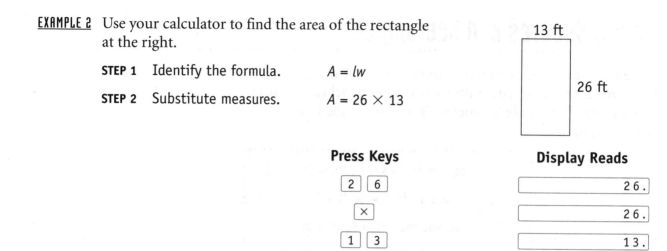

EXAMPLE 2 Use your calculator to find the area of the rectangle at the right.

    STEP 1 Identify the formula. $A = lw$

    STEP 2 Substitute measures. $A = 26 \times 13$

Press Keys	Display Reads
2 6	26.
×	26.
1 3	13.
=	338.

ANSWER: 338 sq ft

You have seen that squaring a number and finding the square root are opposite operations. Using this fact, you can find the side of a square if you know the area. The following formula can be used to find the side of a square.

To find a:

    side of a square $s = \sqrt{A}$, where A = area

EXAMPLE 3 Use your calculator to find the side of a square with an area of 182.25 square yards.

    STEP 1 Identify the formula. $s = \sqrt{A}$

    STEP 2 Substitute measures. $s = \sqrt{182.25}$

Press Keys	Display Reads
1 8 2 . 2 5	182.25
SHIFT √	13.5

ANSWER: 13.5 yd

When the given measures have different units of measure, you need to rename the measure(s) to get a common unit of measure before substituting the measures into the formula.

<u>EXAMPLE 4</u>   Find the area of the rectangle.

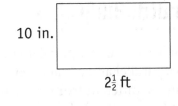

10 in.

$2\frac{1}{2}$ ft

STEP 1	Change feet to inches.	$2\frac{1}{2}$ ft = 30 in. because 1 ft = 12 in.
		$2\frac{1}{2} \times 12$ = 30 inches
STEP 2	Identify the formula.	$A = lw$
STEP 3	Substitute measures.	$A = 30 \times 10$
STEP 4	Solve.	$A = 300$

ANSWER: 300 sq in.

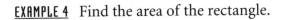

Use your calculator to solve these problems.

1. What is the length of each side of a square tablecloth that covers a
    surface area of 9 square feet?

2. A square table is to be covered with small square ceramic tiles. The
    table has an area of 4 square feet. How many tiles are needed if each
    tile measures 3 inches on one side?

3. The label on a gallon of interior wall paint reads, "Coverage:
    400 square feet." If a wall is 8 feet high, what maximum length of
    wall could be painted with $1\frac{1}{2}$ gallons?

4. A standard piece of typing paper measures 11 inches long by
    $8\frac{1}{2}$ inches wide. Is the area of a piece of this paper greater than
    100 square inches?

Area of Parallelograms

Earlier you learned that a parallelogram is a four-sided figure with opposite sides parallel and equal in length. The terms used with a parallelogram are different from those used with rectangles and squares.

The height (*h*) of a parallelogram is perpendicular to the base (*b*). *Perpendicular* means that the height and base meet to make a right angle. The height is not the same length as the sides.

Look at each of these parallelograms to see the base and height.

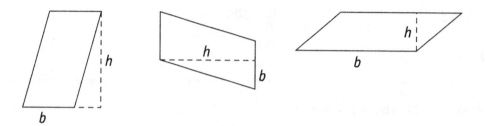

The following is the formula for finding the area of a parallelogram.

The area of a:

parallelogram $A = bh$, where b = base and h = height

EXAMPLE   Use your calculator to find the area of the parallelogram.

STEP 1   Identify the formula. $A = bh$

STEP 2   Substitute measures. $A = 5 \times 3\frac{1}{2}$

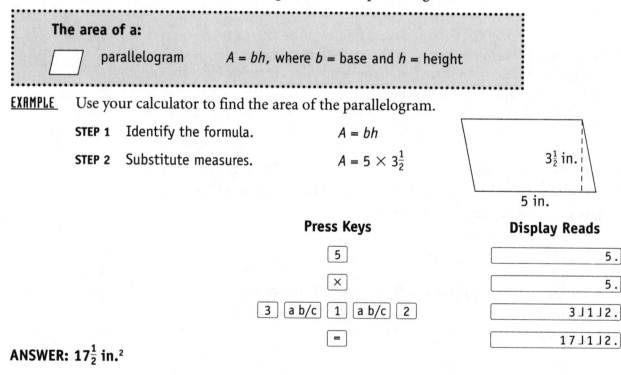

Press Keys	Display Reads
5	5.
×	5.
3 a b/c 1 a b/c 2	3 ⌐1⌐2.
=	17 ⌐1⌐2.

ANSWER: $17\frac{1}{2}$ in.²

Use your calculator to find the area of each figure.

1. $A =$

    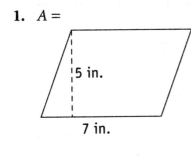

    5 in.

    7 in.

2. $A =$

    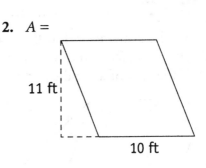

    11 ft

    10 ft

3. $A =$

    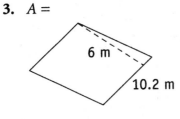

    6 m

    10.2 m

4. $A =$

    6 in.

    $3\frac{1}{4}$ in.

5. A playground in the city park is shaped like a parallelogram. If the base measures 35 meters and the height measures 27 meters, what is the area of this playground?

    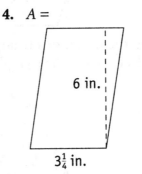

    27 m

    35 m

6. Dave is building a new brick patio. How many square yards is the area of his new patio?

    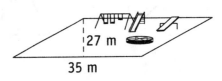

    12 yd

    $7\frac{1}{4}$ yd   8 yd

    12 yd

7. A walkway is built connecting Andy's house to his garage. What is the area of the walkway?

    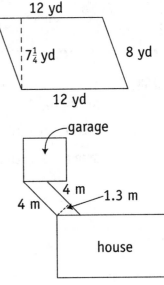

    garage

    4 m   1.3 m

    4 m

    house

8. A piece of steel bar is cut. The cross-section is in the shape of a parallelogram. Find the area of the cross-section.

    $4\frac{1}{2}$ in.

    $3\frac{1}{4}$ in.

Area of Triangles

You can see from the drawings below that a triangle is half of a parallelogram. Using this fact, you can see that the area of a triangle would be one-half the area of a parallelogram.

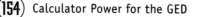

As with parallelograms, the height of a triangle is the perpendicular distance to the base. Look at each of the triangles to see the position of the base and height.

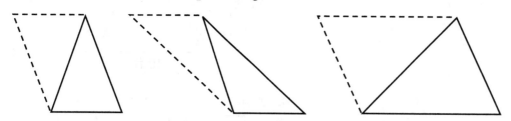

The area of a:

triangle $A = \frac{1}{2}bh$, where b = base and h = height

EXAMPLE   Use your calculator to find the area of the triangle at the right.

STEP 1   Identify the formula. $A = \frac{1}{2}bh$

STEP 2   Substitute measures. $A = \frac{1}{2}(20)(8.5)$

8.5 m

20 m

Press Keys	Display Reads
1 a b/c 2	1⌐2.
×	1⌐2.
2 0	20.
×	10.
8 . 5	8.5
=	85.

ANSWER: 85 sq m

Use your calculator and the formula $A = \frac{1}{2}bh$ to find the area of each triangle.

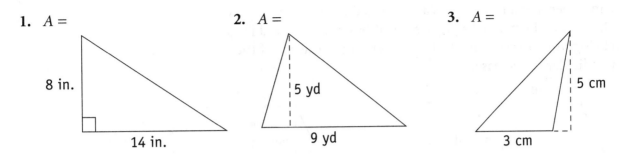

1. $A =$

8 in.

14 in.

2. $A =$

5 yd

9 yd

3. $A =$

5 cm

3 cm

4. A corner counter top is shaped like a right triangle. The two sides forming the right angle have lengths of 3 feet and $5\frac{1}{2}$ feet. What is the surface area of this corner?

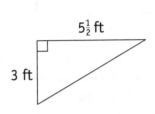

$5\frac{1}{2}$ ft

3 ft

5. Jim cut a piece of plywood into the shape of a triangle. To the nearest square foot, find the area of the plywood if the base measures 8 feet and the height measures $6\frac{1}{4}$ feet.

For problems 6–9, fill in each blank.

	Length	Width	Perimeter	Area
6. square	$8\frac{1}{2}$ ft	$8\frac{1}{2}$ ft	_____	_____
7. rectangle	16.2 m	14.1 m	_____	_____

	Base	Height		Area
8. triangle	6 yd	$9\frac{3}{4}$ yd		_____
9. parallelogram	56 mm	6.8 mm		_____

10. Find the area of the figure at the right.

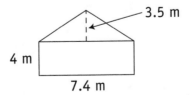

3.5 m

4 m

7.4 m

11. What is the area of a triangle with a base of 2 feet and a height of 8 inches?

Area of Trapezoids

Remember that a trapezoid is a four-sided figure with only two parallel sides. The parallel sides are called **bases**, b_1 and b_2. Like a parallelogram and triangle, the height (h) is the measure of the perpendicular to the base.

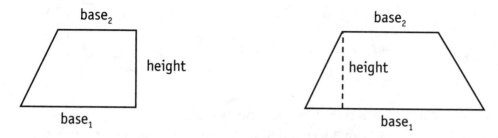

The following is the formula for the area of a trapezoid.

The area of a:

trapezoid $A = \frac{1}{2}(b_1 + b_2)h$, where b_1 = base 1, b_2 = base 2, and h = height

EXAMPLE   Use your calculator to find the area of the trapezoid.

STEP 1   Identify the formula. $A = \frac{1}{2}(b_1 + b_2)h$

STEP 2   Substitute measures. $A = \frac{1}{2}(42 + 20)18$

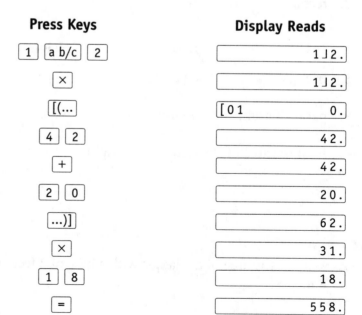

Press Keys	Display Reads
1 a b/c 2	1⌐2.
×	1⌐2.
[(...	[01 0.
4 2	42.
+	42.
2 0	20.
...)]	62.
×	31.
1 8	18.
=	558.

ANSWER: 558 square units

Use your calculator and the formula $A = \frac{1}{2}(b_1 + b_2)h$ to find the area of each trapezoid.

1. $A =$

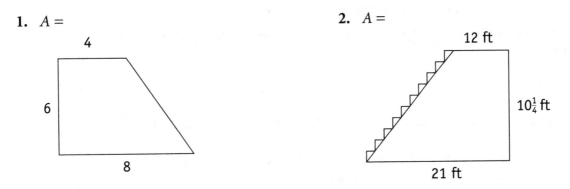

2. $A =$

3. The basement of Stephen White's house is in the shape of a trapezoid. What is the area of the basement if the parallel sides have lengths of 38 feet and 34 feet, and the distance between the parallel sides is 22 feet?

4. The Jones Roofing Co. is going to shingle a section of roof that is in the shape of a trapezoid. The parallel sides measure 54 feet and 46 feet and are 24 feet apart. If a bag of shingles covers 50 square feet, how many bags of shingles are needed to cover this roof?

5. Mark is going to grade and pave the sloping approach from the street to his driveway. The driveway is 12 feet wide. The base of the approach is 20 feet. The distance between the driveway and the street is $8\frac{3}{4}$ feet. How many square feet will be paved?

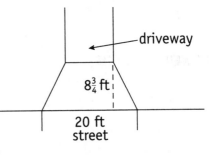

Find the perimeter and area of the figure below.

6. $P =$ $A =$

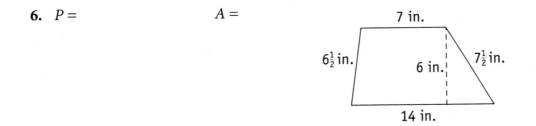

Area of Circles

The following is the formula for finding the area of a circle.

The area of a:

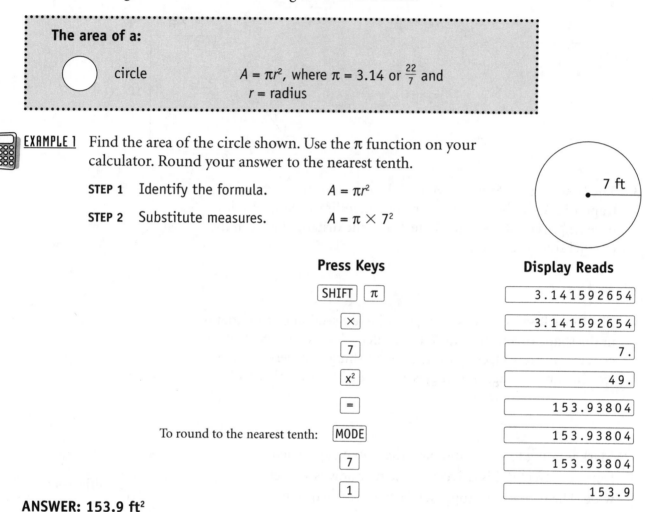

○ circle $\qquad$ $A = \pi r^2$, where $\pi = 3.14$ or $\frac{22}{7}$ and $r =$ radius

EXAMPLE 1 Find the area of the circle shown. Use the π function on your calculator. Round your answer to the nearest tenth.

STEP 1 Identify the formula. $\qquad$ $A = \pi r^2$

STEP 2 Substitute measures. $\qquad$ $A = \pi \times 7^2$

7 ft

Press Keys	Display Reads
SHIFT π	3.141592654
×	3.141592654
7	7.
x^2	49.
=	153.93804
To round to the nearest tenth: MODE	153.93804
7	153.93804
1	153.9

ANSWER: 153.9 ft²

If the diameter of the circle is given, remember to find the radius $(r = \frac{d}{2})$ as your first step in solving for the area.

EXAMPLE 2   To the nearest square meter, what is the area of a circle with a diameter of 4.2 meters?

STEP 1   Identify the formula. $A = \pi r^2$

STEP 2   Find the radius. $r = \frac{d}{2}$

$r = \frac{4.2}{2} = 2.1$

STEP 3   Substitute measures. $A = 3.14 \times (2.1)^2$

Press Keys	Display Reads
SHIFT π	3.141592654
×	3.141592654
2 . 1	2.1
x²	4.41
=	13.8544236

ANSWER: 14 sq m

Use your calculator to find the area of each circle.

1. To the nearest square foot, what is the area of grass watered by a circular sprinkler that has a radius of 17 feet?

2. A round glass mirror measures 1 foot from the center to the edge. How many square inches of glass are in the mirror?

3. If six people share a large pizza that has a 14-inch diameter, how much pizza will each person get? Round your answer to the nearest square inch.

4. The circular flat roof of a water tower has a diameter of 29.5 feet. Estimate the area of this roof.

5. Radio station KNPA broadcasts its signal to all points within an 84 kilometer radius of the station. To the nearest kilometer, what is the area of the region served by this station?

Solving Two-Step Area Problems

Many area problems involve figures that are a combination of common geometrical shapes. These problems are called **two-step area problems.**

To solve a two-step area problem, divide the figure into individual shapes and then solve for each shape separately.

EXAMPLE 1 What is the area of the room pictured at the right?

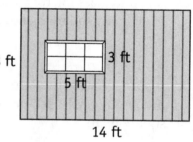

    STEP 1 Divide the room into two rectangles. Label the rectangles I and II. Label the unmeasured long side of rectangle I as l for length. You need to know the value of l before you can find the area of rectangle I.

    STEP 2 To find l subtract 8 from 24.
$$l = 24 - 8 = 16$$

    STEP 3 Find the area of rectangle I and the area of rectangle II.
Area of I = lw = 16 × 10 = 160 sq ft

Area of II = lw = 18 × 8 = 144 sq ft

    STEP 4 Add the areas of rectangles I and II.

ANSWER: The area of the room is 304 sq ft.

160 sq ft
+ 144 sq ft
304 sq ft

Many area problems require that you subtract a smaller area from a larger area.

EXAMPLE 2 How many square feet of wallpaper will be needed to cover the wall at right?

    STEP 1 Find the area of the wall including the window.

Area of wall = 14 × 8 = 112 sq ft

    STEP 2 Find the area of the window.

Area of window = 5 × 3 = 15 sq ft

    STEP 3 Subtract to find the area of the wall.

ANSWER: The amount of wallpaper needed is 97 square feet.

112 sq ft
− 15 sq ft
97 sq ft

Use your calculator to find the area of each figure.

1. $A =$

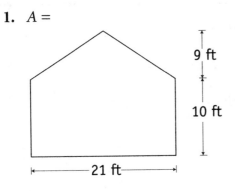

9 ft

10 ft

21 ft

2. $A =$

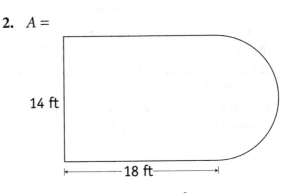

14 ft

18 ft

(Round your answer to the nearest square foot.)

3. Lois's house sits in the middle of her lot. The lot is shaped like a trapezoid. Except for the house and driveway, her lot is covered with grass. How many square feet of grass are on the lot?

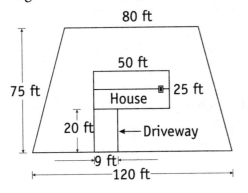

80 ft

50 ft

75 ft

25 ft

House

20 ft   ←— Driveway

9 ft

120 ft

4. Two triangular planters sit in the rose garden. Excluding the planters, how many square feet of garden area remain?

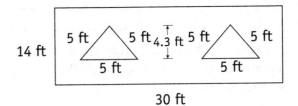

14 ft   5 ft   5 ft   4.3 ft 5 ft   5 ft

5 ft   5 ft

30 ft

5. To the nearest square centimeter, what is the area of the washer below?

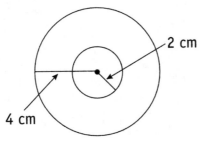

2 cm

4 cm

Pythagorean Theorem

In a right triangle the side opposite the right angle is called the **hypotenuse.** The other two sides are called **legs.** The letters a and b are usually used to denote the legs of a right triangle; c is used to denote the hypotenuse.

You can use squares and square roots to calculate the length of the hypotenuse if you know the length of the two legs.

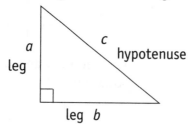

Pythagoras, a famous Greek mathematician, discovered an important relationship between the hypotenuse of a right triangle and the two legs. This relationship is called the **Pythagorean theorem.**

> **The Pythagorean theorem:**
>
> $c = \sqrt{a^2 + b^2}$, where c = the longest side (the hypotenuse),
> a = one leg, and b = one leg

In words, the Pythagorean theorem says, "In a right triangle, the square of the hypotenuse equals the sum of the squares of the two shorter sides."

EXAMPLE 1 A triangular wedge is 4 inches on one side and 3 inches on the other. Use your calculator to find the length of the hypotenuse.

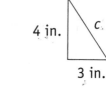

STEP 1 Identify the formula. $c = \sqrt{a^2 + b^2}$

STEP 2 Substitute measures. $c = \sqrt{3^2 + 4^2}$

Press Keys	Display Reads
3	3.
x^2	9.
+	9.
4	4.
x^2	16.
=	25.
SHIFT √	5.

ANSWER: 5 inches

You can also use another form of the Pythagorean theorem to find a missing leg of a right triangle.

To find the missing side:

$a = \sqrt{c^2 - b^2}$, where a = leg, c = hypotenuse, b = leg

OR $b = \sqrt{c^2 - a^2}$, where b = leg; c = hypotenuse, a = leg

<u>EXAMPLE 2</u> Use your calculator to find the missing side of the triangle at the right.

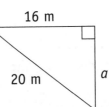

16 m

20 m a

STEP 1 Identify the formula. $a = \sqrt{c^2 - b^2}$

STEP 2 Substitute the measures. $a = \sqrt{20^2 - 16^2}$

Press Keys	Display Reads
2 0	20.
x^2	400.
–	400.
1 6	16.
x^2	256.
=	144.
SHIFT √	12.

ANSWER: 12 m

Find the length of each hypotenuse.

1.

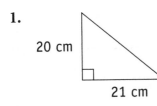

20 cm

21 cm

2.

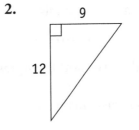

9

12

Find the length of each leg.

3.

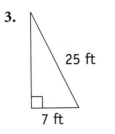

25 ft

7 ft

4.

37 m   12 m

The Pythagorean theorem can also be used to identify a right triangle. Suppose you were constructing a deck and wanted to make sure the corner was a square. You would measure out 4 feet on one side and 3 feet on the other. The diagonal between the two measurements should measure 5 feet if the angle is a right angle.

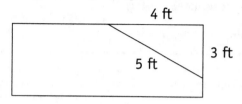

4 ft

3 ft

5 ft

A triangle is a right triangle if:

a, b, and c are the lengths of the sides and $a^2 + b^2 = c^2$.

Using the Pythagorean theorem, substitute the values for a, b, and c.

$$3^2 + 4^2 = 5^2$$
$$9 + 16 = 25$$
$$25 = 25$$

Because the formula is true, the triangle must be a right triangle.

EXAMPLE 3 If a triangle has sides of 5 inches, 12 inches, and 13 inches, is it a right triangle?

STEP 1	Identify the formula.	$a^2 + b^2 = c^2$
STEP 2	Substitute the measures.	$5^2 + 12^2 = 13^2$
STEP 3	Solve.	$25 + 144 = 169$
		$169 = 169$

ANSWER: Yes. The triangle with sides of 5 inches, 12 inches, and 13 inches is a right triangle.

Tell whether these triangles are right triangles.

5. A triangle with sides measuring 6 feet, 7 feet, and 8 feet

6. A triangle with sides 30, 40, and 50

Trigonometric Ratios

The word **trigonometry** comes from Greek words that mean "measuring triangles." Trigonometry is the study of the relationship between pairs of sides in right triangles.

The three most common ratios in trigonometry are the **sine,** the **cosine,** and the **tangent.** The abbreviations for these ratios are *sin, cos,* and *tan.*

In the triangle at the right, angle A is one of the two acute angles in a right triangle. Side AC is the hypotenuse. Side BC, which is across from $\angle A$, is labeled *opposite.* And side AB, which forms one side of $\angle A$, is labeled *adjacent.*

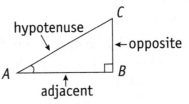

Below are the definitions of the sine, the cosine and the tangent.

$$\sin = \frac{\text{opposite side}}{\text{hypotenuse}} \qquad \cos = \frac{\text{adjacent side}}{\text{hypotenuse}} \qquad \tan = \frac{\text{opposite side}}{\text{adjacent side}}$$

For the triangle at the right, the legs measure 3 and 4, and the hypotenuse is 5. Following are the three trigonometric ratios for angle X:

$$\sin X = \frac{\text{opposite}}{\text{hypotenuse}} = \frac{3}{5} = 0.6$$

$$\cos X = \frac{\text{adjacent}}{\text{hypotenuse}} = \frac{4}{5} = 0.8$$

$$\tan X = \frac{\text{opposite}}{\text{adjacent}} = \frac{3}{4} = 0.75$$

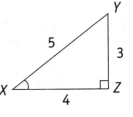

EXAMPLE 1 For the triangle at the right, what is the tangent of $\angle M$ to the nearest thousandth?

The tangent is $\frac{\text{opposite}}{\text{adjacent}}$.

2 is opposite and 3 is adjacent.

The tangent of $\angle M$ is $\frac{2}{3}$ or 0.667.

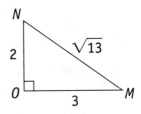

 You can use the Casio *fx–260* to find a trigonometric ratio for an angle when you know the number of degrees in the angle.

EXAMPLE 2 Use a calculator to find the sine of 25°.
Round your answer to the nearest thousandth.

	Press Keys	**Display Reads**
STEP 1 Enter the number of degrees in the angle.	[2] [5]	25.
STEP 2 Press the [SIN] key.	[SIN]	0.422618261

ANSWER: 0.423

EXAMPLE 3 Use a calculator to find the cosine of 50°.
Round your answer to the nearest thousandth.

	Press Keys	**Display Reads**
STEP 1 Enter the number of degrees in the angle.	5 0	5 0 .
STEP 2 Press the COS key.	COS	0.642787609

ANSWER: 0.643

EXAMPLE 4 Write an equation with a trigonometric ratio to express the height x of triangle ABC at the right.

> Side AB is the hypotenuse. Height BC is opposite the 60° angle and base AC is adjacent. The ratio of the height x to the base 15 is the tangent of 60°.

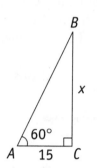

ANSWER: tan 60° = $\frac{x}{15}$

EXAMPLE 5 To the nearest tenth, what is the height of the triangle in the previous example?

STEP 1 Find tan 60° on a calculator.

Press Keys	**Display Reads**
6 0	6 0 .
TAN	1.732050808

Round to the nearest thousandth. tan 60° = 1.732

STEP 2 Multiply both sides of the equation by 15 to solve for x. $1.732 = \frac{x}{15}$

STEP 3 Round 25.98 to the nearest tenth. 25.98 = x

25.98 → 26.0

ANSWER: The height of the triangle is 26.0.

....

For problems 1–3, use the triangle below.

1. Which side, XY, XZ, or YZ is opposite ∠X?

2. Which side in triangle XYZ is the hypotenuse?

3. Does the ratio of $\frac{YZ}{XZ}$ represent the sine, the cosine, or the tangent of ∠X?

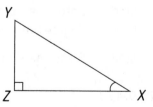

For problems 4–6, use the triangle below. Tell what each of the following ratios represents for ∠M: the sine, the cosine, or the tangent.

4. $\frac{12}{13} =$

5. $\frac{5}{12} =$

6. $\frac{5}{13} =$

For problems 7–9, use triangle *EFG* below. Write a ratio for each of the following.

7. $\sin E =$

8. $\cos E =$

9. $\tan E =$

Use a calculator to fill in the following chart. Where necessary, round each answer to the nearest thousandth.

	angle	sin	cos	tan
10.	30°			
11.	45°			
12.	60°			
13.	75°			

14. The diagram below shows a building that casts a shadow 44 feet long. The angle created by the shadow and an imaginary line from the top of the building to the end of the shadow is 65°. Use your calculator to find the height of the building to the nearest tenth of a foot.

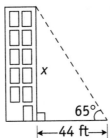

Plane Figures Review

This review covers the material you have just studied. When you finish, check your answers at the back of the book.

Write the formula for the perimeter of each figure.

1.

2.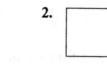

3.

Write the formula for the area and each figure.

4. 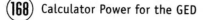 5. 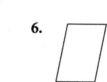 6. 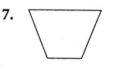 7.

8. If the diameter of a circle is 7, then the area is _____ to the nearest hundredth.

Use your calculator to find the perimeter and area of each figure.

9.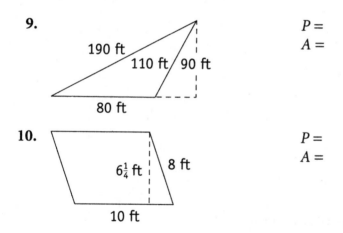

   $P =$
   $A =$

10.
   $P =$
   $A =$

11. If you double the length of the sides of a square room, what happens to the area?

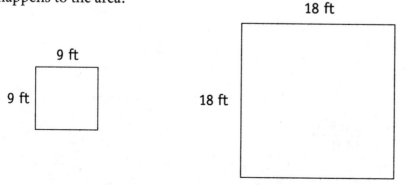

12. To the nearest hundredth, what is the area of the shaded region?

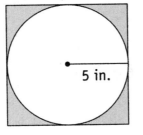

5 in.

13. A farmer has divided his circular garden into four equal plots. How many square feet will be planted with corn? Round your answer to the nearest square foot.

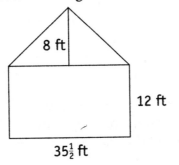

Corn   Beans

50 ft diameter

Potatoes   Tomatoes

14. How many square feet of siding is needed for the side of this house?

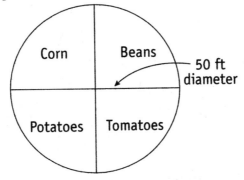

8 ft

12 ft

$35\frac{1}{2}$ ft

15. If the equator of the earth is about 25,000 miles around, what is the diameter to the nearest mile? Use the formula $d = \frac{C}{\pi}$.

Find the area of the shaded parts of the figures to the nearest whole unit.

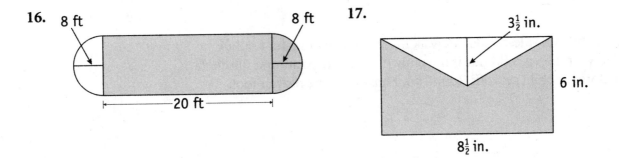

16. 8 ft   8 ft

20 ft

17.

$3\frac{1}{2}$ in.

6 in.

$8\frac{1}{2}$ in.

18. Find the number of square meters of wood used for the side of this form.

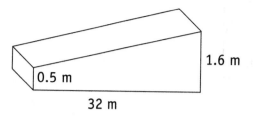

19. What is the area of this concrete retaining wall?

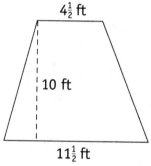

20. Plastic tubing is wrapped around this reel 7 times. To the nearest foot, how much tubing is on the reel?

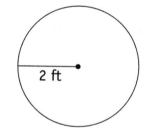

21. Two hundred yards of fencing will be used to fence in a yard. The yard can be made in the shape of a square, a rectangle, or a parallelogram as shown below. Which of the shapes provides the greatest area for a yard?

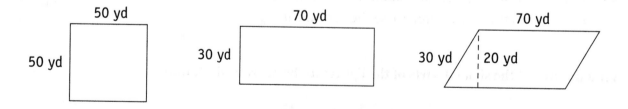

22. In a carnival ride, the ponies walk in a circle with a 14-foot radius. How far does a child ride if the pony makes 10 trips around the circle before the child gets off? Round your answer to the nearest foot.

23. Refer to the drawing below. Which of the following fractions results when the area of triangle *ABC* is divided by the area of the square?

    (1) $\frac{2}{3}$

    (2) $\frac{1}{4}$

    (3) $\frac{1}{3}$

    (4) $\frac{1}{2}$

    (5) $\frac{3}{4}$

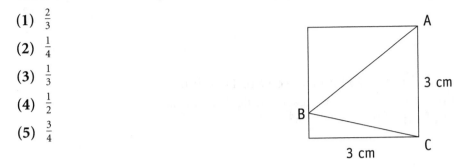

24. Refer to the drawing below. Choose the whole number that is closest to the result of dividing the area of the square by the area of the circle.

    (1) 4
    (2) 5
    (3) 6
    (4) 7
    (5) 8

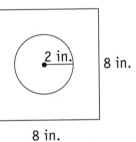

25. To the nearest foot, what is the shortest distance between home plate and second base?

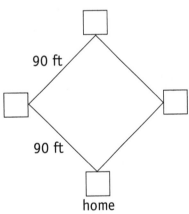

26. How long is the guy wire for this flag pole?

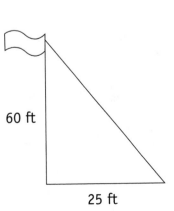

27. A 30-foot ladder is leaning against a wall. The ladder is 8 feet from the base of the wall. To the nearest foot, how high on the wall will the ladder reach?

28. A plane flies from city A due east 230 miles to city B. Then it flies north another 450 miles to city C. To the nearest mile, how far is the return direct flight from City C to City A?

29. Write an equation that can be used to calculate the length of y in the triangle below.

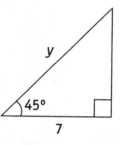

30. Use a calculator to find the length, to the nearest tenth, of y in the triangle above.

Plane Figures Review Chart

Circle the number of any problem that you missed and review the appropriate pages. A passing score is 27 correct answers. If you missed more than three questions, you should review this chapter.

PROBLEM NUMBERS	SKILL AREA	PRACTICE PAGES
1, 2, 3, 9	perimeter	147–148
15	diameter of circles	149–150
20, 22	circumference	149–150
4, 8, 12, 13, 16, 24	area of circles	160–161
11, 12, 14, 16, 17, 21, 23, 24	area of squares or rectangles	151–153
6, 10, 21	area of parallelograms	154–155
5, 9, 14, 17, 23	area of triangles	156–157
7, 18, 19	area of trapezoids	158–159
25, 26, 27, 28	Pythagorean theorem	164–166
29, 30	trigonometric ratios	167–168

SOLID FIGURES

Volume of Cubes and Rectangular Solids

Volume (V) is a measure of the space taken up by a solid figure. The solid figure has three dimensions: length, width and height. Volume is measured in cubic units of measure. Some common volume units are cubic inch, cubic feet, cubic meters, and cubic kilometers. You may see the units abbreviated with an exponent.

> cubic inches = cu in. = in.³
>
> cubic feet = cu ft = ft³
>
> cubic meters = cu m = m³
>
> cubic kilometers = cu km = km³

To find the volume of a rectangular solid, multiply the length times the width times the height. The rectangular solid at the right has a length (l) of 4 meters, width (w) of 3 meters, and height (h) of 2 meters. The volume is 24 cubic meters.

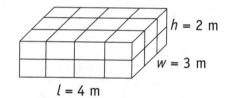

$h = 2$ m
$w = 3$ m
$l = 4$ m

The following are formulas for finding volume.

The volume of a:

cube $V = s^3$, where s = side

rectangular $V = lwh$, where l = length, w = width,
solid h = height

EXAMPLE 1 Find the volume of the cube below. Use the $\boxed{x^3}$ function located above the backspace key $\boxed{\blacktriangleright}$.

$4\frac{1}{2}$ in.

STEP 1 Identify the formula. $V = s^3$

STEP 2 Substitute the measures. $V = (4\frac{1}{2})^3$

Press Keys	Display Reads
4 a b/c 1 a b/c 2	4⌐1⌐2.
SHIFT x³	91.125

ANSWER: V = 91.125 cubic inches

You know that squaring a number and finding the square root are opposite operations. Cubing a number and finding the cube root are also opposite operations. Using this fact, you can find the side of a cube if you know the volume.

> **To find a side:**
>
> $s = \sqrt[3]{V}$, where V = volume

EXAMPLE 2 Find the side of a cube with a volume of 90 cubic inches. Round your answer to the nearest tenth.

STEP 1 Identify the formula. $s = \sqrt[3]{V}$

STEP 2 Substitute measures. $s = \sqrt[3]{90}$

Press Keys	Display Reads
9 0	90.
SHIFT $\sqrt{}$	4.481404747
To round to the nearest tenth: MODE	4.481404747
7	4.481404747
1	4.5

ANSWER: 4.5 inches

EXAMPLE 3 Find the volume of the rectangular solid below.

STEP 1 Identify the formula. $V = lwh$

STEP 2 Substitute measures. $V = 4 \times 3 \times 2$

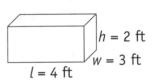

$h = 2$ ft
$w = 3$ ft
$l = 4$ ft

Press Keys	Display Reads
4	4.
$\times$	4.
3	3.
$\times$	12.
2	2.
=	24.

ANSWER: 24 cubic feet

When the measurements of a figure are in different units, change the measurements to a common unit before substituting into a formula.

EXAMPLE 4 Find the volume for the figure below.

STEP 1	Identify the formula.	$V = lwh$	
STEP 2	Substitute measures.	$V = (9)(4)(2)$ $(3 \text{ yd} = 9 \text{ ft})$	
STEP 3	Solve.	$V = 72 \text{ ft}^3$	

ANSWER: 72 ft³

....

Use your calculator and the volume formula to find the volume of each figure.

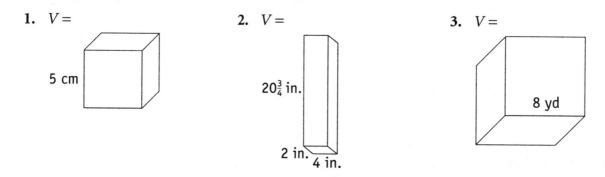

1. $V =$ 5 cm

2. $V =$ $20\frac{3}{4}$ in.   2 in.   4 in.

3. $V =$ 8 yd

Use your calculator and the volume formula to find the length of the side of each cube. Round your answer to the nearest tenth.

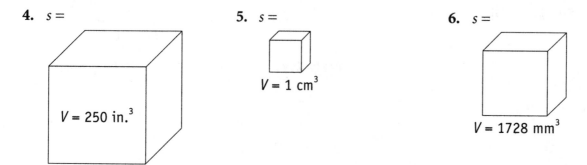

4. $s =$ $V = 250 \text{ in.}^3$

5. $s =$ $V = 1 \text{ cm}^3$

6. $s =$ $V = 1728 \text{ mm}^3$

Solve.

7. A water storage tank in the shape of a cube measures 4.1 meters along each edge. If one cubic meter of water weighs one metric ton, how many metric tons of water can the tank hold?

8. How many cubic feet of water are in a waterbed that is 6 feet long, 5 feet wide, and $\frac{1}{2}$ foot high?

9. Simon's Toy Co. makes plastic blocks that are in the shape of cubes 3 inches on each edge. How many blocks can be put into a cube-shaped mailing box that measures 15 inches on each edge?

10. What is the volume of space in a bedroom that measures 4 meters long, 3 meters wide, and $2\frac{1}{2}$ meters high?

11. The Deluxe Calculator Co. packs calculators in cubical shipping boxes that are 2 feet on each side. How many shipping boxes can be put in a moving van that has a packing volume of 896 cubic feet?

12. How many cubic feet of air can be pumped into an air mattress that is 4 feet wide, 6 feet long, and 8 inches high?

13. One cubic foot holds approximately $7\frac{1}{2}$ gallons of water. How many gallons of water will it take to fill a swimming pool 40 feet long, 20 feet wide, and 6 feet deep?

Volume of Square-Based Pyramids

A **square-based pyramid** has a square base and four triangular faces for sides. If you were to unfold a square-based pyramid, it would look like the figure at the right. You can see there are four triangles and a square.

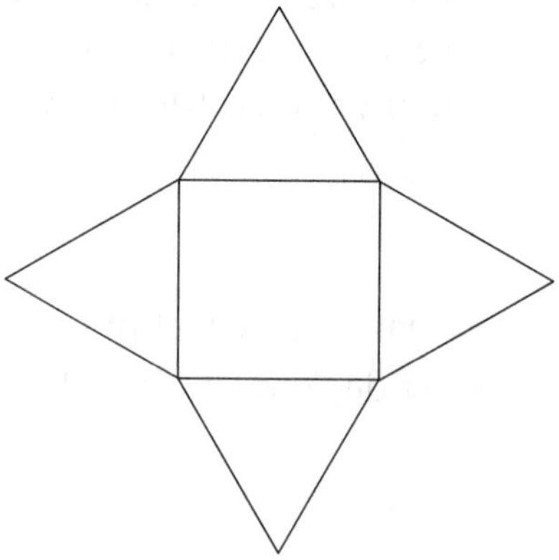

The distance from the top of the pyramid to the center of the base is called the **height** (h). The sides of the base square are represented by b.

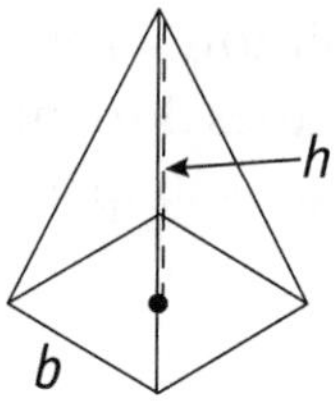

The following is the formula for finding the volume of a square-based pyramid.

The volume of a:

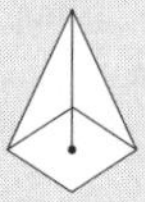

square-based pyramid $V = \frac{1}{3}b^2h$, where b = side of the base, h = height

<u>EXAMPLE</u>   Find the volume of the square-based pyramid at the right.

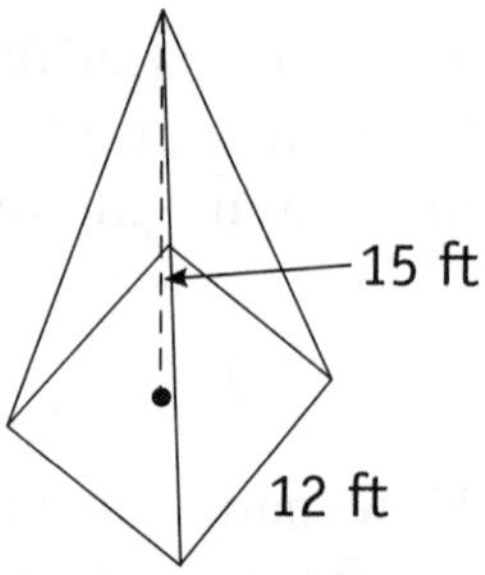

    STEP 1   Identify the formula. $V = \frac{1}{3}b^2h$

    STEP 2   Substitute measures. $V = \frac{1}{3} \times 12^2 \times 15$

Press Keys	Display Reads
1 a b/c 3	1⌐3.
×	1⌐3.
1 2	12.
x²	144.
×	48.
1 5	15.
=	720.

ANSWER: 720 ft³

Use your calculator and the formula $V = \frac{1}{3}b^2h$ to find the volume of each figure.

1. $V =$

2. $V =$

3. $V =$

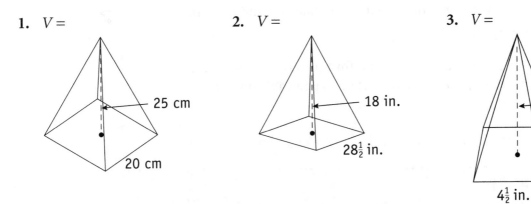

25 cm

20 cm

18 in.

$28\frac{1}{2}$ in.

4 ft

$4\frac{1}{2}$ in.

For problems 4–11, fill in each blank.

	Side	Length	Width	Height	Volume
4. rectangular solid		5 m	3 m	1 m	_____
5. rectangular solid		6 yd	4 yd	2 ft	_____
6. cube	$2\frac{1}{2}$ in.				_____
7. cube	1.2 m				_____
8. square-based pyramid	8 in.			$4\frac{3}{4}$ in.	_____
9. square-based pyramid	3.6 cm			10 cm	_____
10. cube	_____				1000 in.³
11. cube	_____				343 m³

Solve.

12. Find the volume of a rectangular box with a length of 1 foot, a width of 5 inches, and a height of 9 inches.

13. A square building block has a volume of 1,400 cubic inches. To the nearest tenth of an inch, what do the sides measure?

Volume of Cylinders

A **cylinder** is a 3-dimensional figure with a circular top and bottom and rectangular sides.

To find the volume (V) of a cylinder, first find the area of the circular top (or bottom) using πr^2, where r is the radius. Then multiply that number by the height (h).

The following is the formula for the volume of a cylinder.

The volume of a:

cylinder $\qquad V = \pi r^2 h$, where π is 3.14 or $\frac{22}{7}$, r = radius, h = height

EXAMPLE Find the volume of the cylinder below. Round your answer to the nearest tenth of a cubic yard.

STEP 1 Identify the formula. $\qquad V = \pi r^2 h$

STEP 2 Substitute measures. $\qquad V = (3.14)(0.75)^2(2)$

0.75 yd
2 yd

Press Keys	Display Reads
SHIFT π	3.141592654
×	3.141592654
. 7 5	0.75
x^2	0.5625
×	1.767145868
2	2.
=	3.534291735
To round to the nearest tenth: MODE	3.534291735
7	3.534291735
1	3.5

ANSWER: 3.5 cubic yards

Use your calculator and the formula $V = \pi r^2 h$ **to find the volume of each figure. Round your answer to the nearest tenth.**

1. $V =$

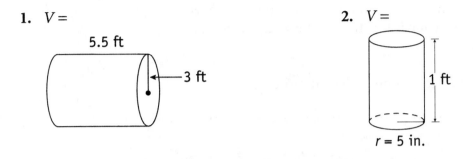

2. $V =$

3. A cylindrical can is $5\frac{1}{2}$ inches across and 8 inches tall. To the nearest cubic inch, what is the volume of the can?

4. A hot water tank is half full. The tank measures $1\frac{3}{4}$ feet across and is 4 feet tall. To the nearest tenth, how many cubic feet of water are in the tank?

5. To the nearest tenth, how many more cubic yards does cylinder B hold than cylinder A?

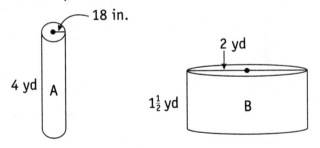

6. Dirt is put in a cylindrical plastic container. The basket is 24 inches across and 30 inches tall. To the nearest cubic foot, how many cubic feet of dirt fill the container?

Volume of Cones

A **cone** has a circular base and a point on the top. The point is called the **vertex.** The **height** (h) of a cone is the distance between the vertex and the center of the circle.

The following is the formula for finding the volume of a cone.

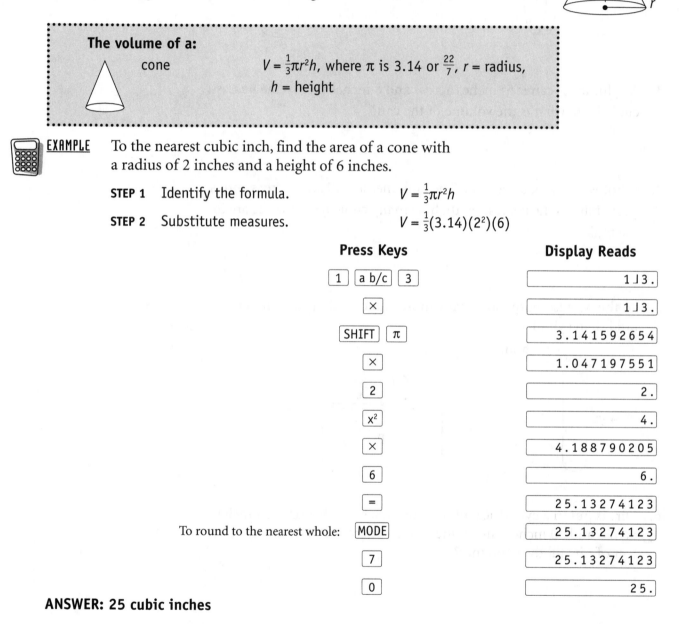

The volume of a:

cone — $V = \frac{1}{3}\pi r^2 h$, where π is 3.14 or $\frac{22}{7}$, r = radius, h = height

EXAMPLE To the nearest cubic inch, find the area of a cone with a radius of 2 inches and a height of 6 inches.

STEP 1 Identify the formula. $V = \frac{1}{3}\pi r^2 h$

STEP 2 Substitute measures. $V = \frac{1}{3}(3.14)(2^2)(6)$

Press Keys	Display Reads
1 a b/c 3	1⌐3.
×	1⌐3.
SHIFT π	3.141592654
×	1.047197551
2	2.
x²	4.
×	4.188790205
6	6.
=	25.13274123
To round to the nearest whole: MODE	25.13274123
7	25.13274123
0	25.

ANSWER: 25 cubic inches

Use your calculator and the formula $V = \frac{1}{3}\pi r^2 h$ to find the volume of each figure. Round your answer to the nearest hundredth.

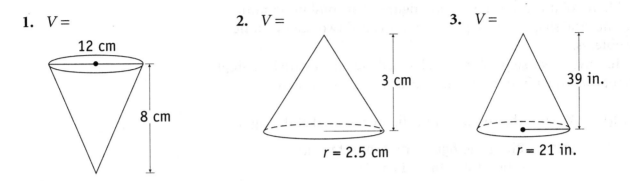

1. $V =$

    12 cm

    8 cm

2. $V =$

    3 cm

    $r = 2.5$ cm

3. $V =$

    39 in.

    $r = 21$ in.

Solve.

4. A pile of sand is in the shape of a cone. The height of the sand is 7 feet and the distance across the pile is 9 feet. To the nearest cubic foot, how many cubic feet of sand are in the pile?

5. A tapered steel part is machined as shown. To the nearest tenth, how many cubic centimeters of steel are contained in the whole part?

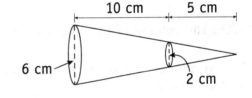

    10 cm   5 cm

    6 cm

    2 cm

6. If the radius of the cone at the right is doubled and the height is unchanged, what will happen to the volume?

    (1) It is doubled.
    (2) It is increased by 2 cubic inches.
    (3) It is quadrupled.
    (4) It is increased by 4 cubic inches.

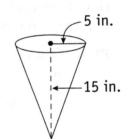

    5 in.

    15 in.

7. A sugar cone is $2\frac{1}{2}$ inches across and $5\frac{1}{2}$ inches long. To the nearest cubic inch, how much ice cream can be packed into the cone?

Solving Two-Step Volume Problems

Many volume problems involve figures that combine common geometrical shapes. These problems are called **two-step volume problems**.

To solve a two-step volume problem, divide the figure into single shapes and then find the volume of each shape separately.

EXAMPLE 1 What is the volume of the figure pictured at the right?

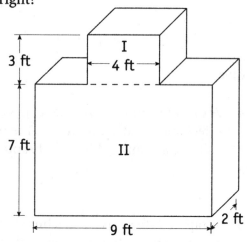

STEP 1 Divide the figure into two rectangular solids. Label these I and II.

STEP 2 Find the volume of each rectangular solid. Volume of I = *lwh*

$$V = 4 \times 2 \times 3 = 24$$

Volume of figure II = *lwh*

$$V = 9 \times 2 \times 7 = 126$$

STEP 3 Add the volumes of I and II.

$$24 + 126 = 150$$

ANSWER: The volume of the figure is 150 cubic feet.

Many volume problems are solved by subtracting a smaller volume from a larger volume.

EXAMPLE 2 How many cubic inches of metal are contained in the rectangular bar at the right?

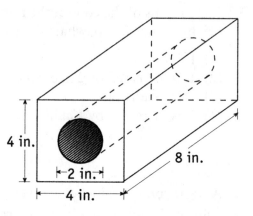

STEP 1 Find the volume of the bar as if it were solid.

Volume of solid bar = *lwh*

$$V = 8 \times 4 \times 4 = 128$$

STEP 2 Find the volume of space taken by the hole drilled through the bar.

Volume of hole = $\pi r^2 h$

$$V = 3.14 \times 1 \times 1 \times 8 = 25.1$$

STEP 3 Subtract to find the volume of metal in the bar.
$$128 - 25.12 = 102.88$$

ANSWER: The amount of metal left in the bar is 102.88 cubic inches.

Use your calculator and volume formulas to solve each problem.

1. What is the volume of the figure drawn below?

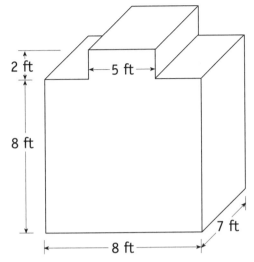

2. Estimate the number of cubic inches of metal that are contained in the cylinder drawn below. Round your answer to the nearest cubic inch.

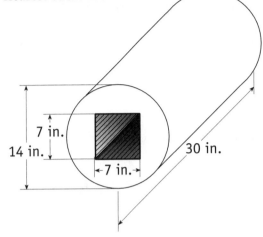

3. What is the volume of the mailbox shown below? (**Hint:** The mailbox can be thought of as a half-cylinder plus a rectangular solid.)

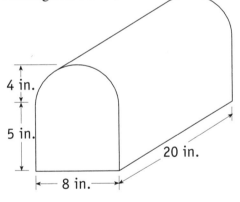

4. The concrete steps below contain how many cubic feet of concrete?

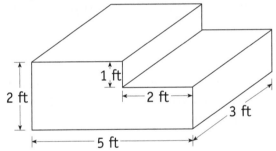

5. To the nearest tenth, what is the volume of the figure below? (**Hint:** The figure can be separated into a cylinder and a cone.)

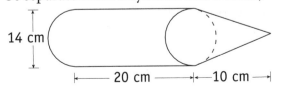

6. What is the volume of the slotted beam below?

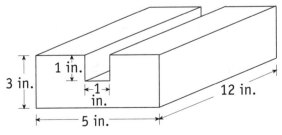

Solid Figures Review

This review covers the material you have just studied. When you finish, check your answers at the back of the book.

Use your calculator to solve the following problems.

1. How many cubic inches are in a block of ice that measures 1 foot by 1 foot by 1 foot?

2. Find the volume of the rectangular solid below.

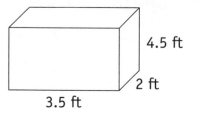

   4.5 ft
   2 ft
   3.5 ft

3. How much feed can be stored in a silo if the silo's radius is 8 feet and its height is 20 feet? Round your answer to the nearest square foot.

4. Find the volume of space left in the carton below after it is filled with the two cylinders shown. Round your answer to the nearest whole number.

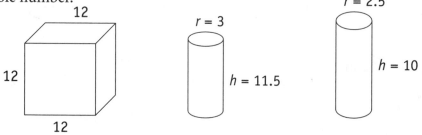

   12
   12
   12
   r = 3
   h = 11.5
   r = 2.5
   h = 10

5. Joe Jones needs a new rectangular sidewalk. One section of the sidewalk needs to be 48 inches long, 40 inches wide, and 3 inches deep. How much concrete does he need?

6. Sherrie is going to fill the plastic container shown below with colored sand. How many cubic centimeters of sand will she need? Round your answer to the nearest cubic centimeter.

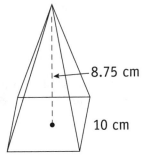

←—8.75 cm

10 cm

7. To the nearest cubic inch, how much oil will this funnel hold?

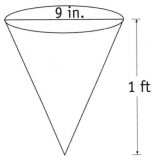

9 in.

1 ft

8. A square-based pyramid has a base *perimeter* of 144 inches and a height of 20 inches. Find its volume.

9. Find the volume of the figure below. Round your answer to the nearest cubic centimeter.

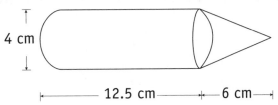

4 cm

←——— 12.5 cm ———→ ←— 6 cm —→

10. A disposable plastic drinking cup is designed in the shape of a cone. The rim base has a diameter of 3 inches. The depth of the cup is 4 inches. How many cubic inches of water will the cup hold? Round your answer to the nearest cubic inch.

11. A hot water tank is 1.8 meters high and has a diameter of 0.5 meter. To the nearest hundredth, how many cubic meters of water can it hold?

Solid Figures Review Chart

Circle the number of any problem that you missed and review the appropriate pages. A passing score is 9 correct answers. If you missed more than two problems, you should review this chapter.

PROBLEM NUMBERS	SKILL AREA	PRACTICE PAGES
1, 4	volume of cubes	176–179
2, 5	volume of rectangular solids	176–179
3, 4, 11	volume of cylinders	182–183
6, 8	volume of square-based pyramids	180–181
7, 10	volume of cones	184–185
9	two-step volume problems	186–187

GED Practice

Use your calculator to solve the following problems.

Questions 1–3 refer to the drawing below.

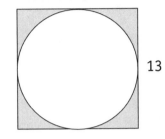

13

1. A circle is drawn inside a square each of whose sides measure 13. What is the diameter of the circle?

   (1)   4.14
   (2)   6.00
   (3) 13.00
   (4) 40.84
   (5) 169.00

2. To the nearest hundredth, what is the circumference of the circle?

   (1)   3.14
   (2) 18.84
   (3) 20.41
   (4) 40.84
   (5) 42.25

3. To the nearest tenth, what is the area of the shaded parts?

   (1)   16.5
   (2)   36.3
   (3) 132.7
   (4) 169.0
   (5) Not enough information is given.

4. What is the thickest measurement the wall of this pipe could be?

   (1) $\frac{1}{16}$ in.

   (2) $\frac{1}{2}$ in.

   (3) $\frac{15}{32}$ in.

   (4) $\frac{15}{16}$ in.

   (5) $1\frac{1}{16}$ in.

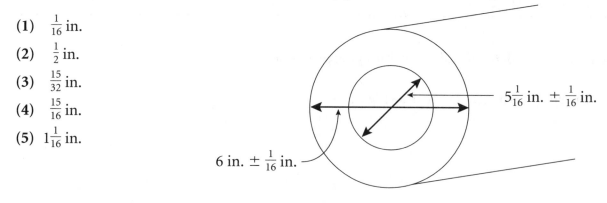

$5\frac{1}{16}$ in. $\pm$ $\frac{1}{16}$ in.

6 in. $\pm$ $\frac{1}{16}$ in.

5. Which expression can be used to find the area of the trapezoid below?

   (1) $\frac{1}{2}(5 + 8)6$

   (2) $\frac{1}{2}(6 + 7)8$

   (3) $\frac{1}{2}(6 + 7)5$

   (4) $\frac{1}{2}(5 + 8)7$

   (5) Not enough information is given.

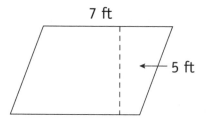

6. Find the area of the parallelogram below. Mark your answer on the number grid.

7 ft

5 ft

7. Which expression can be used to find the length of *b*?

   (1) $b = \sqrt{10^2 + 20^2}$

   (2) $b = \sqrt{20^2 - 10^2}$

   (3) $b = \sqrt{10^2} - \sqrt{20^2}$

   (4) $\sqrt{20^2 - b^2} = 10^2$

   (5) $b = \sqrt{20^2} + \sqrt{10^2}$

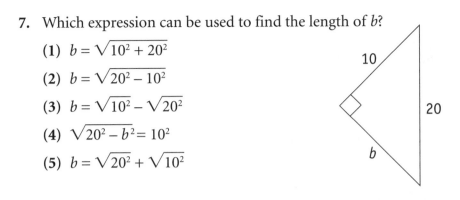

8. Which of the following are the measurements of the sides of a right triangle?

   (1) 10 m, 8 m, 6 m
   (2) 15 in., 20 in., 30 in.
   (3) 7 cm, 11 cm, 9 cm
   (4) 1 mi, 1 mi, 2 mi
   (5) 3 ft, 4 ft, 6 ft

9. How many cubic feet of attic space can be found if the roof is in the shape of a square pyramid? Mark your answer on the number grid.

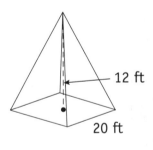

12 ft

20 ft

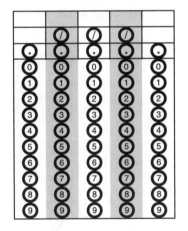

10. A pile of gravel is in the shape of a cone. If the pile is 8 feet high and the diameter of the pile is 10 feet, how many cubic feet of gravel are in the pile? Round your answer to the nearest cubic foot.

   (1) 84
   (2) 209
   (3) 251
   (4) 628
   (5) 838

11. An 8-inch pizza has a diameter of 8 inches. A 12-inch pizza has a diameter of 12 inches. Approximately how many times more pizza is in the larger pizza than the smaller one?

   (1) 2

   (2) $\frac{3}{4}$

   (3) $1\frac{1}{2}$

   (4) 63

   (5) Not enough information is given.

12. To the nearest hundredth of a foot, what is the length of the side of a square that has an area of 1 acre? (1 acre = 43,560 sq ft)

   (1) 65.57
   (2) 208.71
   (3) 208.92
   (4) 211.09
   (5) Not enough information is given.

13. Jeremy installed carpet in a room measuring 12 feet by 8 feet. The cost of carpet is $18.75 per square yard. How much did Jeremy spend to carpet the room? Mark your answer on the number grid.

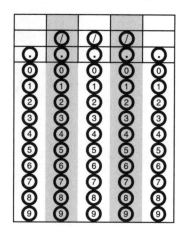

14. A circular pool has a diameter of 18 feet. The gravel walk around the pool is $2\frac{1}{2}$ feet wide. What is the area of the circular walk around the pool? Round your answer to the nearest square foot. Mark your answer on the number grid.

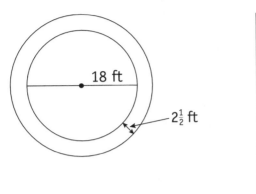

15. Which of the following represents sin X for the diagram below?

(1) $\frac{YZ}{XZ}$

(2) $\frac{XZ}{YZ}$

(3) $\frac{XY}{YZ}$

(4) $\frac{YZ}{XY}$

(5) $\frac{ZX}{XZ}$

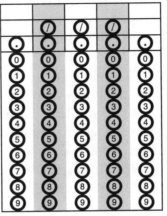

16. A flagpole casts a shadow 20 feet long. The angle created by the shadow and an imaginary line to the top of the pole measures 75°. Find the height (x) of the pole. Round your answer to the nearest foot. Mark your answer on the number grid.

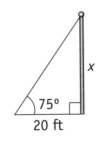

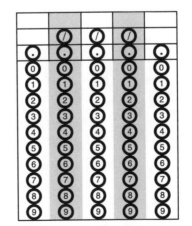

PRACTICE TEST

Directions: The test that follows is similar to the GED Mathematics Test. The test has two parts. On the GED test, you will be permitted the use of a calculator on only the first part. **On this test, however, because this book emphasizes using the Casio *fx*-260, you may use that calculator on both parts.** Each part of the posttest should take no longer than 45 minutes to complete.

At the end of 45 minutes, if you have not completed Part I, mark your place and finish the test. Do the same with Part II. This will give you an idea of whether you can finish the real test in 90 minutes. Mark each answer on the answer grid. Answer as many questions as you can. A blank will be a wrong answer, so make a reasonable guess if you are not sure. Use any formulas on page 222 that you need.

When you finish, check your answers. The evaluation chart at the end of the answers will help you determine which areas to review before you are ready for the actual GED Mathematics Test.

Practice Test Answer Grid, Part I

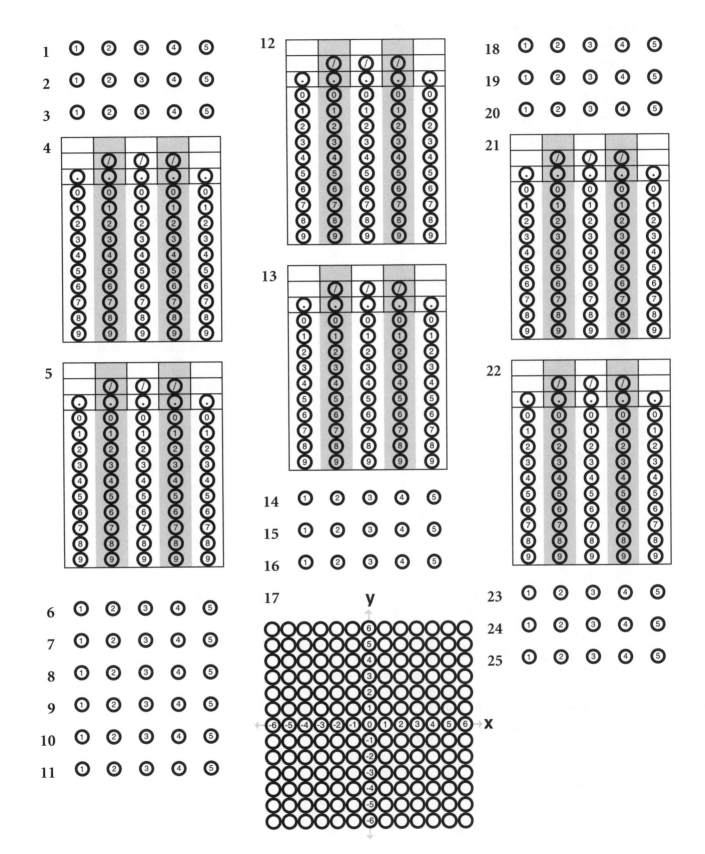

Part I

Directions: Solve each problem. You may use a calculator on any of these problems. Use the formulas on page 222 as needed.

1. What is the distance, in meters, around a rectangular vegetable garden that is 4.5 meters long and 2.3 meters wide?

   (1) 5.2
   (2) 6.8
   (3) 10.3
   (4) 13.6
   (5) 20.3

2. Imani bought 6.5 gallons of gasoline at the price of $1.349 per gallon. How much change will she get from $20?

   (1) $11.23
   (2) $10.23
   (3) $ 9.77
   (4) $ 7.77
   (5) $ 1.23

3. Which of the following is equal to $3(-8) + (-5)^2$?

   (1) −14
   (2) −1
   (3)   1
   (4) 34
   (5) 49

For problems 4 and 5, mark your answers on the corresponding number grid on the answer sheet.

4. At the start of a trip, Tom's odometer (mileage gauge) had a reading of 39,276.4 miles. When he returned from his trip, the reading was 40,083.5 miles. How many miles did he travel?

5. The diameter of a pizza pan is 18.5 inches. What is the radius, in inches, of the pizza pan? Express the answer in decimal form.

6. From a piece of decorative molding that is 24 inches long, Martha cut a section $5\frac{7}{8}$ inches long. Assuming no waste, how many inches long is the remaining piece?

   (1) $18\frac{1}{8}$
   (2) $19\frac{1}{8}$
   (3) $19\frac{7}{8}$
   (4) $29\frac{1}{8}$
   (5) $20\frac{7}{8}$

7. Five brothers each calculated the volume of earth to be removed from a hole that is 36 feet long, 24 feet wide, and 9 feet deep. The answer choices show their calculations. Which brother has the correct answer?

   (1) Jim—54 cu yd
   (2) John—69 cu ft
   (3) Joe—144 cu yd
   (4) Jake—288 cu yd
   (5) Jed—324 cu ft

8. Charlene paid $15.87 for a pork roast that weighs 4.3 pounds. To the nearest cent, what is the unit price (cost per pound) of the meat?

   (1) $1.58
   (2) $1.59
   (3) $2.59
   (4) $3.29
   (5) $3.69

The table below lists the per capita state taxes in selected states. Use the table to answer questions 9–11.

U.S. Average	$1758
New Hampshire	851
New York	1989
California	2073
Pennsylvania	1719
Connecticut	2869
Wisconsin	2135

9. A town in New York with a population of 10,000 pays approximately how much in yearly state tax?

   (1) $ 5,000,000
   (2) $10,000,000
   (3) $15,000,000
   (4) $20,000,000
   (5) $25,000,000

10. The per capita state taxes in Pennsylvania are about how many times that of the per capita state taxes in New Hampshire?

   (1) 2 times
   (2) $2\frac{1}{2}$ times
   (3) 3 times
   (4) $3\frac{1}{2}$ times
   (5) 4 times

11. The per capita state taxes in Wisconsin are about what percent of the per capita state taxes in Connecticut?

   (1) 80%
   (2) 75%
   (3) 70%
   (4) 65%
   (5) 60%

For problems 12 and 13, mark your answers on the corresponding number grid on the answer sheet.

12. In Alma's English as a second language class there are 24 students. Ten of the students are men. Women make up what fraction of the class?

13. To the nearest tenth, what is the value of $(1.6)^3$?

14. What is the distance from point A to point B on the number line?

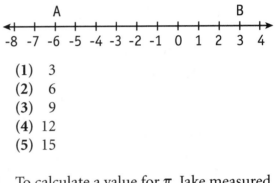

   (1) 3
   (2) 6
   (3) 9
   (4) 12
   (5) 15

15. To calculate a value for π, Jake measured the distance around a plate and the distance across the plate. The distance around the plate was 23.5 inches, and the distance across the plate was 7.5 inches. To the nearest hundredth, what was the value of π?

   (1) 3.02
   (2) 3.09
   (3) 3.10
   (4) 3.13
   (5) 3.19

16. What is the area of the shaded part of the figure below?

   (1) 56
   (2) 64
   (3) 72
   (4) 88
   (5) 96

17. Mark the point (−4, 6) on the corresponding coordinate plane grid on the answer sheet.

18. Max's weight in kilograms is 68. One kilogram equals 2.2 pounds. To the nearest whole number, what is Max's weight in pounds?

    (1) 132
    (2) 144
    (3) 150
    (4) 160
    (5) 168

19. The shaded part of the illustration represents a walkway around a circular pool. The diameter of the pool is 24 feet, and the width of the walkway is 4 feet. Which of the following represents the area of the walkway?

    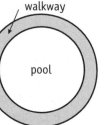
    walkway
    pool

    (1) $\pi(24)^2 - \pi(20)^2$
    (2) $\pi(20)^2 - \pi(16)^2$
    (3) $\pi(16)^2 - \pi(12)^2$
    (4) $\pi(16)^2 - \pi(8)^2$
    (5) $\pi(16)^2 - \pi(4)^2$

20. Which of the following represents the simplified form of the algebraic expression $\frac{8+13}{7} - (5 - 2)$?

    (1) 3
    (2) 2
    (3) 1
    (4) 0
    (5) −1

For problems 21 and 22, mark each answer on the corresponding number grid on the answer sheet.

21. To the nearest tenth of a square meter, what is the area of a square that measures 3.8 meters on each side?

22. Five years ago, Helen bought a car for $23,500. This year the car is worth only $5,875. The value of the car this year is what fraction of the price Helen paid?

23. The illustration shows an above-ground pool. One cubic foot of water is approximately equal to 7.48 gallons. Approximately how many gallons of water does the pool hold if it is filled to the rim?

    (1) 7000
    (2) 6500
    (3) 6000
    (4) 5500
    (5) 5000

    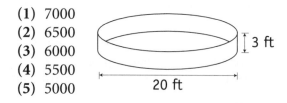
    3 ft
    20 ft

24. One kilowatt hour of electricity costs $0.1508. To the nearest cent, what is the cost of 470 kilowatt hours of electricity?

    (1) $ 7.88
    (2) $ 31.17
    (3) $ 70.88
    (4) $311.67
    (5) $708.76

25. The illustration shows a large window. To the nearest square foot, how much glass is required to make the window?

    (1) 35
    (2) 40
    (3) 45
    (4) 50
    (5) 55

    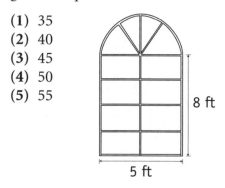
    8 ft
    5 ft

Practice Test Answer Grid, Part II

26 ① ② ③ ④ ⑤

27 ① ② ③ ④ ⑤

28 ① ② ③ ④ ⑤

29 ① ② ③ ④ ⑤

30 ① ② ③ ④ ⑤

31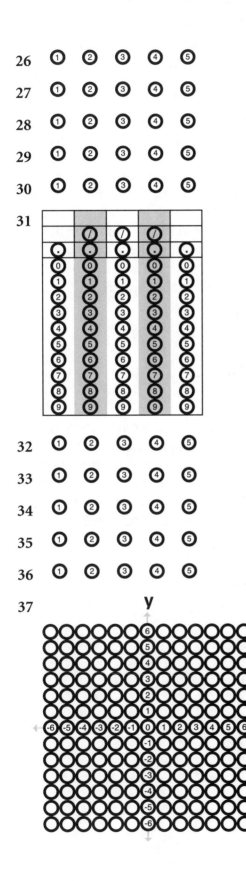

32 ① ② ③ ④ ⑤

33 ① ② ③ ④ ⑤

34 ① ② ③ ④ ⑤

35 ① ② ③ ④ ⑤

36 ① ② ③ ④ ⑤

37

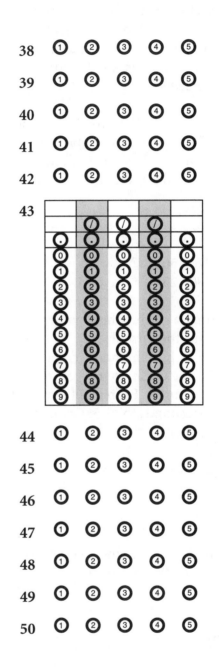

38 ① ② ③ ④ ⑤

39 ① ② ③ ④ ⑤

40 ① ② ③ ④ ⑤

41 ① ② ③ ④ ⑤

42 ① ② ③ ④ ⑤

43

44 ① ② ③ ④ ⑤

45 ① ② ③ ④ ⑤

46 ① ② ③ ④ ⑤

47 ① ② ③ ④ ⑤

48 ① ② ③ ④ ⑤

49 ① ② ③ ④ ⑤

50 ① ② ③ ④ ⑤

Part II

Directions: On Part II of the GED test, you will not be permitted to use a calculator. On this test, however, you may use a calculator to solve these problems. Use the formulas on page 222 as needed.

26. Fred borrowed $2500 from his cousin Mike. Fred agreed to pay Mike 7% interest in 18 months. How much money will Fred owe Mike at the end of 18 months?

    (1) $2626
    (2) $2675
    (3) $2718
    (4) $2762.50
    (5) $2806.25

27. To estimate a Fahrenheit temperature, Rosa used the formula $F \approx 2C + 30$ where F is the Fahrenheit temperature and C is the Celsius temperature. What is the approximate Fahrenheit temperature that corresponds to 18.5° Celsius?

    (1) 47°F
    (2) 52°F
    (3) 57°F
    (4) 62°F
    (5) 67°F

28. Which of the following is equal to the expression $10^2 - 5 \times 9 + 6$?

    (1) 61
    (2) 55
    (3) 51
    (4) 45
    (5) 41

The table below tells the rates for calculating the cost of a taxi ride in a big city. Use the table to answer questions 29 and 30.

$2.00 for the first $\frac{1}{5}$ mile
$0.30 for each additional $\frac{1}{5}$ mile
$0.50 surcharge after 8:00 P.M.

29. Charles and Janice decided to take a taxi from their hotel to the theater where they had tickets to see a play. They left their hotel at 7:15 in the evening. The theater was 2.8 miles from the hotel. Not including a tip, what was the cost of the taxi ride to the theater?

    (1) $6.20
    (2) $5.90
    (3) $4.90
    (4) $4.20
    (5) $3.90

30. After the play, Charles and Janice walked half a mile to a pizzeria. Then they took a taxi back to the hotel. The distance from the pizzeria to the hotel was 2.4 miles. Not including a tip, what was the cost of the taxi ride back to the hotel?

    (1) $3.60
    (2) $4.80
    (3) $5.30
    (4) $5.80
    (5) $6.10

For problem 31, mark the answer on the corresponding number grid on the answer sheet.

31. For the illustration below, the area of triangle *ACE* is what fraction of the area of rectangle *ABDE*?

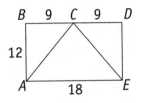

The circle graph shows how each dollar of an international relief agency spends its funds. Use the graph to answer questions 34 and 35.

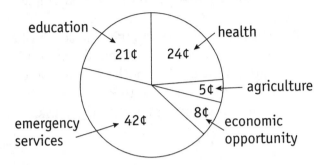

32. A batting average is the number of hits a baseball player gets divided by the number of times the player is at bat. The result is rounded to the nearest thousandth. Carlos got 28 hits in 89 times at bat. What was his batting average?

   (1) .276
   (2) .298
   (3) .315
   (4) .319
   (5) .327

33. The number of night school students at the Oakwood Community Center increased from 185 in the fall term to 259 in the spring term. By what percent did the number of students increase?

   (1) 35%
   (2) 40%
   (3) 45%
   (4) 50%
   (5) 55%

34. Together, emergency services and economic opportunity programs make up what fraction of the agency's expenditures?

   (1) $\frac{1}{2}$
   (2) $\frac{1}{3}$
   (3) $\frac{1}{4}$
   (4) $\frac{1}{5}$
   (5) $\frac{1}{6}$

35. The yearly budget for the agency is $98,000,000. How much is spent in a year on agricultural projects?

   (1) $ 4,900,000
   (2) $ 9,800,000
   (3) $24,500,000
   (4) $49,000,000
   (5) $98,000,000

36. Simplify the following equation: $(-3.8) + (-4.3) - (-7.1)$.

   (1) −14.2
   (2) −7.1
   (3) −1
   (4) +1
   (5) +7.1

37. Solve for y in the equation $y = 3x + 5$ when $x = 0$. Then mark the coordinates of the solution (x, y) on the corresponding coordinate plane grid on the answer sheet.

38. The illustration shows the first sketch of a deck that Jamal wants to build behind his house. If he doubles both the length and the width of the deck, the area will be how many times the area of the original sketch?

    (1) $1\frac{1}{2}$ times
    (2) 2 times
    (3) 3 times   12 ft
    (4) 4 times
    (5) 8 times

    15 ft

39. The illustration shows the dimensions of the square, fenced-in area where Mary lets her dog play. She decided that a rectangular shape would permit the dog more exercise. If she uses the same amount of fencing and the rectangle is only eight feet wide, what will be the length, in feet, of the rectangular space?

    (1) 12
    (2) 16
    (3) 20   20 ft
    (4) 24
    (5) 32

    20 ft

40. The table shows the relative number of various types of cars sold in one year in the United States. Al's Auto dealership follows the national pattern. In a year, Al sold 392 cars. About how many of the cars that he sold were midsize?

    (1) 50
    (2) 75
    (3) 125
    (4) 150
    (5) 200

Car Sales	
Luxury	17%
Large	8%
Midsize	52%
Small	23%

41. Charlene works as a waitress. In a week when she worked 30 hours, she made a total of $527.50 in tips. What was the average, or mean, amount of her tips for each hour that she worked?

    (1) $ 5.27
    (2) $10.54
    (3) $13.19
    (4) $17.58
    (5) $35.16

42. Rodolfo drove for 5 hours. For the first 3 hours he maintained an average speed of 62 miles per hour. A sudden, heavy rainstorm forced him to drive at an average of 37 miles per hour for the last two hours. How many miles did he travel altogether?

    (1) 310
    (2) 260
    (3) 198
    (4) 185
    (5) 99

For problem 43, mark the answer on the corresponding number grid on the answer sheet.

43. The illustration shows the dimensions of a large rectangular container. How many rectangular boxes, each 3 feet long, 2 feet wide, and 1 foot high, can fit inside the large container?

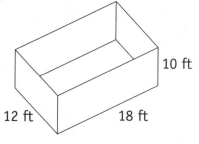

10 ft

12 ft   18 ft

Use the illustration below to answer questions 44 and 45.

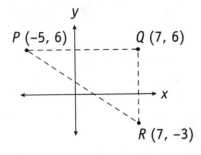

44. What is the distance from point P to point Q?

(1) 10
(2) 11
(3) 12
(4) 15
(5) 19

45. What is the distance from point P to point R?

(1) 9
(2) 10
(3) 12
(4) 15
(5) 20

46. Which of the following is *not* equal to $(3\frac{1}{2})^2$?

(1) 3.5×3.5
(2) $\frac{7}{2} \times \frac{7}{2}$
(3) 2×3.5
(4) $\frac{49}{4}$
(5) 12.25

47. Katharine drove 24 miles east on Highway 2 and 10 miles south on Highway 1. How many miles was she from her starting point?

(1) 14
(2) 24
(3) 26
(4) 34
(5) 40

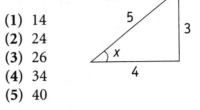

48. Which of the following represents the sine of angle x for the diagram below?

(1) $\frac{3}{5}$
(2) $\frac{5}{3}$
(3) $\frac{4}{5}$
(4) $\frac{5}{4}$
(5) $\frac{3}{4}$

49. If c represents the list price of an item, which of the following represents the final cost of the item if it is on sale for 10% off the list price in a state where there is a sales tax of 5%?

(1) $0.9c$
(2) $0.945c$
(3) $0.95c$
(4) $1.05c$
(5) $1.1c$

50. What is the slope of the line that passes through points S and T in the illustration?

(1) $\frac{1}{5}$
(2) $\frac{1}{4}$
(3) $\frac{1}{3}$
(4) $\frac{1}{2}$
(5) $\frac{2}{3}$

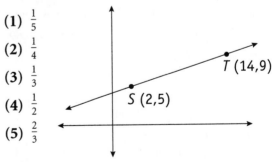

Practice Test Answer Key

Part I

1. (4) 13.6 $P = 2l + 2w$

$P = 2(4.5) + 2(2.3)$

$P = 9 + 4.6 = 13.6$ m

2. (1) $11.23 $c = nr$

$c = 6.5 \times \$1.349 = \$8.7685 \approx \$8.77$

$\$20.00 - \$8.77 = \$11.23$

3. (3) 1 $3(-8) + (-5)^2 = -24 + 25 = 1$

4. 807.1 $40{,}083.5 - 39{,}276.4 = 807.1$

5. 9.25 $r = \frac{d}{2} = \frac{18.5}{2} = 9.25$

6. (1) $18\frac{1}{8}$ $24 - 5\frac{7}{8} = 23\frac{8}{8} - 5\frac{7}{8} = 18\frac{1}{8}$ in.

7. (4) Jake – 288 cu yd

Change each measurement to yards.

$l = \frac{36}{3} = 12$ yd, $w = \frac{24}{3} = 8$ yd, and

$h = \frac{9}{3} = 3$ yd

$V = lwh = 12 \times 8 \times 3 = 288$ cu yd

8. (5) $3.69 $r = \frac{c}{n} = \frac{\$15.87}{4.3} = \$3.6907\ldots \approx \$3.69$

9. (4) $20,000,000

New York $1989 per capita

$\$1989 \times 10{,}000 = \$19{,}890{,}000 \approx$
$\$20{,}000{,}000$

10. (1) 2 times

$\dfrac{\text{Pennsylvania}}{\text{New Hampshire}} = \dfrac{\$1719}{\$851} = 2.0199\ldots \approx 2$

11. (2) 75%

$\dfrac{\text{Wisconsin}}{\text{Connecticut}} = \dfrac{\$2135}{\$2869} = 0.7441\ldots \approx 0.75 = 75\%$

12. $\frac{7}{12}$ $24 - 10 = 14$ women

$\frac{14}{24} = \frac{7}{12}$

13. 4.1 $(1.6)^3 = 1.6 \times 1.6 \times 1.6 = 4.096 \approx 4.1$

14. (3) 9   Point A is 6 units to the left of 0, and point B is 3 units to the right of 0.

The distance between them is $6 + 3 = 9$.

15. (4) 3.13 $\pi = \frac{\text{circumference}}{\text{diameter}} = \frac{23.5}{7.5} = 3.1333\ldots \approx 3.13$

16. (2) 64   The shaded part is a trapezoid.

$\text{base}_1 = 5$ and $\text{base}_2 = 3 + 5 + 3 = 11$

$A = \frac{1}{2}(5 + 11) \times 8 = \frac{1}{2}(16) \times 8 = 64$

17. The point is 4 units left of the vertical axis and 6 units above the horizontal axis.

18. (3) 150 $2.2 \times 68 = 149.6 \approx 150$

19. (3) $\pi(16)^2 - \pi(12)^2$

The radius of the pool is $\frac{24}{2} = 12$ feet.

The radius of the walkway is $12 + 4 = 16$ feet.

The area of the large circle formed by the walkway is $A = \pi(16)^2$, and the area of the pool is $A = \pi(12)^2$.

The area of the walkway is the difference between the two areas.

20. (4) 0 $\qquad \frac{8+13}{7} - (5-2) = \frac{21}{7} - 3 = 3 - 3 = 0$

21. 14.4 $\qquad A = s^2 = (3.8)^2 = 3.8 \times 3.8 = 14.44 \approx$

14.4 sq m

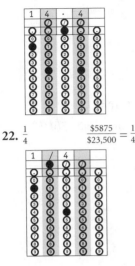

22. $\frac{1}{4}$ $\qquad \frac{\$5875}{\$23,500} = \frac{1}{4}$

23. (1) 7000 $\qquad$ The radius is $\frac{20}{2} = 10$ ft, and the height is 3 ft.

$V = \pi r^2 h = 3.14(10)^2 \times 3 = 3.14(100)(3) = 942$

$942 \times 7.48 = 7046.16 \approx 7000$ gallons

24. (3) \$70.88 $\qquad 470 \times \$0.1508 = \$70.876 \approx \$70.88$

25. (4) 50 $\qquad$ The top of the window is a half circle with an area of $\frac{\pi r^2}{2}$.

The radius of the circle is $\frac{5}{2} = 2.5$ ft.

The bottom of the window is a rectangle.

The length of the rectangle is 8 ft and the width is 5 ft.

$A = \frac{\pi r^2}{2} + lw = \frac{3.14 \times (2.5)^2}{2} + (8 \times 5) = 9.8125 + 40 = 49.8125 \approx 50$

Part II

26. (4) \$2762.50

18 months = 1 year 6 months = 1.5 years

7% = 0.07

$i = prt = \$2500 \times 0.07 \times 1.5 = \$262.50$

$\$2500 + \$262.50 = \$2762.50$

27. (5) 67°F $\qquad$ F $\approx$ 2C + 30

F $\approx$ 2(18.5) + 30 = 37 + 30 = 67

28. (1) 61 $\qquad 10^2 - 5 \times 9 + 6 = 100 - 45 + 6 = 61$

29. (2) \$5.90 $\qquad \frac{1}{5}$ mile = 0.2 mile

2.8 − 0.2 = 2.6 miles which cost \$0.30 for every 0.2 mile

$2.6 \div 0.2 = 13$

$13 \times \$0.30 = \$3.90$

total = \$2.00 + \$3.90 = \$5.90

30. (4) \$5.80 $\qquad$ 2.4 − 0.2 = 2.2 miles which cost \$0.30 for every 0.2 mile

$2.2 \div 0.2 = 11$

$11 \times \$0.30 = \$3.30$

total = \$2.00 + \$3.30 + \$0.50 (surcharge) = \$5.80

31. $\frac{1}{2}$ $\qquad$ Area of triangle $ACE = \frac{1}{2}bh = \frac{1}{2}(18)(12) = 108$

Area of rectangle $ABDE = lw = (18)(12) = 216$

$\frac{108}{216} = \frac{1}{2}$

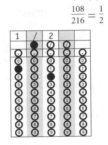

32. (3) .315 $\qquad \frac{\text{hits}}{\text{times at bat}} = \frac{28}{89} = 0.3146\ldots \approx .315$

33. (2) 40% $\qquad 259 - 185 = 74$

$\frac{\text{change}}{\text{original}} = \frac{74}{185} = 0.4 = 40\%$

34. (1) $\frac{1}{2}$ $\qquad \$0.42 + \$0.08 = \$0.50$

$\frac{\$0.50}{\$1} = \frac{1}{2}$

35. (1) \$4,900,000

agricultural projects = 5% = 0.05

$0.05 \times \$98,000,000 = \$4,900,000$

36. (3) −1 $\qquad (-3.8) + (-4.3) - (-7.1) =$

$-3.8 - 4.3 + 7.1 =$

$-8.1 + 7.1 = -1$

37. The point (0, 5) is on the vertical axis and 5 units above the horizontal axis.

When $x = 0$, $y = 3(0) + 5 = 0 + 5 = 5$

The solution is (0, 5)

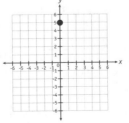

38. (4) 4 times

The area of the original sketch is
$A = lw = (15)(12) = 180$ sq ft.

The new length is $2(15) = 30$, and the new width is $2(12) = 24$.

The area of the new plan is
$A = lw = (30)(24) = 720$ sq ft.

$\frac{720}{180} = 4$ times

39. (5) 32

The perimeter of the square is
$P = 4s = 4(20) = 80$ ft.

Solve for l in $P = 2l + 2w$ where
$P = 80$ and $w = 8$.

$80 = 2l + 2(8)$

$80 = 2l + 16$

$64 = 2l$

$32 = l$

(Or you can substitute the answer choices for l.)

40. (5) 200

Round the number of cars sold, 392, to 400.

Round 52% (midsize cars) to 50% $= \frac{1}{2}$.

$\frac{1}{2}$ of $400 = 200$

41. (4) $17.58 $527.50 \div 30 = \$17.583\ldots \approx \$17.58$

42. (2) 260

$d = rt + rt$

$d = (62)(3) + (37)(2)$

$d = 186 + 74 = 260$ miles

43. 360

Volume of container $= lwh = (18)(12)(10) = 2160$ cu ft

Volume of one box $= lwh = (3)(2)(1) = 6$ cu ft

$\frac{2160}{6} = 360$ boxes

44. (3) 12

P is 5 units left of the vertical axis.

Q is 7 units right of the vertical axis.

The distance between P and Q is $5 + 7 = 12$.

45. (4) 15

$PR = \sqrt{(7-(-5))^2 + (-3-6)^2}$

$PR = \sqrt{(12)^2 + (-9)^2}$

$PR = \sqrt{144 + 81}$

$PR = \sqrt{225}$

$PR = 15$

46. (3) 2×3.5 The other choices all equal 12.25 or $12\frac{1}{4}$.

47. (3) 26

$d = \sqrt{(24)^2 + (10)^2}$

$d = \sqrt{576 + 100}$

$d = \sqrt{676}$

$d = 26$ miles

48. (1) $\frac{3}{5}$ $\text{sine} = \frac{\text{opposite}}{\text{adjacent}} = \frac{3}{5}$

49. (2) $0.945c$ 10% = 0.1 and 5% = 0.05

sale price $= c - 0.1c = 0.9c$

sales tax on sale price $= 0.05(0.9c) = 0.045c$

total $= 0.9c + 0.045c = 0.945c$

50. (3) $\frac{1}{3}$ $\text{slope} = \frac{9-5}{14-2} = \frac{4}{12} = \frac{1}{3}$

Practice Test Evaluation Chart

On the chart below, circle the number of each problem you got wrong. To the right of the problem numbers, you will find the section and starting pages that cover the skills you need to solve the problems. Use this chart to determine the skills on which you need more practice.

	PROBLEM	SECTION	STARTING PAGE
Number Sense and Operations	9, 10, 41	Whole Numbers	7
	2, 4, 8, 18, 29, 30, 32	Decimals	35
	6, 12, 22, 34	Fractions	53
	11, 33, 35, 40, 49	Percent	70
Algebra	14, 36	Signed Numbers	90
	13, 46	Powers and Roots	100
	3, 20, 28	Operations with Numbers	110
	2, 8, 24, 26, 27, 42	Formulas	118
	17, 37, 44, 45, 50	Coordinate Grids	128
Geometry and Measurement	5, 15	Plane Figures	143
	1, 5, 39	Perimeter and Circumference	147
	16, 19, 21, 25, 31, 38	Area	151
	47	Pythagorean Theorem	164
	48	Trigonometric Ratios	167
	7, 23, 43	Volume	180

Answer Key

Pages 3–4

1. 123
2. 123.45
3. 9,999,999,999
4. Clear Key
5. subtract

6. 4.19; 6.12
7. 0.27; 0.42
8. 0.01; 0.08
9. 1.06; 2.07

Page 6

1. 2,450
2. 875
3. 4,056
4. 39,450
5. 1,832
6. 29,609
7. $18.32
8. $2,471.60
9. $649.09
10. $5,038.18

11. **b.** three hundred forty
12. **c.** nine hundred
13. **c.** three dollars and seven cents
14. **a.** twenty cents
15. 95.
16. 243.
17. 3529.
18. 8406.
19. 15.82
20. 204.09

Pages 8–9

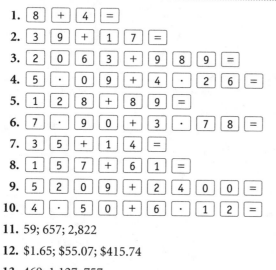

11. 59; 657; 2,822
12. $1.65; $55.07; $415.74
13. 469; 1,127; 757
14. $1,413; $6.68; $11.51
15. 5,418 pounds

Page 10

1. $\boxed{2}\ \boxed{7}\ \boxed{+}\ \boxed{1}\ \boxed{8}\ \boxed{=}$
2. $\boxed{2}\ \boxed{0}\ \boxed{+}\ \boxed{3}\ \boxed{9}\ \boxed{=}$
3. $\boxed{1}\ \boxed{5}\ \boxed{3}\ \boxed{+}\ \boxed{8}\ \boxed{9}\ \boxed{=}$
4. $\boxed{\cdot}\ \boxed{6}\ \boxed{7}\ \boxed{+}\ \boxed{\cdot}\ \boxed{4}\ \boxed{9}\ \boxed{=}$

	Wrong Key	Double Keying	Transposed Digits
1.		✓	
2.			✓
3.	✓		
4.			✓

Page 12

1. 700
2. $13.00
3. $108

4. 6,600
5. $2,400
6. 10,218; 11,875

Problems 9, 10, 11, and 14 are incorrect.

9. $12.98
10. $635

11. 390
14. 8,001

Page 14

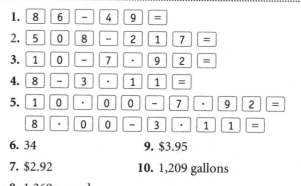

6. 34
7. $2.92
8. 1,269 pounds

9. $3.95
10. 1,209 gallons

Page 16

1. the sticker price of the car; how much the salesman lowered the sticker price; the trade-in allowance
2. Round $23,450 to $20,000; round $1,875 to $2,000; round $7,250 to $7,000.
3. subtraction
4. $23,450 − $1,875 = $21,575; $21,575 − $7,250 = $14,325
6. A
7. larger numbers

Pages 18–19

1.	90	50	90
	+ 70	+ 30	− 40
	160	80	50

2.	500	900	$700
	− 200	+ 100	− 300
	300	1,000	$400

3.	5,000	8,000	12,000
	+ 2,000	+ 5,000	− 8,000
	7,000	13,000	4,000

4. d. 90   **6. a.** 50   **8. c.** 700

5. e. 60   **7. b.** 100

Estimates will vary. Example answers are given below.

	9. Estimate	Exact
	700 miles	696 miles

10.	Estimate	Exact
	100 miles	118 miles

11.	Estimate	Exact
	$56.00	$56.11

12.	Estimate	Exact
	40	42

13.	Estimate	Exact
	$180.00	$177.60

Page 20

1 and 2 (See completed register below.)

Page 22

1. [7] [6] [×] [4] [0] [=]
2. [1] [0] [6] [×] [8] [8] [=]
3. [9] [.] [0] [4] [×] [7] [=]

4. Exact	Estimate	5. Exact	Estimate
1,536	1,500	10,944	12,000
3,953	4,200	9,248	9,000
1,672	1,800	15,318	14,000

6. 280; 912; 1,955   **8.** $140.70; $254.80; $937.62

7. 6,216; 2,002; 98,298   **9.** $85.44

Pages 24–25

1. dividend = 152; divisor = 19

[1] [5] [2] [÷] [1] [9] [=]

2. dividend = $19.68; divisor = 8

[1] [9] [.] [6] [8] [÷] [8] [=]

3. dividend = 361.56; divisor = 23

[3] [6] [1] [.] [5] [6] [÷] [2] [3] [=]

4. dividend = 576; divisor = 27

[5] [7] [6] [÷] [2] [7] [=]

5. Estimate: 400 ÷ 20 = 20; 700 ÷ 20 = 35; 300 ÷ 20 = 15

Exact: 418 ÷ 19 = 22; 693 ÷ 21 = 33; 288 ÷ 18 = 16

6. 45; 26; $48; 61   **12.** $33,677.50

7. 32 tables   **13.** $268 × 52 = $13,936

8. $35   **14.** $330 × 52 = $17,160

9. $341.25   **15.** $330 ÷ 40 = $8.25

10. $2,219,200   **16.** $34,580 ÷ 52 = $665

11. 244 boxes

Number	Date	Description of Transaction	Payment/ Debit (−)		✓ T	Fee (−)	Deposit/ Credit (+)	Balance $1568 43	
202	6/1	North Street Apartments	$ 825	00	✓	$	$	743	43
203	6/4	Amy's Market	39	74				703	69
204	6/8	Import Auto Repair	109	66	✓			594	03
	6/15	Payroll Deposit					1442 45	2036	48
205	6/19	Value Pharmacy	13	29	✓			2023	19
206	6/21	Gazette Times	18	75				2004	44
207	6/23	Nelsen's	39	83	✓			1964	61
208	6/24	Hi-Ho Foods	63	79	✓			1900	82
	6/26	Check Reorder Charges	26	50				1874	32
	6/30	Payroll Deposit					1442 45	3316	77

Page 28

1. $23.35 [1] [5] [·] [7] [5] [M+] [2] [4] [−] [1] [6] [=] [8] [×] [·] [9] [5] [M+] [MR]

2. $121.75 [3] [×] [2] [8] [·] [7] [5] [M+] [2] [×] [1] [7] [·] [7] [5] [M+] [MR]

3. $87.75 [1] [2] [·] [4] [8] [×] [6] [M+] [4] [·] [2] [9] [×] [3] [M+] [MR]

4. $1,363.09 Add the numbers for Mon–Sun. Put in memory [M+] key. Enter $85,283.28. Press [−]. Press [MR]. Press [=].

Page 29

	CURRENCY	2803	00
CASH	COIN	70	50
LIST CHECKS SINGLY			
24 – 72		44	89
31 – 29		39	85
42 – 16		120	00
TOTAL FROM OTHER SIDE		—	
TOTAL		3078	24
LESS CASH RECEIVED		0	
NET DEPOSIT		3078	24

Page 30

1. [4] [7] [5] [÷] [8] [0] [=] [5.9375]
   5 full buses, 1 more bus = 6 buses

2. [4] [5] [0] [÷] [3] [5] [=] [12.85714286]
   12 full disks, 1 more disk = 13 disks

Page 32

1. 15 r3
2. 9 r17
3. 18 r11
4. 39 r5
5. 15 r45
6. 228 r20

7. 47 ÷ 3 = 15.66666667
   15 costumes with 2 yards left.

8. 114 ÷ 12 = 9.5
   The last load will contain 6 cubic yards.

9. 3,185 ÷ 350 = 9.1
   She drove 35 miles on the final day.

10. 1,497 ÷ 75 = 19.96
    19 boxes were filled with 72 parts left to start a new box.

Pages 33–34, Whole Numbers and Money Review

1. 950
2. 376
3. 152 r 22

4.

Number	Date	Description of Transaction	Payment/ Debit (−)		✓ T	Fee (−)	Deposit/ Credit (+)		Balance	
									$ 186	40
110	5/6	Dr. William Tuff	$ 45	43					140	97
	5/10	Deposit					220	15	361	12
111	5/15	Allen's Hardware	83	56					277	56
112	5/16	Amherst Insurance	176	45					101	11

5. $14,120

6. 1,905 parts

7. $31.50

8. a. 16 assemblies
   b. 2 more bolts

9.

DICK'S SPORTING GOODS

Sold to: R. J. Cleary
32 Maplewood
Cottonwood, NY 13111

Invoice no. 3361
Date: March 15, 20____

Quantity	Description	Unit Price	Total Amount
50	Jump Ropes	$2.49	124.50
1	Shuffleboard Set	$49.98	49.98
10	Pkg. Golf Balls	$11.95	119.50
5	Basketballs	$15.95	79.75 ✓
2	Jump Suits #N-395	$31.75	63.50
	Total:		437.23

Page 36

1. five hundredths
2. five tenths
3. five millionths
4. five thousandths
5. five hundred-thousandths
6. five ten-thousandths
7. c. 206 thousandths
8. c. 47 thousandths
9. a. 7 tenths
10. a. 15 hundredths

11. 1 ÷ 8 = 0.125
    b. 125 thousandths
12. 9 ÷ 100 = 0.09
    b. 9 hundredths
13. 30 ÷ 8 = 3.75
    b. 3 and 75 hundredths
14. 5 ÷ 16 = 0.3125
    c. 3,125 ten-thousandths

Page 39

1. $0.30
2. $1.00
3. $7.90
4. $0.60
5. 3.5; 3.46
6. 8.01; 8.007
7. 14.4; 14.38
8. 24.00; 24.005

9. 1.2307692 ≈ 1.2; 1.375 ≈ 1.4; 3.428571429 ≈ 3.4

10. $1.9375 ≈ $1.94; 1.875 ≈ 1.88; $1.888888889 ≈ $1.89

11. 1.4375 ≈ 1.438; 2.045454545 ≈ 2.045; 2.285714286 ≈ 2.286

12. 33 ÷ 7 = 4.714285714 ≈ 4.71 inches

13. 2.54 × 36 = 91.44 ≈ 91.4 centimeters

Answer Key **211**

Page 41

1. 1.36; 0.99; 3.95

2. 0.16; 2.5; 11.65

3.
Estimate	Exact	Estimate	Exact	Estimate	Exact
8	8.3	6	6.3	10	9.7
+ 6	+ 5.6	+ 7	+ 7.1	+ 7	+ 6.5
14	13.9	13	13.4	17	16.2

4.
Estimate	Exact	Estimate	Exact	Estimate	Exact
30	25.8	30	27.85	80	75.60
+ 10	+ 13.6	+ 10	+ 12.4	+ 20	+ 24.83
40	39.4	40	40.25	100	100.43

5.
Estimate	Exact	Estimate	Exact	Estimate	Exact
300	328.65	900	900	500	547.69
200	211.06	400	375.8	200	243.63
+ 100	+ 123	+ 200	+ 245.18	+ 200	+ 181.8
600	662.71	1,500	1,520.98	900	973.12

6. 37; 95; $204

7. 387; 318; $58

8. 3.74 inches

Page 43

1. 0.81

2. 0.11

3. 0.035

4. 0.23; 0.175; 0.019

5. 0.044; 0.01; 0.026

6. 0.153

7. $4.65

8. $0.70

9. 5.4°F

Pages 44–45

1. ÷ $510 ÷ 12 = $42.50

2. + 2.89 + 19.4 = 4.83 meters

3. − 6.2 − 4.79 = 1.41 pounds

4. × 22.5 × 16 = 360 miles

5. ÷ 142 ÷ 5 = 28.4 pounds

6. 2.37 seconds

7. $14.17

8. 0.89 mile

9. 1.8 gallons

10. 0.4375 inch

Pages 47–48

1. 46.8; 7.71; 5.628; 72.05; .7688

2. 144

3. 345.0

4. $111.32

5. $283.98

6. $20.32

7. 143 pounds

8. 1.1 pounds

9. Drills: $389.40

Chests: $199.95

Hammers: $116.55

Shovels: $320.96

Vises: $123.92

Ladders: $337.74

Screwdrivers: $154.40

10. TOTAL PURCHASES: $1,642.92

11. $1,526.37 ($1,642.92–$116.55)

12. $1,206.50; $1,286

13. Super Kids would be $79.50 less for three months.

Pages 49–50

1. dividend 6.54; divisor 3.1; quotient 2.109677419

2. dividend 8; divisor 2.7; quotient 2.962962963

3. dividend 604.86; divisor 12; quotient 50.405

4. dividend 130.41; divisor 13.8; quotient 9.45

5. 44.8; 24.3; 7.2; 8.2

6. 33.91; $3.09; $23.81; 2.41

7. $5.65

8. $1.08

9. 2.7 pounds

Pages 51–52, Decimals Review

1. $3.68

2. $16.32

3. 398.4 pounds

4. 5 pieces

5. 3.5 inches

6. $377.60

7. $14.16

8. $448.40

9. 4.71 inches

10. $21.90

11. $5.98

12. $1,002.63

Pages 54–55

1. $\frac{5}{6}$

2. $2\frac{3}{8}$

3. $\frac{12}{5}$

4. $13\frac{1}{3}$

5. $\frac{25}{10}$

6. $\frac{15}{16}$

7. $\frac{4}{100}$

8. $\frac{200}{2}$

9. $1\frac{8}{9}$

10. $\frac{10}{10}$

11. I M I P

12. M I P P

13. $\frac{1}{2}$; $\frac{3}{4}$

14. $2\frac{1}{2}$; $\frac{7}{8}$

15. $6\frac{5}{8}$; $\frac{3}{8}$

16. $3\frac{1}{4}$

17. $\frac{2}{6}$ or $\frac{1}{3}$

18. $2\frac{7}{8}$

19. $1\frac{2}{8}$ or $1\frac{1}{4}$

20. $\frac{2}{3}$

21. $\frac{2}{8}$ or $\frac{1}{4}$

22. $1\frac{1}{5}$

Page 57

1. 0.375

2. 0.9

3. 25.8

4. 0.0625

5. 0.266666666

6. 3.875

7. 0.76; $\frac{5}{8}$; 0.4; 0.865

8. $\frac{2}{3}$; $\frac{9}{17}$; $\frac{2}{3}$; $\frac{8}{10}$

9. $\frac{3}{16}$; $\frac{19}{32}$; $\frac{3}{4}$; $\frac{7}{8}$

Page 59

1. $\frac{1}{4}$ $\frac{1}{2}$ $\frac{1}{25}$
2. $\frac{4}{5}$ $\frac{3}{4}$ $\frac{26}{29}$
3. $\frac{1}{3}$ $11\frac{2}{5}$ $2\frac{2}{9}$
4. $12\frac{1}{25}$ $1\frac{9}{11}$ 1
5. $\frac{3}{8}$ $\frac{15}{16}$ $2\frac{1}{4}$

Pages 60–61

1. $1\frac{1}{16}$
2. $1\frac{7}{24}$
3. $1\frac{1}{15}$
4. $1\frac{1}{5}$
5. $8\frac{23}{24}$
6. $21\frac{7}{15}$
7. $8\frac{25}{32}$
8. $23\frac{1}{4}$
9. $17\frac{5}{8}$ pounds
10. John worked $25\frac{1}{4}$ hours; Al worked $23\frac{1}{12}$; Jim $24\frac{3}{4}$; John worked more hours.
11. $113\frac{11}{24}$ yards
12. $1\frac{17}{32}$ inches
13. $215\frac{5}{8}$ feet

Pages 62–63

1. $\frac{3}{8}$
2. $\frac{3}{20}$
3. $\frac{11}{80}$
4. $5\frac{17}{32}$
5. $14\frac{5}{8}$
6. $\frac{27}{140}$
7. $13\frac{7}{16}$
8. $1\frac{3}{8}$
9. $\frac{3}{8}$ inch
10. $2\frac{1}{4}$ gallons of water
11. underestimated by 1 hour
12. $4\frac{1}{6}$ feet
13. $9\frac{3}{4}$ inches
14. $15\frac{19}{32}$ feet

Page 65

1. $1\frac{1}{2}$
2. $\frac{1}{4}$
3. $\frac{4}{15}$
4. $\frac{1}{16}$
5. 2
6. $12\frac{1}{3}$
7. $32\frac{1}{2}$
8. $38\frac{2}{5}$
9. 29 yards
10. $w = 4\frac{4}{5}$ inches; $h = 6$ inches
11. $\frac{45}{64}$ inch
12. $9\frac{3}{8}$ inches
13. no
14. 40 minutes

Page 67

1. $\frac{8}{45}$
2. 24
3. $\frac{32}{35}$
4. $\frac{3}{5}$
5. $\frac{15}{256}$
6. $1\frac{1}{2}$
7. 400
8. $3\frac{59}{72}$
9. $1.39
10. Twelve 2 x 4's
11. 64 miles per hour
12. $9\frac{23}{24}$ inches
13. 16 studs

Pages 68–69, Fractions Review

1. $\frac{7}{8}$ inch
2. $15\frac{13}{32}$ inches
3. $\frac{1}{16}$ teaspoon paprika
   $\frac{1}{6}$ cup mayonnaise
4. $47\frac{3}{8}$ inches
5. $41.25
6. $3\frac{7}{16}$ inches
7. 38 chairs
8. $11.06

Page 71

1. percent, division
2. part, multiplication
3. whole, division

Page 73

1. 18; 84; $2.04; 66
2. 0.02; 0.595; $1.65; 2.108
3. 0.075; $10.75; 103.$\overline{3}$; 22.6
4. 45; $174; 135; $56
5. $36.54
6. $11.50

Page 75

1. 20%
2. 80%
3. 38%
4. 40%
5. 32%
6. 51.7%
7. 25%; 60%; 45%; 70%; 40%
8. 37.5%; 31.3%; 33.3%; 9.4%; 66.7%
9. 16%
10. 40%

Page 77

1. 268
2. 1,000
3. 150
4. 250
5. $2,000
6. 400
7. $2,500
8. 600
9. 20 pounds
10. $660
11. $128, 700

Page 79

1. 60,264
2. $1,992.90
3. $129.22
4. $12,290.28
5. $62.79
6. $72.80
7. $101.12
8. No, a 35% discount would yield a final price of $97.37.

Page 81

1. The percents are as follows:
   Housing 32%
   Other 17%
   Clothing 7%
   Transportation 12%
   Food 18%
   Savings 5%
   Medical Care 9%

2. $7,139.84
3. 44%
4. 23%
5. 22%
6. $558
7. $803.25
8. $2,788.75

Page 82

1. 8%
2. 27%
3. 29%
4. 15%
5. 25%
6. 22%

Page 83–84, Percent Review

1. 2000 square feet
2. $2000
3. 87%
4. 16.2%
5. $1050 - 350 = 700 \div 350 = 200\%$ increase
6. 20.48 ounces
7. $25,789.31
8. Bridget; she received a 41% discount
9. $231.20

Pages 86–88, GED Practice

1. (3) $2.00
2. $30.12

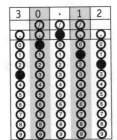

3. (4) 459
4. (3) 293
5. 12

6. (3) 27.35°
7. (2) B
8. (3) $271.50
9. (4) 17%
10. $\frac{15}{38}$

Page 90

1. ← ┼─┼─•─┼─•─┼─┼─┼─•─┼─•─┼─┼ →
   $-\frac{5}{2}$ -1 0 $-\frac{5}{2}$ 3 4.5

2. A −4   B 2   C $-\frac{1}{2}$ D $5\frac{1}{2}$ E $6\frac{1}{2}$

Page 91

1. −   −   +
2. +   −   +
3. −   −   −

Page 92

1. +   −   −
2. +   +   −
3. −   −   −

Page 93

1. 10   −0.75 $-\frac{3}{4}$
2. −5 $\frac{2}{3}$ −15.55
3. −56   −1.6   −1
4. −1.75 $2\frac{5}{12}$ −7
5. 0   35   13

Page 94

1. −   −   +
2. +   −   −
3. +   −   +

Page 95

1. −   −   +
2. +   −   +
3. −   +   −

Page 96

1. −24	−27	$-\frac{5}{72}$
2. −6	−16	+25
3. −20	−9	−96
4. $-1\frac{1}{2}$	$+\frac{1}{6}$	+7
5. −4	−2.1	+50

Pages 97–99, Signed Numbers Review

1.

2. $A = -2\frac{1}{2}$

3. c.	−8	1.1	6
4. 2	−22	−5	2
5. 4	−18	−4	−3
6. −32	54	28	0
7. −3	16	−9	$\frac{7}{8}$

8. 34 + 7 − 13 = 28°F

9. $10

10. 24 − 13 − 8 = 3 yards

11. maximum = 35.8 + 0.01 = 35.81 mm
minimum = 35.8 − 0.01 = 35.79 mm

12. 20,300 − (−1290) = 21,590 feet

13. 18°F

14. −8 and −5

15. 70 points

Page 101

1. 7^5	1^3
2. $(\frac{1}{4})^3$	$(0.3)^4$
3. 10^2	$(-5)^2$
4. 2^4	$inch^3$
5. $feet^3$	$meter^2$
6. 3×3	$5 \times 5 \times 5$	$1 \times 1 \times 1 \times 1$
7. $2 \times 2 \times 2$	7.5×7.5	$2 \times 2 \times 2 \times 2 \times 2$
8. 1×20	-6×-6	$\frac{1}{2} \times \frac{1}{2} \times \frac{1}{2}$
9. 100^3	30^1
10. 15^3	10^3
11. 5^2	$(-3)^5$
12. $(\frac{2}{10})^4$	$(\frac{2}{100})^2$
13. $(\frac{3}{8})^5$	8^0

Page 102

1. 10,000	25	144
2. 0.01	169	$\frac{4}{9}$ or 0.444...
3. 6.25	169	$\frac{1}{9}$ or 0.111...
4. 0.140625	$\frac{9}{64}$	
5. 0.694...	$\frac{25}{36}$	

Page 103

1. 27	−8	0.09
2. 0.125 or $\frac{1}{8}$	−3,375	1,024
3. 0.04	279,936	4,096
4. 1,000,000	100,000,000	100
5. 3,125	81	64

Page 104

1. $\sqrt{25} = 5$; $\sqrt[3]{1,728} = 12$

2. $\sqrt[5]{32} = 2$; $\sqrt[10]{59,049} = 3$

3. $\sqrt[3]{15.625} = 2.5$; $\sqrt{\frac{1}{4}} = \frac{1}{2}$

4. 1.5; 1

5. 0.3; 4

Page 106

1. 2.2	4.5	5.5
2. 12.04	8.9	10.2
3. 10.5	7.4	6.7

	estimate	calculator
4.	7	7.1
5.	0.2	0.2
6.	10	9.9
7.	1	1
8.	0.1	0.1
9.	50	50
10.	4.5	4.5
11.	100	100

Page 107

1. 24.49	0.6	1
2. 17.54	20	1
3. 4.64	16	25
4. 0.3	0.2	14.42
5. 105 ft		
6. 11.2 in.		

Pages 108–109, Powers and Roots Review

1. $6^2 = 36$ $1.5^3 = 3.375$ $100^2 = 10,000$

2. $(\frac{1}{2})^2 = \frac{1}{4}$ or 0.25 $(-4)^6 = 4,096$ $a^2 = a^2$

3. $\sqrt{81} = 9$ because $9^2 = 81$
$\sqrt[3]{1,331} = 11$ because $11^3 = 1,331$

4. $\sqrt{100} = 10$ because $10^2 = 100$
$\sqrt{169} = 13$ because $13^2 = 169$

5. $\sqrt{1,000}$

6. $\sqrt[3]{512}$

7. $\sqrt[4]{6,561}$

8. 0.5   8.66   12.60

9. 3.11   21   441

10. 9.26   100   1,000,000

11. 133 yd

12.

Volume	Length of Side(s)
27 cm³	3 cm
1,000 cu ft	10 ft
1 m³	1 m
216 cu ft	6 ft
8 cu yd	2 yd

Page 110

1. division   14

2. multiplication $1\frac{1}{3}$

3. multiplication   16

4. division   0

5. division   29

Pages 112–113

1. 600   5

2. 7   31.3

3. $20.61   2

4. 6   10

5. 392   6

6. 4,785   −20

7. 25   7

8. $5.38   61

9. $19.03   5.5

10. $11\frac{1}{2}$ $5\frac{1}{2}$

11. $2\frac{1}{2}$ 2

12. 2   5

Page 115

1. $(300 \times \$21) + (150 \times \$15.25)$ $8,587.50

2. $(5 \times \$1.79) + \$0.67$ $9.62

3. $2(5 \times 1.9) + 10(0.2)$ 21 miles

4. $20 - (4 \times 4.3)$ 2.8 pounds

5. $(\$329.99 - \$44.99) \div 3$ $95

6. $(6.4 \times \$8.75) - (4.5 \times \$3.08)$ $42.14

7. $50(\$0.19) + 10(\$13.95) + \$7.25$ $156.25

Page 116

1. 73   143   45

2. 7   1.25   −8

3. 2   −1   9

4. 144   0   85

5. 84   25   289

Page 117, Operations with Numbers Review

1. 8

2. 0.09

3. $(24 \times \$25.00) + (24 \times \$5.30) = \$727.20$

4. $\frac{1}{6}(\$2400) + \frac{1}{12}(\$2400) = \$600$

5. $(10,510 + 15,898 + 18,892)\$5.25 + (1,775 + 3,065 + 5,215)\$2.00 = \$257,935$

Page 118

1. Home Foods $14.35 for 15 pounds of grapes

2. Marcy's $12.43 for 12 quarts of skim milk

Page 119

1. a. $0.48   **2. a.** $0.19   **3. a.** $0.112   **4. a.** $0.283
   b. $0.49   **b.** $0.20   **b.** $0.104   **b.** $0.273
   c. $0.47   **c.** $0.21   **c.** $0.099   **c.** $0.297

Page 121

1. $r = \frac{d}{t} = \frac{182}{14} = 13$ mph

2. $d = rt = 59 \times 7 = 413$ miles

3. $t = \frac{d}{r} = \frac{3255}{620} = 5\frac{1}{4}$ hours

4. $d = rt = 65 \times 9 = 585$ miles

5. $r = \frac{d}{t} = \frac{572}{11} = 52$ mph

6. $t = \frac{d}{r} = \frac{275}{55} = 5$ hours
   8:00 A.M. $+$ 5 hours $=$ 1:00 P.M.

7. $r = \frac{d}{t} = \frac{265}{5} = 53$ mph

Page 123

1. $\frac{3}{4}$

2. $3\frac{2}{12}$

3. $4\frac{1}{6}$

4. $\$2{,}500 \times 3 \times 3\frac{1}{3}\% = \$250$

5. $\$1{,}500 \times 2 \times 10\frac{1}{8}\% = \$303.75$

6. $750 \times 2\frac{1}{6} \times 4\frac{1}{4}\% = \$69.06$

7. $i = (\$375 \times 2\frac{5}{12} \times 3.75\%) = \$33.98$
   total saved $= \$375.00 + \$33.98 = \$408.98$

8. $i = \$650 \times \frac{15}{12} \times 14.50\% = \$117.81$
   total owed $= \$650.00 + \$117.81 = \$767.81$

Page 125

1. -48 0.4 $\frac{1}{6}$

2. -20 64 -4

3. -32 2 -0.025 or $-\frac{1}{40}$

4. -2 0.02 64

5. 2 $-\frac{1}{2}$ or -0.5 -0.2 or $-\frac{1}{5}$

6. $°C = 15°$ $°C = \frac{5}{9}(59 - 32)$

7. $°F = 32°$ $°F = \frac{9}{5}(0) + 32$

8. $150°F = \frac{5}{9}(150 - 32) = 65\frac{5}{9}°C$ or $66°C$
   $180°F = \frac{5}{9}(180 - 32) = 82\frac{2}{9}°C$ or $82°C$

9. $-57\frac{7}{9}°C$ $\frac{5}{9}(-72 - 32)$

Pages 126–127, Formulas in Algebra Review

1. $\$1100$ $V = \$2000 - (\$2000 \times 0.15 \times 3)$

2. 62.5 milligrams   child's dose $= 4 \div (4 + 12) \times 250$

3. $\$12.50$ $P = \$1.00 \div 8\%$

4. $\$550$ $r = \$4840 \div 8\frac{4}{5}$

5. $\$112.50$ $i = \$1500 \times 5\% \times \frac{18}{12}$

6. 411 tickets $n = \frac{\$3596.25}{8.75}$

7. 2,400 miles $d = 20 \times 120$

8. $40°C$ $C = \frac{5}{9}(104 - 32)$

9. -13

10. 13

Page 128

1. $(4, -2)$ 2. $(-3, 5)$ 3. $(2, 6)$ 4. $(-4, -7)$

Page 129

1.
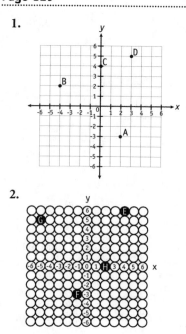

2.

Page 132

1. positive

2. negative

3. undefined

4. zero slope

5. undefined

6. negative slope

7. $\frac{-4 - 0}{3 - 0} = \frac{-4}{3}$

8. slope $= \frac{-1 - 4}{3 - 5} = \frac{-5}{-2} = -\frac{5}{8}$

9. slope $= \frac{-4 - 4}{-1 - 3} = \frac{-8}{-4} = \frac{2}{1} = 2$

10. slope $= \frac{4 - 2}{1 - 0} = \frac{2}{1} = 2$

11. slope $= \frac{5 - 2}{-2 - 1} = \frac{3}{-3} = -1$

12. slope $= \frac{6 - 1}{4 - 3} = \frac{5}{1} = 5$

Page 134

1. $\sqrt{(-1 - (-1))^2 + (6 - 1)^2} = 5$

2. $\sqrt{(1 - 4)^2 + (1 - 1)^2} = 3$

3. $\sqrt{(4 - 4)^2 + (5 - 1)^2} = 4$

4. $\sqrt{(4 - 1)^2 + (5 - 1)^2} = 5$

5. $\sqrt{(-5 - 3)^2 + (-4 - 2)^2} = 10$

6. $\sqrt{(3 - 6)^2 + (6 - 1)^2} = 5.8$

7. $\sqrt{(-3 - 5)^2 + (3 - 1)^2} = 8.2$

8. $\sqrt{(5 - (-2))^2 + (1 - (-5))^2} = 9.2$

Page 135–136, Coordinate Grids Review

1.

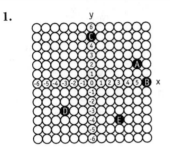

2. slope $= \frac{-2-1}{6-0} = \frac{-3}{6} = -\frac{1}{2}$

3. AB $= \sqrt{(-5-0)^2 + (3-0)^2} = 5.8$

  AC $= \sqrt{(-5-3)^2 + (3-(-5))^2} = 11.3$

  DE $= \sqrt{(5-(-2))^2 + (5-(-1))^2} = 9.2$

  CD $= \sqrt{(3-5)^2 + (-5-5)^2} = 10.2$

  BE $= \sqrt{(0-(-2))^2 + (0-(-1))^2} = 2.2$

4. ST $= \sqrt{(2-0)^2 + (-3-0)^2} = 3.6$

Pages 137–141, GED Practice

1. (1) −3

2. (4) 5

3. 2.75

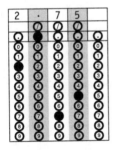

4. (5) 50(5 + 3 + 8)

5. (3) 40($1.00) + 75($0.80) + 25($1.25)

6. 50 $40^2 + 30^2 = \sqrt{1,600 + 900} = \sqrt{2,500} = 50$

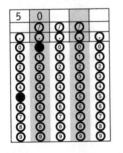

7. (4) (40 × $10.50) + (5 × $10.50 × 1.5)

8. (2) 1

9. (3) 0.38 (31,555 − 30,950)

10. (3) 24

11. (2) B

12. 225 $90 + 15(26 - 17) = 90 + 15(9) =$
     $90 + 135 = 225$

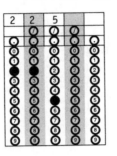

13. (1) −37

14. (4) $\frac{6}{5}$(1,250)

15. $3,876
     ($94,000 + $84,500 + $79,900) × 0.015 = $3,876

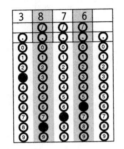

16. (4) D

17. (2) $\frac{1}{6}$

Page 146

1. 19 in.

2. 24.2 m

3. $13\frac{3}{4}$ in.

4. 30 ft

5. 6 ft

6. $75\frac{3}{4}$ ft

7. 6 ft

8. 4.5 m

9. 28.4 cm

10. 72 in.

11. 480 cm

12. 18 cm

13. 80 in.

Page 148

1. 12.6 mi

2. 20 ft

3. 314 yd

4. 9.7 m

5. 30.2 m

Page 151

1. 81 sq ft

2. 64 tiles

3. 75 ft

4. no

Page 153

1. 35 sq in.
2. 110 sq ft
3. 61.2 sq m
4. $19\frac{1}{2}$ sq in.
5. 945 sq m
6. 87 sq yd
7. 5.2 sq m
8. $14\frac{5}{8}$ sq in.

Page 155

1. 56 sq in.
2. $22\frac{1}{2}$ sq yd
3. $7\frac{1}{2}$ sq cm
4. $8\frac{1}{4}$ sq ft
5. 25 sq ft

6. $P = 34$ ft $A = 72.25$ sq ft
7. $P = 60.6$ m $A = 228.42$ sq m
8. $A = 29\frac{1}{4}$ sq yd
9. $A = 380.8$ sq mm
10. 42.55 sq m
11. 96 sq in. or $\frac{2}{3}$ sq ft

Page 157

1. 36 square units
2. $169\frac{1}{8}$ sq ft
3. 792 sq ft
4. 24 bags
5. 140 sq ft
6. $P = 35$ in.; $A = 63$ sq in.

Page 159

1. 908 sq ft
2. 452 sq in.
3. 26 sq in.
4. 675 sq ft
5. 22,167 sq km

Page 161

1. $304\frac{1}{2}$ sq ft
2. 329 sq ft
3. 6,070 sq ft
4. 398.5 sq ft
5. 38 sq cm

Pages 163–164

1. 29 cm
2. 15
3. 24 ft
4. 35 m
5. no
6. yes

Pages 166–167

1. YZ
2. XY
3. $\frac{YZ}{XZ} = \tan X$
4. $\frac{12}{13} = \cos M$
5. $\frac{5}{12} = \tan M$
6. $\frac{5}{13} = \sin M$
7. $\sin E = \frac{1}{\sqrt{5}}$
8. $\cos E = \frac{2}{\sqrt{5}}$
9. $\tan E = \frac{1}{2}$

	angle	sin	cos	tan
10.	30°	0.5	0.866	0.577
11.	45°	0.707	0.707	1.0
12.	60°	0.866	0.5	1.732
13.	75°	0.966	0.259	3.732

14. $\tan 65° = 2.145$
$2.145 = \frac{x}{44}$
$x = 94.38 \approx 94.4$ feet

Pages 168–172, Plane Figures Review

1. $P = a + b + c$
2. $P = 4s$
3. $P = 2l + 2w$ or $2(l + w)$
4. $A = \pi r^2$
5. $A = \frac{1}{2}bh$
6. $A = bh$
7. $A = \frac{1}{2}(b^1 + b^2)h$
8. 38.48

9. $P = 360$ ft $A = 4,400$ sq ft
10. $P = 36$ ft $A = 62\frac{1}{2}$ sq ft
11. The area quadruples or gets 4 times larger.
12. 21.46 sq in.
13. 491 sq ft
14. 568 sq ft
15. 7,958 mi
16. 420 sq ft
17. 36 sq in.
18. 33.6 sq m
19. 80 sq ft
20. 88 ft

21. The square that is 50 yards on each side
22. 880 ft
23. (4) $\frac{1}{2}$
24. (2) 5
25. 127 ft
26. 65 ft
27. 29 ft
28. 505 mi
29. $\cos 45° = \frac{7}{y}$
30. 9.9

Pages 176–177

1. 125 cu cm
2. 166 cu in.
3. 512 cu yd
4. 6.3 in.
5. 1 cm
6. 12 mm
7. 68.921 metric tons
8. 15 cu ft
9. 125 blocks
10. 30 cu m
11. 112 boxes
12. 16 cu ft
13. 36,000 gal

Page 179

1. $3,333\frac{1}{3}$ cm³
2. 4873.5 in.³
3. 324 cu in.
4. 15 m³
5. 432 ft³ or 16 yd³
6. 15.625 in.³
7. 1.728 m³
8. $101\frac{1}{3}$ in.³
9. 43.2 cm³
10. 10 in.
11. 7 m
12. 540 in.³
13. 11.2 in.

Page 181

1. 155.5 ft³
2. 942.5 cu in.
3. 190 in.³
4. 4.8 cu ft
5. 1.6 cu yd
6. 8 cu ft

Page 183

1. 301.59 cm³
2. 19.63 cm³
3. 18,010.75 cu in.
4. 148 cu ft
5. 141 cu cm
6. (3) quadrupled
7. 9 cu in.

Page 185

1. 518 cu ft
2. 2,940 cu in.
3. 1,302.65 cu in.
4. 24 cu ft
5. 3,591.9 cu cm
6. 168 cu in.

Pages 186–188, Solid Figures Review

1. 1,728 in.³
2. 31.5 ft³
3. 4,021 ft³
4. 1,207 in.³
5. 5,760 in.³
6. 292 cm³
7. 254 in.³
8. 8,640 in.³
9. 182 cm³
10. 13 in.³
11. 0.35 m³

Pages 189–193, GED Practice

1. (3) 13.00
2. (4) 40.84
3. (2) 36.3
4. (5) $1\frac{1}{16}$ in.
5. (5) Not enough information is given.

6. 35 sq ft

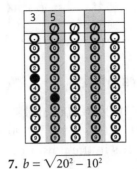

7. $b = \sqrt{20^2 - 10^2}$
8. (1) 10 m, 8 m, 6 m
9. 1,600 sq ft

10. (2) 209
11. (1) 2
12. (2) 208.71
13. $200

14. 161 sq ft

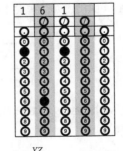

15. (4) $\frac{YZ}{XY}$
16. 75 ft

Using Mental Math

Multiplying by Powers of Ten

The numbers 10, 100, 1,000, 10,000, and so on are called **powers of ten.** (They are so-named because $10 = 10^1$, $100 = 10^2$, $1,000 = 10^3$, $10,000 = 10^4$, and so on.) To multiply any number by a power of ten, count the zeros in the power of ten and write that number of zeros to the right of the other factor.

EXAMPLES

$$\begin{array}{r} 21 \\ \times\ 1,000 \leftarrow 3\text{ zeros} \\ \hline 21,000 \leftarrow \text{product} \end{array} \qquad \begin{array}{r} 1,525 \\ \times\ \ \ \ 100 \leftarrow 2\text{ zeros} \\ \hline 152,500 \leftarrow \text{product} \end{array}$$

To multiply a decimal number by a power of ten, count the zeros in the power of ten. In the other factor, move the decimal point *to the right* that number of places.

EXAMPLES $\quad 13.52 \times 1,\underset{\text{3 zeros}}{\underline{000}} = 13\underset{\text{3 places}}{\underline{520}}.$

$$0.05238 \times 1\underset{\text{2 zeros}}{\underline{00}} = 05\underset{\text{2 places}}{\underline{.238}}$$

To multiply two factors with zeros at the right, count the zeros in both factors. Ignoring all the zeros, multiply the two numbers. Then write that number of zeros to the right of the product.

EXAMPLES

$$\begin{array}{r} 130 \\ \times\ \ 200 \\ \hline 26,000 \end{array} \quad \text{3 zeros}$$

$13 \times 2 \quad$ 3 zeros

$$\begin{array}{r} 1500 \\ \times\ \ 4000 \\ \hline 6,000,000 \end{array} \quad \text{5 zeros}$$

$15 \times 4 \quad$ 5 zeros

Dividing with Zeros at the Right

To divide by a power of ten, count the zeros in the power of ten. In the numerator (the dividend), move the decimal point *to the left* that number of places.

EXAMPLES $\quad \dfrac{575.2}{100} = 5.752 \qquad \dfrac{1.32}{10,000} = 0.000132$

2 zeros   2 places   4 zeros   4 places

To divide two numbers with zeros at the right, cancel the same number of zeros in the numerator as in the denominator.

EXAMPLES $\quad \dfrac{600}{30} = \dfrac{60\cancel{0}}{3\cancel{0}} = \dfrac{60}{3} = 20$

$$\dfrac{7000}{400} = \dfrac{70\cancel{00}}{4\cancel{00}} = \dfrac{70}{4} = 17.5$$

Using Estimation

In **front-end estimation,** you round each number to its left-most digit. Then you can use mental math to calculate with the rounded values.

EXAMPLE   Round each number to its left-most digit. Then add the rounded values.

Exact Problem		Rounded Values
687	→	700
4,435	→	4,000
+ 393	→	+ 400
		5,100 ← Estimate

EXAMPLE

Exact Problem		Rounded Values
385	→	400
+ 57	→	+ 60
		24,000 ← Estimate

In division, you round to **compatible numbers** that make the mental math easier.

EXAMPLE   Instead of rounding to the left-most digit, replace the numbers with approximate values that make the new problem divide evenly.

Exact Problem		Approximate Values	Estimate
$\dfrac{529{,}420}{710}$	→	$\dfrac{490{,}000}{700}$ because 7 divides evenly into 49 → 700	

Decimal problems may ask you to **round to the nearest** tenth, hundredth, thousandth, and so on.

EXAMPLE

Exact Number	Rounded to the Nearest Tenth	Rounded to the Nearest Hundredth
72.578	72.6	72.58

Fraction problems my ask you to **round to the nearest** whole.

EXAMPLE

Exact Problem	Rounded Number
$7\frac{2}{3}$	8

Formulas

AREA of a:

square	Area = side^2
rectangle	Area = length × width
parallelogram	Area = base × height
triangle	Area = $\frac{1}{2}$ × base × height
trapezoid	Area = $\frac{1}{2}$ × (base$_1$ + base$_2$) × height
circle	Area = π × radius^2; π is approximately equal to 3.14.

PERIMETER of a:

square	Perimeter = 4 × side
rectangle	Perimeter = 2 × length + 2 × width
triangle	Perimeter = side$_1$ + side$_2$ + side$_3$

Circumference of a circle

Circumference = π × diameter; π is approximately equal to 3.14.

VOLUME of a:

cube	Volume = edge^3
rectangular solid	Volume = length × width × height
square pyramid	Volume = $\frac{1}{3}$ × (base edge)^2 × height
cylinder	Volume = π × radius^2 × height; π is approximately equal to 3.14.
cone	Volume = $\frac{1}{3}$ × π × radius^2 × height; π is approximately equal to 3.14.

COORDINATE GEOMETRY

distance between points = $\sqrt{(x_2 - x_1)^2 + (y_2 - y_1)^2}$; (x_1, y_1) and (x_2, y_2) are two points in a plane.

slope of a line = $\frac{y_2 - y_1}{x_2 - x_1}$; (x_1, y_1) and (x_2, y_2) are two points on the line.

PYTHAGOREAN RELATIONSHIP

$a^2 + b^2 = c^2$; a and b are legs and c the hypotenuse of a right triangle.

TRIGONOMETRIC RATIOS

$\sin = \frac{\text{opposite}}{\text{hypotenuse}}$　$\cos = \frac{\text{adjacent}}{\text{hypotenuse}}$　$\tan = \frac{\text{opposite}}{\text{adjacent}}$

MEASURES OF CENTRAL TENDENCY

mean = $\frac{x_1 + x_2 + \ldots + x_n}{n}$, where the x's are the values for which a mean is desired, and n is the total number of values for x.

median = the middle value of an odd number of *ordered* scores, and halfway between the two middle values of an even number of *ordered* scores.

SIMPLE INTEREST

interest = principal × rate × time

DISTANCE

distance = rate × time

TOTAL COST

total cost = (number of units) × (price per unit)

Glossary

A

all clear key   The key that clears any value displayed by the calculator

and   The word that represents the decimal point in a decimal number or amount of money. For example, 4.054 is read "four *and* fifty-four thousandths"; $12.43 is read "twelve dollars *and* forty-three cents."

area   Measure of the amount of surface of a plane figure

arithmetic expressions   Expressions that involve numbers, parentheses, and the operations +, −, ×, and ÷. For example, $(34 + 23) \div 3$.

C

circle   Plane figure, each point of which is an equal distance from the center

circumference   Distance around a circle

clear key   The key that clears the value displayed by the calculator. It does not affect any value stored in memory.

common fraction   A number expressed as a ratio of two integers. For example, $\frac{3}{4}$, $\frac{-7}{10}$, and $\frac{115}{-8}$ are common fractions.

cone   A 3-dimensional figure with a circular base and a vertex at a height from the center of the base

coordinate grid   A grid on which points are identified by an ordered pair of numbers called coordinates

cosine   In trigonometry, a ratio of the adjacent side to the hypotenuse of a right triangle

cubed number   Number with a exponent of 3. The number is multiplied times itself three times.

cylinder   A 3-dimensional shape with a circular top and bottom and rectangular sides

D

decimal   A number between zero and one expressed with a decimal point. 0.15 and 0.1119 are decimals.

decimal places   Places to the right of a decimal point. The decimal places are tenths, hundredths, thousandths, ten-thousandths, hundred-thousandths, millionths, ten-millionths, and so on.

diameter   Distance across the center of a circle

difference   The answer to a subtraction problem. In the problem $14 - 9 = 5$, the difference is 5.

digit keys   The keys for the digits 0, 1, 2, 3, 4, 5, 6, 7, 8, 9

display   The panel on a calculator that shows the current value calculated by the calculator

distance formula   Formula to find how far something travels when the speed and time taken are known

dividend   The number you are dividing into in a division problem. In the division problem $35 \div 7 = 5$ or $7\overline{)35}$, the dividend is 35.

divisor   The number you are dividing by in a division problem. In the division problem $35 \div 7 = 5$ or $7\overline{)35}$, the divisor is 7.

E

error symbol   An indication in a calculator that it has been asked to do something it cannot do. A calculator displays an error symbol if the number being calculated is too large to be shown in the display window (this is called an **overflow**) or if it has been asked to divide by zero.

estimating   Using rounded values to find an approximate answer to a problem

exponent   Number that tells how many times the base is to be multiplied times itself

G

grouping symbols   Parentheses and brackets used to isolate arithmetic expressions and show their order of operations

I

improper fraction   A fraction that is greater than or equal to 1. $\frac{15}{11}$ and $\frac{7}{7}$ are improper fractions.

interest formula   Formula to find the money earned or paid for the use of money when the rate of percent and time are known

K

keying error   The act of making incorrect keystrokes. For example, entering $\boxed{8}\,\boxed{2}$ instead of $\boxed{2}\,\boxed{8}$, entering $\boxed{1}\,\boxed{0}\,\boxed{3}$ instead of $\boxed{1}\,\boxed{\cdot}\,\boxed{3}$, entering $\boxed{7}\,\boxed{7}\,\boxed{4}$ instead of $\boxed{7}\,\boxed{4}$, and so on

M

memory keys   Keys for storing and retrieving values entered by the user or calculated by the calculator

mental math   Performing a calculation in your mind, without writing it down or using a calculator

mixed number   The sum of a whole number and a proper fraction. $3\frac{2}{7}$ and $113\frac{67}{70}$ are mixed numbers.

N

number line   Line used to represent both positive and negative numbers

O

on key   The key that clears any value stored in memory. It can be used to clear the display or to turn the calculator on.

operation keys   The keys used to add, subtract, multiply, or divide

order of operations   Set of rules for finding the value of arithmetic expressions
1. Do operations within parentheses.
2. Do exponents and roots.
3. Do multiplication and division.
4. Do addition and subtraction.

P

parallelogram   Plane figure with two pairs of parallel sides; opposite sides are equal and opposite angles are equal

part   In the percent problem "25% of 200 is 50," the value 50 is the part.

percent   In the percent problem "25% of 200 is 50," the value 25% is the percent.

percent circle   A device that can be used to help remember which operation to perform to solve various kinds of percent problems

percent key   The key that shows the results of a calculation as a percent.
$\boxed{5}\,\boxed{6}\,\boxed{\times}\,\boxed{2}\,\boxed{5}\,\boxed{\text{SHIFT}}\,\boxed{\%}$ displays 14.

perfect square   A number that is the product of some number times itself. For example, 64, 100, and 225 are perfect squares because $64 = 8^2$, $100 = 10^2$, and $225 = 15^2$.

perimeter   Distance around a plane figure

pi   Ratio of circumference to diameter for any circle

place value   Places to the left or right of a decimal point. To the left of the decimal point the place values are ones, tens, hundreds, thousands, and so on. To the right of the decimal point the place values are tenths, hundredths, thousandths, ten-thousandths, hundred-thousandths, millionths, ten-millionths, and so on.

placeholding zero   Using the digit zero to help digits line up in a calculation. The addition problem at the right uses placeholding zeros.

$$
\begin{array}{r}
24.58 \\
112.046 \\
+\ 78.3 \\
\hline
\end{array}
\qquad
\begin{array}{r}
24.580 \\
112.046 \\
+\ 78.300 \\
\hline
\end{array}
$$

plane figure   Geometric figure of 2-dimensional shape

power   Product of a number multiplied by itself one or more times

problem-solving steps
1. Read the problem and find the key information.
2. Estimate an answer.
3. Choose the operation and set up a calculation.
4. Perform and check the calculation(s).
5. Reread the problem and verify your answer.

product   The answer to a multiplication problem. In the problem $3 \times 6 = 18$, the product is 18.

proper fraction   A fraction in which the numerator (top number) is smaller than the denominator (bottom number). $\frac{2}{3}$, $\frac{177}{178}$, and $\frac{5}{358}$ are proper fractions.

Pythagorean theorem   Relationship between the legs and hypotenuse of a right triangle

Q

quotient   The answer to a division problem. For example, in the division problem $35 \div 7 = 5$ or $7\overline{)35}^{5}$, the quotient is 5.

R

radius   Distance from the center of a circle to any point on the circle's edge

rectangle   Plane figure with two pairs of parallel sides and four right angles

reciprocal   A fraction with 1 in the numerator and a particular number in the denominator. The reciprocal of 3 is $\frac{1}{3}$; the reciprocal of 12 is $\frac{1}{12}$; the reciprocal of $\frac{3}{4}$ is $1 \div \frac{3}{4}$ or $1 \times \frac{4}{3}$ or $\frac{4}{3}$.

remainder   In a division problem, the part of the quotient that is not a whole number. For example, in the division problem $41 \div 7 = 5 \, r \, 6$ or $7\overline{)41}^{\,5r6}$, the remainder is 6.

root   The opposite operation of finding a power

rounded number   A number with zeros to the right of a given place value. 700 is the rounded number for 742.

S

signed numbers   Positive and negative numbers

sine   In trigonometry, the ratio of the opposite side to the hypotenuse of a right triangle

slope   Ratio of a line that compares the rise to the run

solid figure   Geometric figure of a 3-dimensional shape

square   Plane figure with four equal sides, two pairs of parallel sides, and four right angles

square root   One of two equal factors of a number

square-based pyramid   A 3-dimensional shape with a square base and four triangular faces for sides

square root key   The key that finds the square root of a displayed number. $\boxed{3}$ $\boxed{6}$ $\boxed{\text{SHIFT}}$ $\boxed{\sqrt{}}$ displays 6.

squared number   Number with an exponent of 2; the number is multiplied times itself

sum   The answer to an addition problem. In the problem $4 + 9 = 13$, the sum is 13.

T

tangent   In trigonometry, the ratio of the opposite side to the adjacent side of a right triangle

terms   Numbers, products, and quotients in an arithmetic expression. In the expression $\frac{27 + 2 \times 7}{13} + 23 \times 5 - 16.4$, there are three terms: $\frac{27 + 2 \times 7}{13}$, 23×5, and 16.4.

total cost   Formula to find the cost of purchasing several items

trapezoid   Plane figure with four sides, one pair of which is parallel

triangle   Plane figure with three sides and three angles

trigonometry   Study of the relationship between pairs of sides of right triangles

U

unit price   Formula to find the amount paid for a single item

V

volume   Measure of the space taken up by a solid or 3-dimensional figure

W

whole   In the percent problem "25% of 200 is 50," the value 200 is the whole.

X

***x*-axis**   Horizontal axis of a coordinate grid

Y

***y*-axis**   Vertical axis of a coordinate grid

Index